Wild Blue Yonder

Terry Gwynn-Jones was born in England. He served as a fighter pilot and jet instructor with the British, Canadian and Australian air forces before joining Australia's Department of Civil Aviation in 1969 as an Examiner of Airmen. In 1975, with another ex-RAF pilot, he set an around-the-world speed record for piston-engined aircraft. In 1988 he gave up flying to pursue a full-time writing career.

Since 1972 he has published sixteen books and hundreds of magazine articles. He was a consultant and writer for Time-Life's *Epic of Flight* and *How Things Work* series. Following resident writing assignments with the Smithsonian Institution's National Air & Space Museum, he was appointed to the Board of Advisors of the Smithsonian Institution's History of Aviation book project. In 1995 he wrote the children's book *Discoveries: Flight* for Time-Life Books and co-authored *The Greatest Flight*, the story of the recreation of the Smith Brothers 1919 England–Australia epic, sponsored by the National Geographic Society.

Wild Blue Yonder

FLYING STORIES OF AMAZEMENT AND WONDER

TERRY GWYNN-JONES
aviation writer par excellence

University of Queensland Press

First published 1996 by University of Queensland Press
Box 42, St Lucia, Queensland 4067 Australia

© Terry Gwynn-Jones 1996

Typeset by University of Queensland Press
Printed in Australia by McPherson's Printing Group, Victoria

Distributed in the USA and Canada by
International Specialized Book Services, Inc.,
5804 N.E. Hassalo Street, Portland, Oregon 97213–3640

Cataloguing in Publication Data
National Library of Australia

Gwynn-Jones, Terry, 1933– .
  Wild blue yonder.

  1. Air pilots — Biography. 2. Aeronautics — History.
  I. Title.

629.130922

ISBN 0 7022 2751 X

To Australia's great pioneer airwoman
Lores Bonney (1897–1994)
who helped conquer the wild blue

"First Europe, and then the globe, will be linked by flight, and nations so knit together that they will grow to be next-door neighbours. This conquest of the air will prove, ultimately, to be man's greatest and most glorious triumph. What railways have done for nations, airways will do for the world."

English pioneer aviator
Claude Grahame-White
(reported by aviation writer
Harry Harper in 1914)

Contents

Preface

The great names of aviation history and their flights can rarely be matched one against the other on a competitive scale. Each must stand alone and be judged on individual merit. The stories in this book recall just a few of those remarkable aviation pioneers, some famous, some forgotten.

Some chased records for fame and glory. Others were driven by that inexplicable challenge ... to do it because it was there. The more far-sighted pioneered the future air routes of the world. Over the horizon they saw a day when their seemingly unimportant efforts would be recognised as the first faltering steps of the great airlines that would surely come. Many gave their lives for the dream. A fortunate few lived to ride in the modern airliners that eventually travelled the routes they had helped pioneer.

To chronicle all who played a part would take a library full of books. For every headline hero, a hundred forgotten fliers helped define aviation's future. This accolade should extend to the pilots who were the contemporaries of the Wright brothers, to the record breakers and trail blazers between the wars, to barnstormers in their tumble-down biplanes, to bush pilots and outback aviators, to airline pilots in open cockpits cringing from the noise and wind, to all those pilots of the past who with high spirits, flouted gravity and daily put their lives on the line. They all played their part in the growth of aviation.

Terry Gwynn-Jones

1
Escape from Paris

The young Prussian soldier crouched behind the gun. A strange-looking affair it was, rather like a giant rifle. It swivelled on a shoulder-high pedestal, and the whole contraption was mounted on top of a wooden-wheeled horse-drawn cart. As he carefully took aim, the gunner's fingers rested near a metal plate embossed with the name Krupps, the famous Prussian arms manufacturer.

The target floating high above, across the gun's open sights, was a huge balloon. Dangling beneath, suspended by a mass of ropes, was a small wicker basket containing two men. The Prussian's finger slowly closed on the trigger and with the final squeeze there was a loud explosion. A small shell whistled skywards, reached the top of its trajectory, and fell harmlessly to explode in the French countryside.

To the world's first anti-aircraft gunner, the target seemed, as usual, to be out of range. Yet another French balloon had escaped from Paris. Ever since the siege had begun three months earlier they had been crossing the Prussian lines every few days.

The Franco–Prussian War had reached its climax in September 1870, when Paris was surrounded and communications were cut with the rest of France. With the Prussian Army dug in at the outskirts and intent on starving the city into submission, the scene was set for a desperate and daring gamble. It was vital that the beleaguered citizens maintained some communication link with the provisional French government which had set up its headquarters 120 kilometres to the south in Tours. With no hope of breaking the blockade on the ground, the inventive French turned to a new and relatively untried medium — the sky.

Less than a hundred years earlier, in 1783, Paris had been the setting for the world's first flight by humans, when a hot-air balloon, invented by France's Montgolfier brothers, had carried two noblemen aloft over the city. By 1870 gas had supplanted hot air as the lifting medium for balloons. Now safer and more efficient, they had become a fashionable pastime and were a common sight on the world's horizons.

Parisians were about to put their invention to a new use — operating the world's first air transport service. Balloons would carry passengers and urgent mail out of the city. Their pilots would also observe and report on Prussian army positions — a prophetic demonstration of the part aircraft would play in wars of the future.

When the last ground escape route was closed by the enemy, six experienced French aeronauts (as the balloon pilots were called) were still in the city. They were Gaston Tissandier, one of the greatest balloonists of the era; Eugene Godard, a veteran with eight hundred ascents to his credit; Godard's sons Jules and Louis; Jules Durouf and Georges Mangin.

The aeronauts approached the authorities and advised that there were already several balloons in the city and enough materials to build and inflate many more. They were confident that, under the right wind conditions, their hydrogen-filled aircraft could ascend over the city and be out of range of the Prussian muskets before crossing the enemy lines. With a good breeze they could easily reach the unoccupied zones or even carry on to England if need be.

The city's military commander acted with remarkable haste, and approval to commence preparations for the first flight was given within a few days. The group, managed by businessman Gaspard Tournachon, was named Compagne d'Aerostiers Militaires and balloon factories were established at the Gare du Nord and Gare d'Orléans, where Eugene Godard and his wife supervised the work. The huge covered platforms at the stations were ideal for the delicate task. British journalist Henry Vizetelly described the production line at the Gare d'Orléans:

Under the vast iron and glass roof — on the long metal rafters on which sailors balanced themselves or sat astride, engaged in suspending long strips of coloured calico reaching almost to the ground — scores of women were occupied, either spreading out and ironing long pieces of material or else soaking the calico to get rid of its stiffness. Having been hung up to dry, the material was then cut out to the various patterns, marked out to their full size upon the ground, and after a preliminary varnishing a hundred or more work girls, seated at long tables and superintended by Madame Godard, proceeded to sew the seams with mechanical exactitude.

Each balloon took about twelve days to complete and was equipped with a wicker basket, a barometer for gauging the height, a compass, a thermometer and a small cage to carry messenger pigeons.

On 23 September all was ready for the first flight and Durouf was chosen to crew the balloon *La Neptune*. Shortly after dawn the inflation process began on the hill of Montmartre. By 8 a.m. 125 kilograms of mail and military despatches had been loaded aboard and the aeronaut took his place in the basket. On his command the ground crew released the retaining ropes and he lifted quickly over the city.

With a steady wind from the south-east *La Neptune* moved out over the city, following roughly in the direction of the River Seine. As it crossed the Prussian lines the enemy troops watched in stunned surprise as the balloon drifted high overhead. They had never expected such a novel method of breaking their stranglehold on the city. The Prussians eventually sent a ragged volley of rifle-fire skywards as *La Neptune* drifted towards the horizon. Not equipped to retaliate, the disdainful Duroff coolly showered choice curses and his visiting cards on the enemy troops.

Three hours later Durouf landed 130 kilometres away at Evreux in unoccupied territory. The authorities in Paris had no way of knowing whether or not *La Neptune* had reached safety. However, when last spotted it was flying steadily and had cleared the immediate danger of the Prussian guns. Thus there seemed no reason to believe that Duroff had not got through and delivered the despatches. It was decided to continue with the flights.

Two days later Mangin carried 300 kilograms of mail from the city in the balloon *Ville-de-Florence*, landing safely in a field just on the other side of enemy territory. Louis Godard followed only four days later in *Les Etats-Unis*, an unusual balloon made up of two small gas bags tied together.

Both Godard and Mangin had attracted ragged musket fire as they crossed the enemy lines, but had not been hit. There was talk about flights being conducted at night should the Prussians become effective at hitting the balloons. In the meantime they would continue to fly by day so as not to face the additional hazard of night flying.

Gaston Tissandier chose to make the next flight, and lifted off on 30 September carrying 25 000 letters and three messenger pigeons in an old balloon called *Le Celeste*. Fired on a number of times, Tissandier crossed occupied territory without the gas bag being punctured by bullets, although he was alarmed to discover that the ageing balloon had "a whole constellation of [natural] punctures". Recalling the battle-scarred countryside around Paris, Tissandier wrote:

Not a soul on the roads, not a carriage or a train. All the demolished bridges offer the appearance of abandoned ruins. Not a soldier, not a sentinel, nothing. You might think yourself on the outskirts of an ancient city destroyed by time.

At one stage, forced down by cooling temperatures, Tissandier came perilously close to making a forced landing near a troop of Prussian cavalry. Luckily he managed to throw out sufficient ballast, including bundles of anti-Prussian leaflets, to make the balloon climb back out of range. However, two hours later, with the gas leaking slowly away, he was again skimming the treetops near the town of Dreux. Tissandier was already looking for an open field for landing when *Le Celeste* went into a sudden and uncontrollable descent. Dropping violently from fifty feet, the basket crashed into the ground and the luckless aeronaut was thrown out, breaking an arm.

With the "gas-bag airline" having proved it could safely overfly the Prussian positions, passengers were now carried out of the city. The first, and by far the most important, to leave was Léon Gambetta, France's Minister of the Interior. Gambetta's mission was of vital importance. He was charged with talking to the faltering French government in its temporary headquarters at Tours. Gambetta hoped to raise an army in the unoccupied provinces and lead them to the relief of Paris.

Thousands of Parisians flocked to the Place Saint-Pierre on 7 October to see him off. Clad in a long overcoat and fur cap, and accompanied by his secretary, Gambetta climbed aboard the basket of the balloon *Armand Barbes*. It was commanded by Trichet — one of the two remaining trained aeronauts. A second balloon, the *George-Sand*, took off at the same time as the *Armand Barbes*. It was commanded by a plucky Paris hotelier and carried two escaping Americans. The event was recorded in the Tours edition of *Le Moniteur Universal*:

> Borne along by a very slight wind, the two balloons left Saint Denis behind them to their right, but scarcely had they passed the line of fortifications when they were welcomed by a fusillade from the Prussian outposts. They also received some cannon-fire.
>
> At this time the balloons were at 600 metres and the aerial travellers heard bullets whistling around their heads; they then rose to a height where they were out of the soldiers' range; but by some accident, or by some mistake in manoeuvring, the balloon carrying the Minister of the Interior began to go down rapidly and landed in a field across which, only a few hours before, enemy troops had marched, and which was very close to a German post. When ballast had been jettisoned they rose again and continued on their way.
>
> The balloon was only at an altitude of 200 metres when, near Creil, a second salvo was fired in their direction by soldiers from Wurtemburg. At this time they were in great peril: luckily, the arms of the enemy were piled; before they could take hold of them, the balloon, rid of some of its ballast, was climbing to 800 metres. The bullets, as on the first occasion, did not find their target, but they passed very close to the travellers, and M. Gambetta even had his hand grazed by a projectile.

With all its ballast gone and the gas running out, the *Armand Barbes* slowly descended. An hour later it was again fired on as it passed low over a Prussian encampment on the edge of a forest near Montdidier. Minutes later the basket became entangled in the topmost branches of a huge oak. Aeronaut Trichet and his passengers clung there until nearby villagers arrived and helped them down. The second balloon also ran the gauntlet of Prussian fire before landing safely forty kilometres away from its companion.

Following his arrival at Montdidier, Gambetta was able to get a message back to Paris. Before the flight it had been suggested that the balloon be equipped with carrier pigeons for return communication to Paris. The following day a pigeon arrived at its loft in the embattled city. From the message cylinder on the bird's leg, the following message was extracted:

> Arrived after accident in forest at Epineuse. Balloon deflated, we were able to escape from the Prussian rifle fire and, thanks to Mayor of Epineuse, come here, from whence we leave in one hour for Amiens, from there railway to Le Mans and Tours. The Prussian lines end at Clermont, Compiegne and Breteuil in the Somme. Everywhere the people are rising. The government of La Defense Nationale is acclaimed on all sides — Leon Gambetta.

Pigeons were used by other balloons and, although only a few returned to Paris with vital information, they provided an invaluable link. When the supply of birds ran out, trained dogs were used to carry despatches back to the capital.

On 14 October architect Albert Tissandier, the brother of balloonist Gaston, took off in the balloon *Jean-Bart* from a clearing adjacent to the Gare d'Orléans railway station. In all probability he had previously flown with his brother. He most surely would have had a long briefing from Veteran Eugene Godard, who had left from the same spot a little earlier in the balloon *General Cavaignac*. Both drifted slowly east across the Prussian lines. Tissandier recalled his first ever flight in control of a balloon:

> Besides two travellers [passengers] who had been entrusted to my care I carried 100 000 letters, 100 000 tokens of remembrance sent from Paris by 100 000 anxious families! The sun beat down; we soon passed over the line of fortifications at a height of a 1000 metres. We made out the enemy and saw hordes of Prussians preparing to shoot us down, but we were too far from the ground to be really concerned about the possibility of being hit by bullets; however we could hear them humming like flies passing below our car [basket] as we continued on our way above the forest of Armanvilliers. At this moment I notice that

our balloon is imperceptibly deflating, the lower part of the fabric is folding and making a noise similar to flapping silk. I throw over a bag of ballast to stop us from drawing closer to the ground for I can see a Prussian encampment in the forest below.

One could see their defences ably deployed to avoid any possibility of a surprise attack, the tents forming two parallel lines at the end of which had been erected fascines and gabions. Further on we see a huge convoy of munitions covering the road. Behind the convoy are an incalculable number of small carts protected by white covers. Uhlans escort the vehicles. When they see the aerostat they halt, and we can make out, despite the distance which separates us, that they are throwing glances full of hatred and resentment in our direction.

After three hours of flight the *Jean-Bart* had travelled nearly seventy kilometres. With dusk approaching, the balloon had descended below 1000 feet, when Tissandier and his passengers heard voices calling from below. He recalled:

Peasants are running from all directions. We can hear their cries: "There are no Prussians here, come down, come down. You are at Nogent-sur-Seine, at Montpotier, come down". ... I decide to land. The car, in a manner of speaking, falls into the arms of our compatriots. They surround us full of emotion, welcoming us, eager for news from Paris.

Tissandier's report does not mention (not surprisingly) that his first landing in command of a balloon is heavy and one of his passengers is injured. Anxious to get well away from the enemy, Tissandier and his passengers were taken by carriage to Tours where they delivered the mail.

With five of the six trained balloonists gone, the authorities were faced with a grave problem. Once the balloons left Paris, they and their pilots were of no further use. It was strictly a one-way operation. There was no shortage of balloons coming off the production lines and there was no problem manufacturing hydrogen at the city's gas works. But they were running out of pilots. The remaining expert would be needed to supervise the training of new pilots as well as oversee the construction of balloons.

Finding the new trainee aeronauts was the critical problem. No one was available with any experience whatsoever and, with the city surrounded, there was no area suitable for flight training. The best they could give was rudimentary instruction in a balloon tethered to the ground.

Someone came up with the idea of conscripting a team of high-wire acrobats who were currently appearing at the Paris Hippodrome. The assumption was that at least they would have no fear of height and standing on small platforms. Against their will, the team was pressed into service. It was not surprising that the scheme failed on the very first flight. Seconds after lift-off the unwilling balloonist shinned down the dragline — a rope which at low level was trailed from the basket and dragged along the ground. The balloon — now considerably lightened — shot skywards and disappeared over the enemy lines. High wires were one thing, but to be at the mercy of the vagaries of the wind in an uncontrollable aerial contraption was a different matter!

Next the authorities turned to another source of one-way, one-flight pilots — a detachment of French naval seamen who were stationed in the capital. It was felt that they would at least have a good working knowledge of the changeable winds from their sailing-ship training. Furthermore, the sailors were disciplined, accepted danger as part of their job and, most important of all, were already subject to government orders. They turned out to be excellent balloon pilots. What they lacked in skill they made up in courage, and, in all, thirty-two seamen eventually took to the air.

The seamen were the first to come under fire from a

special anti-balloon gun built by Krupps to deter the escaping balloons. Even though it did not bring down or even damage a balloon, the gun certainly worried the French authorities. Late in November 1970, concerned about its potential, they decreed that all further flights should take place under cover of night.

One of the first to fly at night was Seaman Prince, who took off from the Gare d'Orléans on 30 November 1870, carrying urgent despatches. Before his ascent he had made a prophetic remark to his friends, "I shall make an immense voyage and people will talk about my flight."

The gallant sailor certainly made an immense flight. But it cost him his life. Caught in a strong westward wind, his balloon *Le Jacquard* was carried over the English Channel during the night. The next day it was sighted over the southern coast of Cornwall more than five hundred kilometres away, and heading for the Atlantic Ocean. The unfortunate Prince, seemingly unable to get the balloon down, coolly dropped his bundles of despatches near Land's End. Then the wind carried him rapidly out over the ocean towards America and oblivion.

It seems that Prince, like most of the one-way, one-shot airmen had only been given sufficient training to get his charge in the air. They were not really conversant with the delicate and tricky process of "valving off" (releasing) gas to make the balloon descend near a given point. They were probably told to wait until the balloon's natural leakage of gas brought them down. This would have allowed for a safer descent than having an inexperienced aeronaut "valve-off" too much gas, which could cause a balloon to drop too fast and kill its crew.

Night operations were responsible for the problem that faced an engineer named Rolier who gallantly volunteered to fly the balloon *Ville-d'Orléans*. He became uncertain of his position during the night and by daylight was appalled to find that the balloon was out over the North Sea. After a terrifying 15-hour 1280-kilometres flight, which included being shot at by a British gunboat, Rolier and his passenger came down in snow-covered central Norway. The men were carrying vital communiques informing Gambetta and his commanders of a plan to break the siege. However, by the time Rolier finally reached Tours the break out had taken place and had failed.

The unreliability of wind forecasting added to the balloonists' problems. Two balloons were blown hundreds of kilometres into Prussia, where their crews were taken prisoner, and three others landed in enemy-held territory to the east of Paris.

A second fatality occurred when Seaman Le Gloennec was severely injured in a crash-landing in the Loire Valley. He died eight days later in a hospital in Tours. Seven others were injured during heavy landings, being dashed into high trees and thrown from the wicker baskets.

With the balloon production lines at full strength, the factories were producing an average of four each week. There were insufficient Naval personnel to man them all, so a call went out for volunteers. Balloons were crewed by daring men from all walks of life, including a writer, a mechanic, a merchant, a tradesman and several gymnasts.

One Parisian, desperate to escape the siege, organised his own privately funded balloon which he named *La Bretagne* (Britain) after his intended destination. He chose the wrong day to leave, for the wind took him towards Germany, and he was captured near Verdun three hours later by the Prussians.

As the frigid winter of 1870 moved into the New Year of 1871 the situation in Paris was becoming desperate. Gambetta's army had not materialised and the city was starving. Food reserves were rapidly diminishing, and the city's famous restaurants were mostly closed. Maxims had only one meat dish left on the menu. Its rich and fashionable patrons were reduced to eating stewed rat! *"C'est la guerre,"* they exclaimed with the characteristic Gallic shrug.

In an effort to have some control over their eventual destination, a balloon was built with a hand-operated propeller attached to the basket. On 9 January 1871 it took off from Gare d'Orleans, commanded by Quarter-Master Richard with a crew of three sailors. By hand-turning the airscrew, the sweating seamen hoped to control the balloon's course. The scheme failed and the balloon came down way off-course near Reims eight hours later.

On 28 January 1871, the sixty-sixth and last balloon departed from Paris when Seaman Tristan rose high above the city in his balloon *Général Cambronne* and drifted slowly out over the Prussian lines. On board was only one despatch — the sad message that France had capitulated. The war was over. A month later Prussian troops paraded through Paris.

The Paris airlift had taught the French government a valuable lesson and the ballooning school, closed by Napoleon seventy years earlier, was reopened. During its five months of operation France's makeshift balloon service carried nine tonnes of mail and 155 pilots and passengers out of Paris, for the loss of only three airmen. It was a remarkable achievement, considering the haste with which it was all organised and that only six of those sixty-six long-forgotten heroes of France had previously piloted a balloon.

2

The Andree Expedition

In August 1930, the world's first perplexing aviation mystery was solved by the million-to-one chance discovery of three skeletons. Searching for water on barren White Island in the Arctic Ocean, the crew of a Norwegian sealing ship stumbled on the pitiful remains of the Andree Polar Balloon Expedition. Thirty-three years earlier, long before the advent of powered aircraft, three courageous Swedish explorers had set off in a balloon to reach the North Pole.

In the history of flight no men had placed their faith so implicitly in a balloon and the vagaries of the wind. Their leader, Salamon August Andree, was a noted aeronaut and engineer.

It is too easy, with hindsight, to ridicule Andree's plan as a crank's dream, doomed as it was to failure from its inception. For without such brave "fools" human beings might still be gazing in ignorant envy at soaring birds. The flight of the *Eagle* was surely fanned by the gentle breeze of folly, but her crew personified the spirit of every great aviation pioneer who came after them.

Salamon Andree was an intense and individualistic man with the tenacity of a terrier. He had only two interests in life: ballooning, and the unexplored Arctic regions. The flight was the culmination of twenty-one years of planning and training.

In 1876, at the age of twenty-two, Salamon Andree had worked his way over to America and taken a job at the Philadelphia World's Fair. There he had his first taste of ballooning and from that moment flying became his only aim in life. He studied under the world's leading balloonist, John Wise, who was amazed at Salamon's natural ability and utter lack of fear. "I am going to reach the North Pole in a balloon one day," Andree told his astonished teacher. "Ships have failed, sleds have failed, the best of men have failed. How else but by balloon can man reach there?"

For the next twenty years the young Swede worked towards this single goal. He joined an overland polar expedition, collected weather information, charted winds and tried to raise money for his dream. He persuaded the publishers of the Stockholm newspaper *Aftonbladet* to buy him a balloon "to promote public welfare and science". Andree named it *Svea* and made many pioneering flights, including several over the Baltic Sea.

In 1895 he publically announced his intention to fly to the North Pole as soon as he could obtain the backing. He presented his idea to the Swedish Academy of Science: "It is not only possible, but feasible, for a balloon to fly to the North Pole," he said. Andree told the august gathering, "The winds are steady and from Spitzbergen you can almost count on a northerly wind of two weeks duration. It will carry a balloon across the roof of the world and beyond to Alaska."

Andree went on to explain that the permanent daylight of the Arctic summer would keep temperature variation to a minimum. This would prevent gas expansion and thus the common problem of having to "valve-off" precious gas. He estimated that with the right balloon he could stay aloft for two to three weeks, which was more than enough for the journey. He also planned to attach sails to the gas bag to increase its speed.

To his delight the academy immediately endorsed his scheme and a year later his expedition team had arrived at Danes Island, Spitzbergen. His new balloon, the *Oren* ("Eagle") was manufactured by Europe's leading maker, Henri Lachambre. The bag, hand-sewn from 600 pieces of pongee silk, had a volume of seven million cubic litres which would lift an astonishing 30 000 kilograms. Andree estimated that this would be sufficient to carry a crew of three, their scientific instruments, survival equipment and food.

For six weeks the expedition waited for favourable weather and the rest of the world waited with anticipation for news. Because by mid August the weather had not improved, and the summer was ending, the balloon was deflated and the dejected team returned quietly to Sweden. Overnight, Andree the "hero" was labelled a fraud, and newspapers suggested the whole thing had been a publicity stunt. Opinion was that the whole idea had been a wild dream, and that no balloonist would ever set out for the Pole.

By the spring of 1897 Andree had recovered from his depression and was determined to mount a further expedition. He gained the financial backing of Alfred Nobel, the inventor of dynamite and famed scientist-philanthropist, who would later donate the Nobel prizes. King Oscar II of Sweden also contributed to the $36 000 needed to finance Andree's second attempt at the Pole.

Andree's crewmates had been carefully selected from a flood of volunteers. Knut Fraenkel, an engineer, had considerable Arctic experience. The husky 27-year-old was a mountaineer and fitness fanatic. The third member of the team, 24-year-old Nils Strindberg, was a university professor and expert photographer. He designed a special sealed camera to record their polar adventure.

By mid-June the Andree expedition was back at Danes Island preparing the balloon and its equipment. The *Eagle*'s basket, made of wood and wicker, was double-decked. The upper level, two metres in diameter, was an open observation deck containing a maze of scientific and navigation instruments. From this area the crew would manipulate the maze of ropes controlling ballast, gas valves, steering sails and drag lines. The enclosed lower compartment, which contained a mattress and reindeer-skin sleeping bag, was also designed to double as Strindberg's dark room. Andree planned to send back photos of their progress by the thirty-six homing pigeons the balloon carried.

The walls of both compartments were crammed with supplies such as food, clothing, guns, maps, cooking utensils, sledges and a collapsible boat. The expedition's large store of rations were described in a report to America's Smithsonian Institution:

> The Andree expedition has provisions for nine months. All the boxes in which the conserved food is kept were made of copper, as iron would have had a disastrous effect on the magnetic instruments carried by the expedition. To occupy as little space as possible they were made square. The food consisted of every kind of steaks, sausages, hams, fish, chickens, game, vegetables and fruit.
>
> The expedition is also furnished with a new kind of lozenges of concentrated lemon juice … it is expected they will absolutely prevent every attack of scurvy. Finally it is provided with twenty-five kilos of thin chocolate cakes mixed with pulverised pemmican. Nansen's expedition was also provided with this food, and it was found to be both nourishing and pleasant to taste.

Experts estimated that Andree and his crew could survive two years in the Arctic if they augmented their rations by hunting and fishing.

During the final week of preparation the balloon was assembled in a huge wooden hangar specially built close to the water. After the gas bag was fully inflated with hydrogen, the crew awaited the right winds for take-off. Andree then made a frightening discovery.

Despite the careful attention lavished during manufacture, the *Eagle* leaked! The rate was about thirty-five cubic metres a day — equivalent to about forty-five kilos of lifting power. Lachambre, and almost everyone connected with the venture, pleaded with Andree to postpone the attempt until the bag was rebuilt. Determined not to relive the humiliation of the previous year, the aeronaut responded, "I do not have the courage to postpone the flight again." He and his companions turned a deaf ear to all advice, insisting they could still reach the Pole even if the gas would not hold out long enough to take them on to Alaska. It seems they were already prepared to struggle out on foot. Possibly the trio had decided that death held no fear, so long as they were the first to raise the flag at the top of the world.

On 11 July 1897 conditions were right. A strong steady wind blew in the direction of their target 1600 kilometres to the north. Andree and his companions came ashore from their quarters on board the Swedish naval gunboat *Svensksund*. Aeronauts and groundcrew wept openly as they made their farewells. From the basket the trio made their final handshakes, then Andree shouted for the ropes to be cut.

"Oh hell," muttered a sailor as he nicked a finger while knifing through a hemp mooring rope. Andree, leaning out over the basket, exclaimed, "Hell — that is where we are going to ..."

The *Eagle* rose suddenly as the last rope was cut. The Captain of the *Svensksund*, Count Ehrensvard, called for three cheers from the groundcrew as the balloon caught the wind. The aeronauts called down, "Long live old Sweden."

The steering sails billowed as the breeze took hold and the *Eagle* drifted out over Virgo Bay. Shouts and cheers spurred the adventurers on their way. But the yelling stopped when the balloon was seen to dip erratically and head for the water. One of the three long trailing ropes used to control direction had snagged on a rock. Andree and his crew struggled to control the plunging basket. Actually touching the water, it bounced as the line broke free, and the *Eagle* rose once more into the northern sky.

The base party watched as it grew smaller and finally disappeared into the mists that shrouded the polar horizon.

The three balloonists were never seen alive again.

In the weeks that followed, people in the scattered communities of the remote reaches of Siberia, Canada and Alaska waited for a sighting of the balloon. As an anxious world watched the papers for news, reports from these furthermost outposts of civilisation recorded vague sightings from widely scattered and highly unlikely areas.

The crew of the barque *Ansgar* — two days out of Norway's North Cape — reported seeing a "downed balloon just above the water line", 1300 kilometres south of Andree's take-off point. It was later found to be a dead whale!

A housewife in a remote Swedish village insisted she had seen a balloon with one man on board drift over the trees near her home.

Crewmen on board the steamer *Kong Halfdan* claimed to have seen the *Eagle* pass so close to their ship that its drag lines were visible. They were just off the Norwegian coast!

As the weeks dragged into months, the world speculated on the whereabouts of Salamon Andree.

A Norwegian sealer, the *Alxen*, arrived back in port with the first tangible news since the *Eagle*'s disappearance. A carrier pigeon had alighted on the rigging. Its message, dated 13 July, read:

12.30 Midday. Latitude 82 deg. 2 Longitude
15 deg. 5. Good speed. All on board well.
This is the third pigeon post. Andree

Of the thirty-six carrier pigeons taken with the

expedition, this was the only one ever recovered. Two of the balloons sixteen message buoys were found later, one off the coast of Iceland in 1899 and the other on a Norwegian beach in 1900. Both had been dropped within hours of take-off and told only of their good progress and high spirits.

Over the next two years, three search parties set off to scour the Arctic wastes. A sentimental public believed that the missing heroes were probably isolated on the polar ice pack, still alive and awaiting rescue. They all returned with the same disappointing news that no evidence had been found as to the expedition's fate. The only information arrived from a wandering band of Eskimos who had seen strange birds flying about. They had caught and eaten one. A piece of paper attached to its leg had been thrown away!

In 1910 an old Canadian trapper was told by Eskimos in Hudsons Bay that the balloon had landed there and the crew had been killed in a fight. The report was never verified. The *Eagle*'s disappearance faded from the public's mind, just as it had faded from sight in the mists of Virgo Bay thirteen years earlier. Only in the forecastles of ships plying the northern seas was the mystery kept alive. Seamen told and retold the story. The mystery surrounding the fate of the Andree party became a part of Arctic legend.

Midway through the summer of 1930 the sealing ship *Bratvaag* nosed its way cautiously through the icebergs surrounding the north-east coast of Spitzbergen. On White Island the captain noticed a large herd of walrus and decided to land. A fresh blanket of snow hid most of the rocky surface. While some of the crew were engaged in the hunt, another party surveyed the small island. They were led by Dr Gunnar Horn, a geologist studying Arctic land masses. As the Norwegian scientist poked around collecting geological specimens, two seamen — Olaf Salen and Carl Tusvik — were searching for fresh water. They found a small fast-flowing stream, and as one bent low over the crystal clear water to take a drink, a dull metallic glint from between two rocks caught his eye. As an aluminium saucepan lid came to light, they called out to Horn to join them.

The scientist inspected their find, shaking his head in wonder. To his knowledge no one had visited the island for decades. Horn began poking around the rocks and dug into a large hillock of melting snow. His pick struck something solid. The trio dug into the snow and uncovered the prow of a small canvas boat.

The *Bratvaag*'s captain, Pedar Eliassen, joined the group and closely inspected the tiny boat. Scratching at a marking on the prow Eliassen gasped, "Andree"!

The words were quite clear: "Andree Polar Expedition 1897". They next uncovered a brass boat hook and, moments later, an ammunition box.

A thorough search of the area uncovered the lost expedition's main campsite. Andree's skeleton, the first found, showed that he had died crumpled over a sloping rock wall. Inside his rotted jersey jacket two diaries were visible. Although frozen solid, with careful handling they would later tell the full story of the party's gallant failure. A few metres away lay a rifle, ammunition, a large cache of supplies and a sled. This had been the site of their tent. Close to the cooking stove, beneath a frozen reindeer skin, lay the remains of Fraenkel. Strindberg's body was discovered some days later. He had obviously died earlier than his companions, for his body was found carefully buried beneath a cairn of rocks. Around his neck was a gold locket containing the still discernible picture of his fiancee, Anna Chaslier.

Among the frozen equipment the searchers discovered a pile of exposed photographic plates. Taken by Strindberg, they had lain unprocessed, entombed in ice, for thirty-three years. Photographic experts later described as a miracle the news that the plates had been successfully developed back in Sweden. They produced a graphic record of the final landing of the *Eagle* and the crew's tortuous wanderings over the Arctic icepack.

The remains of the three explorers and their equipment were taken home to Sweden. Andree's diaries were carefully analysed. They gave a moving account of the trio's terrible ordeal. Shortly after take-off, the *Eagle* had lost its main drag line and from then on the airmen had little steering ability. Nevertheless, for the first two days they had made good progress, covering 400 kilometres of their journey to the Pole. Andree's comments showed they were in high spirits and confident of reaching their objective. The diary did not, however, reflect the fears that Andree had privately expressed to his close friend and fellow explorer Fridtjof Nansen. Before the *Eagle* had left Kings Island, Andree had told his friend that he doubted if they would ever get back. Possibly he dreamed of reaching the Pole and sending out one final glorious message by pigeon post before vanishing forever.

Late during the second day their problems had started. Andree had not anticipated striking trouble so soon on the flight. The *Eagle* approached a bank of mist and cloud and, despite dropping ballast, they were unable to climb above it. The temperature dropped and the gas cooled, shrinking the bag. They steadily dropped down from 2500 feet to a scant forty feet above the ice.

More precious ballast had to be jettisoned to keep them in the air. Soon afterwards light freezing rain began falling. It formed a cap of ice over the huge silk gas bag, increasing the weight and pushing the *Eagle* back down towards the ice. They descended until the bottom of the basket skipped on the top of a small hummock of ice. Like a giant rubber ball, the *Eagle* bounced back to about 600 feet, then slowly started to settle again.

The process was repeated time after time as they skipped over the ice like a flat stone on water. Throughout the night and next day they desperately emptied the basket of every bit of non-essential weight, in an effort to stay airborne. The last of their sandbag ballast went over the side. Next to go was their supply of spare rope, anchors and message buoys. The gondola was scraping along the ice when Andree tossed their heavy tarpaulin overboard. The *Eagle* lifted a few feet, steadied, then to their relief climbed slowly to hold a steady thirty feet above the ragged surface.

By the evening of the third day the situation was again critical. In the twilight of the Arctic night the gondola was again scraping and bouncing its way over the ice. A check on their position, recorded in the diary, showed that the *Eagle* had drifted 185 kilometres since the last check, but this time due west — away from their target!

On the fourth and final day of their flight a slight increase in the temperature helped clear a little of the ice from the top of the bag and the gas expanded. The *Eagle* rose again and the basket ceased its bumping, bouncing ride. As the day passed they drifted east and regained their original path. Then the breeze turned into a northerly direction pushing them steadily on again to the Pole.

Obviously, the combination of ice and the leaking balloon meant there was now little hope that they would reach their destination. By late afternoon their luck ran out completely. Andree and his companions heard an ominous hissing sound above their heads. An inspection showed that the constant jolting had loosened an escape valve and gas was draining at a rapid rate. In desperation they tossed their medicine cabinet out. It helped for only a little while. The die was cast and with sinking hearts the airmen realised that their magnificent gamble was over. Following a long drag across the ice, which was obviously damaging the basket, Andree gave the order to open the rip valves and release the gas.

At 7.30 p.m. on 17 July the *Eagle* settled forever on to the Arctic wastes. They had covered 800 kilometres in sixty-five hours flight time. But the Pole was still a further 800 kilometres away. Once camped on the ice the men slept for the first time in four days, wrapped in canvas and sleeping bags. For the next week they remained fogbound at the landing site and prepared their equipment for the long trek back to civilisation.

Realising it was too late in the season for a rescue mission to reach them, Andree decided they must survive the winter. Beforehand they would head for a landmass on which they could build a safe camp. They had two alternatives. The best was a group of islands north-east of Spitzbergen, where there were known to be caches of food and supplies. The second choice was barren Franz Josef Land, which for some inexplicable reason, Andree decided upon. Possibly he believed that the drift of the ice pack would assist by taking them in the direction of Franz Josef Land, which lay 500 kilometres to the south-east.

Eleven days after they started on their glorious adventure, the three men began their return journey. Each was harnessed to a sledge loaded with 230 kilograms of supplies. They left behind the *Eagle*, her giant bag now just a flabby blob on the ice. Inside the deserted gondola, the leftover supplies were stowed away. These included a collection of absurd and useless items the men had taken with them: Russian and American silver and gold money, a white dress tie, a porcelain bowl, a heavy silver vase, a starched white shirt, a weighty collection of towels, newspapers and letters. There were even two tickets to the 1897 Stockholm Exposition which, though adding nothing to the weight the *Eagle* had carried, exemplified the mystery of parasite collection.

The airmen struggled south over the frozen ocean for

a week. The summer sun had partially melted the icepack and they had to contend with huge pools of slushy water and a web of cracks and crevices. They preserved their food supplies by hunting seagull and walrus. On the sixth day of back-breaking travel, Strindberg made an accurate sun-sighting and computed their position. The young Swede then made the shattering announcement that they had actually only progressed a few kilometres towards their destination. During their journey southwards, the huge floating ice pack had been drifting northwards at an almost identical speed! They were on a giant Arctic treadmill.

Thus they concluded that, unless they could increase speed, they would "walk on the spot" until they dropped. The long Arctic night was fast approaching. They lightened their loads and cut down their sleeping and eating stops to a minimum. Constantly they changed their direction to overcome the drifting of the fickle ice floe. Slowly they laboured southwards.

By September they were heading south-west towards Spitzbergen. Frostbitten, with their feet cut and bodies bruised from slips and falls on the ice, they finally reached open water. They stowed the sledges and gear in the collapsible canvas boat and continued by sea. For a week they alternated between open water and ice packs. They had changed direction and were headed for Seven Islands but, with a change in the currents, watched in anguish as their objective faded away.

A few days later, sighting White Island on the far horizon, they inched towards it on foot and by boat, battling against the drifting ice pack. On the way they killed a seal and a polar bear. Andree called these bears "the wandering meat shops of the Arctic". After butchering it, they stored the meat for later. The seal they ate immediately, holding a strange polar feast to celebrate their sighting of White Island. The remains of a diary found on Strindberg's body recorded the menu, "seal steaks, seal liver, seal brains, seal kidneys, butter, Swedish rye bread, gateaux aux raisin, with raspberry sauce and port wine for dessert". The port wine, vintage 1836, had been presented to them by King Oscar to be drunk to celebrate their arrival over the Pole. They could think of no better occasion to open the bottle than that evening. Only a few kilometres away stood land. In addition they had plenty of supplies and now a large stock of polar bear meat. Once on the island, they had only to make camp until the winter ice firmed, then sled the 75 kilometres to the inhabited North East Land.

The trio toasted the King, broke out a Swedish flag, and standing proudly to attention sang their national anthem at the top of their lungs.

Their exhilaration turned to terror early next morning when the ice floe on which they were camped began to break up. A huge crack opened up right through their camp and part of their supplies fell into the sea. They managed to salvage most of the equipment.

During the final two weeks of tortuous travel to reach the island, harnessed to their sleds and dragging the canvas boat, the three men had been slowed by a strange illness. They suffered stomach cramps, diarrhoea and were so severely weakened that they were often too exhausted to cook the polar bear meat they ate each night. Pains in their joints and muscles became so excruciating that the men began taking morphine and opium. This proved to be the final stage of their trek. Probably two of the sleds were dumped at this time. For when they finally reached the rocky shore of White Island on 6 October their supplies were lashed to one sled and the canvas boat.

Within a few hours of their reaching safety, Strindberg collapsed and died. His distraught companions believed the young photographer had suffered a heart attack.

Andree and Fraenkel lived on a further two weeks

but, from the appearance of the campsite when uncovered thirty-three years later, were too ill to do little more than rest in their tent. Horn and his party found equipment strewn everywhere, and much of it still lashed to the sledge. No attempt had been made to use loose rock, which littered the area, to build a proper wall for shelter against the bitter wind.

The final entries in Andree's diaries were indecipherable and the last recognisable date was 17 October. Some time shortly after the Swede made the final agonised scrawl, he staggered out of the tent and died propped against a rock. Fraenkel met his end resting in a sleeping bag.

Little more than three months after the *Eagle* had left Virgo Bay, the great feat of endurance was over.

Following the discovery of the remains of the expedition in 1930 many theories were advanced as to why they had died. From the abundance of supplies at the camp, it was obvious they had not starved. Little attention was paid to Andree's brief notes reporting their illness, as it was concluded that the men had suffered ailments generally associated with cold and exposure. Suggestions ranged from suicide, or death from extreme cold, to the most popular — that Andree and Fraenkel had suffocated when their tiny stove consumed the oxygen in their tent. Asphyxiation in similar circumstances had caused the death of several earlier polar explorers.

Just before the outbreak of World War II a Danish scientist, Dr Ernst Adam Tryde, became interested in the mystery surrounding the death of Andree and his companions. He studied every available shred of evidence. As a former doctor he knew that the symptoms that Andree had written in his diary seemed to be those of a severe cold and he was also aware that such an ailment did not exist above the Polar Circle.

It was not until 1948 that he found an answer while

studying a report concerning a strange disease that had broken out among a tribe of Eskimos. It had eventually been diagnosed as trichinosis. This is a severe illness caused by eating walrus and bear meat contaminated with the trichina bacteria. The symptoms described were exactly the same as reported in Andree's diary, "burning eyes, running noses, diarrhoea, cramps and pains, and severe exhaustion". Tryde devoted all his spare time to a private study of the disease. Then he discovered that a group of German soldiers on Franz Joseph Land had been stricken with these symptoms after eating improperly cooked bear meat!

These clues all fell into place but the evidence was still circumstantial. In 1949 Tryde visited the small museum that had been built at Granna — Andree's birthplace — to house the relics of the expedition. Among the equipment brought back to Sweden by the *Bratvaag* had been the explorer's sleeping bag. During the nightmare on the ice, Andree had patched it with a part of the skin of the polar bear they had shot and eaten. Tryde found tiny particles of dried meat still attached to the bearskin patches.

His diagnosis was irrefutably confirmed a few days later when the bacteriological laboratory of the Copenhagen Veterinary School positively identified trichina capsules which were still in the 52 year-old scraps of meat.

Andree and his companions had not been defeated by the savage Arctic geography. They would almost certainly have survived but for the tiny bacteria in the improperly cooked meat that they had eaten to conserve their tinned rations. The irony was that they already had sufficient food on their sledges to have survived for many weeks, maybe even long enough to have reached North East Land.

In 1930 Sweden paid a final tribute to its three brave

sons. At a state funeral King Gustav V spoke these words:

> In the name of the Swedish nation I greet the dust of the Polar explorers who, more than three decades ago, left their native land to find answers to questions of unparalleled difficulty. A country's hope to honour them in their lifetime after a successful journey was disappointed. We must submit to its tragic result. All that is left us is to express our warm thanks to them for their self-sacrifices in the service of science. Peace be to their memory.

As late as 1953 the ramshackle walls of Salamon Andree's balloon hangar still stood on the shores of barren Danes Island. It was a stark symbol that personified the courage, daring and futility of aviation's most magnificent gamblers.

3
Alberto Santos-Dumont

It was a warm and windless Paris morning in the early summer of 1901. The sun was high. It was a perfect day to promenade. As usual the Champs Elysees was crowded. Elegant women, twirling their parasols, window-shopped from the arms of their top-hatted escorts. There was hardly an empty seat in the boulevard's famed street cafes.

The endless parade of hansom cabs climbed slowly up the hill towards the Arc de Triomphe, their clattering hoof-beats disturbed only by the occasional bellow of a newfangled automobile. At their pavement tables Parisians chatted, flirted, read the papers and watched the world pass by. It was a scene repeated day after day, year after year. But on this morning something new arrived, a foretaste of their city of the future.

At first a gentle buzzing some way off, the insistent sound then grew slowly but steadily louder. Heads popped up above the morning paper, aperitifs were lowered in mid-sip, conversations were cut short, window-shoppers dragged their eyes from the latest Paris mode, and ten thousand heads turned inquiringly towards the Place de la Concorde.

There, floating slowly up the boulevard, almost brushing the tops of the chestnut trees, was a cigar-shaped balloon. Suspended beneath it by a forest of wires dangled a long, fragile metal framework. Sitting near the front, a diminutive figure operated the controls attached to the machine's tiny petrol engine. A slowly rotating propeller and sail-like rudder brought up the rear.

The crowds enjoying the Champs Elysees that morning had their first sight of a powered air machine. For bemused French citizens it was merely the latest escapade of the "Toast of Paris" — Brazilian born Alberto Santos-Dumont, the father of European aviation.

The son of a wealthy Brazilian coffee planter, Santos Dumont epitomised "those magnificent men". Dumont's pioneering flying machines spanned a ten-year period, starting with the world's first powered airships and culminating, in 1906, with Europe's first successful aeroplane.

As a child, Santos-Dumont had avidly read the futuristic stories of Jules Verne. His inquisitive mind was channelled towards things mechanical and by the age of ten his favourite pastime was driving the engines on the railway that circled and served his father's huge plantation.

He was fifteen years old when he first came into contact with aviation. While on a visit to Sao Paolo he witnessed a balloon ascent. Completely entranced by the sight of the huge gas-filled sphere floating lazily over the city, he begged for a flight. Fearing for Alberto's safety, his father refused permission. But the die was cast. The young Brazilian started reading every book and article he could find on aviation. Recalling those early days, when he first dreamed of flight, Santos-Dumont wrote:

> In the long sun-bathed Brazilian afternoons I would lie in the shade of the verandah and gaze into the fair sky of Brazil where birds fly so high and soar with such ease on their great outstretched wings, where the clouds mount so gaily in the pure light of day, and you have only to raise your eyes to fall in love with space and freedom. So, musing on the exploration of the vast aerial ocean, I, too, devised air-ships and flying machines in my imagination.

Three years passed before the young Brazilian had another chance to fly. He had been sent to Paris to complete his schooling and there he met a group of French balloonists who took him for a flight. Afterwards he wrote a vivid description of the great moment:

> At 11 a.m. all was ready. The basket rocked prettily beneath the balloon, which a mild fresh breeze was caressing. Impatient to be off I stood in my corner of the narrow wicker basket with a bag of ballast in my hand. In the other corner M. Machuron gave the word: "Let go all!".
>
> Suddenly the wind ceased. The air seemed motionless around us. We were off, going at the speed of the air current in which we now lived and moved. Indeed, for us there was no more wind; and this is the first great fact of all in spherical ballooning. Infinitely gentle is this unfelt movement forward and upward. The illusion is complete: it seems not to be the balloon that moves, but the earth that sinks down and away.

Over the following twelve months Santos-Dumont made a number of exciting flights. He ordered his own balloon and quickly mastered the intricacies of handling the lighter-than-air craft. In his new balloon he experienced the first of many mishaps that would punctuate his flying career. He made an ascent at the Mediterranean resort of Nice, and after floating majestically over the millionaire's playground he drifted inland and decided it was time to come down. Valving-off gas from the huge bag, the aeronaut descended slowly, only to find a strong breeze carrying him towards a stand of trees. He wrote:

> I was dragged through the small trees and yielding shrubbery, my face a mass of cuts and bruises, my clothes torn from my back, in pain and strain, fearing the worst, and able to do nothing to save myself. Just as I had given myself up for lost the guide rope wound itself round a tree and held. I was precipitated from the basket and fell unconscious. When I came to I had to walk some distance until

I met some peasants. They helped me back to Nice, where I went to bed, and had the doctor sew me up.

Reading the young Brazilian's account of the crash-landing it is easy to understand why he quickly turned his attention to airships. He had realised that, though a delightful pastime, ballooning did little for man's dream of controlled flight.

Within months he designed and built a small airship. It comprised a sausage-shaped balloon from which was suspended a similar to ones used on conventional balloons basket. To this Santos-Dumont attached a petrol engine taken from his De Dion motor tricycle which was modified to drive a small propeller.

He chose the Paris Zoological Gardens as the site for his first flight. On 18 September 1898 *Number One*, as he called the airship, was ready. On the advice of ballooning experts he took off downwind. He should not have listened: within seconds, trees again loomed large in the young Brazilian's life. Desperately trying to out-climb a line of them, *Number One*'s maiden flight ended in the treetops. Two days later he tried again, this time into the wind. With its tiny engine puttering away, the airship made a controlled climb to a height of 1500 feet.

To descend, Alberto had to release gas from the long thin balloon, and in doing so it lost its shape and rigidity. It folded in the middle and fell rapidly towards a large field where some boys were flying kites. The alarmed Brazilian yelled at them to catch hold of the long handling rope that dangled below, and run into wind.

The boys seemed to realise the desperate situation, probably because of their understanding of kites, and quickly caught the line and towed the falling airship into the wind. It then reacted like a giant kite and stopping descending, which probably saved Santos-Dumont's life. They then gently pulled *Number One* back to earth.

Scared by his narrow escape, yet undeterred, Santos-

Dumont decided to fly at lower altitudes until he had perfected his design. Over the next five years he built a succession of airships. Each was an improvement in design and added to his flying experience. However, with every flight and every new machine the Brazilian faced the element of risk inherent in those try-it-and-see days of flying. More often than not, trees destroyed his fragile contraptions and forced him to build a new model.

Dirigible *Number 2* ended as a tangle of wreckage in a large tree. *Number 3* lost its rudder and was severely damaged. *Number 4* incorporated a narrow keel suspended beneath the balloon which enabled Santos-Dumont to adjust the fore and aft trim of the balloon. If it flew nose-heavy, for instance, he could simply move his pilot's position back towards the tail end. To save weight he used a bicycle saddle as his pilot's seat!

Throughout the summer of 1900 Santos Dumont flew *Number 4* almost daily. Its success encouraged him to modify it into an even larger and more powerful model — *Number 5*. Occasionally he still had tree-trouble and on one occasion was found sitting in the branches, refusing to come down until lunch was sent up to him. Only after cold chicken and champagne did the aeronaut decide it was time to untangle his crippled airship.

The daring young man captured the imagination of France. In the glittering night spots of Paris talk often centred on the dashing Brazilian and his exploits. A lover of music, Santos-Dumont was often seen at the theatre and concerts. He was easily recognised by his diminutive stature. Only 1.5 metres tall, he never let his weight exceed fifty kilograms. "An aeronaut cannot afford to be very heavy," he explained to admirers.

Many of the dazzling array of royalty, titled families, and the rich and influential people who inhabited or regularly visited Paris at the turn of the century befriended the dapper young airman. He rapidly became one of the city's personalities and his company was eagerly sought.

In 1900 Henri Deutsch de la Meurthe, a wealthy oil magnate, offered a huge prize of 125 000 francs for the first aeronaut to fly around the Eiffel Tower. Deutsch also stipulated that the flight must commence and end at St Cloud some five kilometres away. By today's standard a flight of less than eleven kilometres sounds laughable. However, in 1900 the difficulty lay not merely in the distance but in steering an air machine in a set direction. Santos-Dumont accepted the challenge.

First he decided to improve the steering system of *Number 5*. It was too vague for the Deutsch flight. He redesigned the system and on 13 July 1901 decided to test its manoeuvrability by making a series of circuits around Longchamps race course. A report published by America's Smithsonian Institution described the pre-dawn journey through the empty Paris streets.

> As early as 3 o'clock in the morning a curious procession emerged from a hillside enclosure on the bank of the Seine and proceeded toward the silent race course of Longchamps across the river. Besides several correspondents, this party was composed mostly of young Parisians, who slowly steered their automobiles while they bent their heads back and looked upward.
>
> Following them, a few yards in the air, there floated a strange mysterious shape, dim and yellowish against the hazy dawn. Several men on foot guided the aerial contrivance by ropes which they clung to jealously. Their care was natural, for they held in leash the first flying machine; and by "fly- ing machine" is meant one that has really flown, and which deserves its name literally, being far, far removed from the monotony of the many failures gone before.

It is obvious that reporter Eugene P. Lyle Jr considered Santos Dumont's airship the first worthy of being called a flying machine. Though historians will argue that earlier machines of Frenchmen Giffard, Renard and Krebbs, and Germany's Heinlein, were to a degree successful, there is little doubt that Santos Dumont's machine was the first to execute precisely controlled flight. He was thus later to be called "the truest and greatest pioneer of air navigation".

Lyle went on to describe the events of this memorable July morning:

At the race track the balloon was pulled down till the framework rested on the ground. A young man, 25 years of age, went hurrying about the airship, tinkering at it here and there till the very last moment, while his comrades of the Automobile and Aero clubs looked on respectfully and let him have his way. He was a very little man in shirt sleeves and a high collar, with an almost effeminate speech, and very amiable, but he seemed to know pretty well what he was about.

When he had examined the tube which connects the cigar-shaped gasoline tank with the motor, he wrapped a strap around the wheel of the motor, pulled the strap off again with a sharp jerk, and thus set the motor going. Involuntarily the spectators jumped back, for the gasoline engine with its four cylinders starts with a crashing explosion so closely followed by others that the deafening bursting combustion is almost continuous; yet through the framework there is scarcely any vibration at all, only a slight quivering.

Before climbing into his basket, the slender little aeronaut took a final look at the sky. He had spent the last two nights near his balloon patiently waiting for favourable weather. He seemed satisfied now, and climbed into his tiny car, which is just a narrow crating of willow fixed into the forward nose of the triangular framework. The guide rope slackened and the balloon lifted slowly from the ground. He gave a signal and the rope was released. The balloon bounded into the calm air. Those below bending back their necks saw the two big fans, the screw of the vessel begin to turn.

Santos-Dumont made history that morning. At his command *Number 5* neatly circled the race track and on reaching the starting point descended with the pilot's guidance to a gentle landing. Dumont's normally pink face was aflame with excitement. His dark eyes glistened with joy. At long last he had total control of his airship. He didn't even have to resort to ballast and gas to climb and descend. To prove the point he took off again and repeated the manoeuvre, not once but five times. By the next day his name would echo around Europe. Man had achieved controlled flight.

Santos-Dumont decided to make an immediate attempt on Deutsch's Grand Prix. By mid-morning he had left the Aero Club Park at St Cloud and was skimming the city towards the Eiffel Tower. The five kilometres took only ten minutes. He rounded the huge steel structure waving cheerily to hundreds of spellbound spectators who, unaware of his flight, had been quietly viewing the city from the Tower's eagle-perch look-outs.

He was well on his way home when one of the gear cords to the rudder broke. Unable to steer, he was forced to make an unscheduled landing in the Trocadero Gardens. He quickly repaired the break and continued the flight back to St Cloud. But as one of the rules of the contest was that the machine was not to touch the ground during the flight, the Brazilian did not qualify for the 125 000 francs.

The next day — the unlucky thirteenth — he made another attempt. All Paris was there to watch. A special committee had now been set up, whose members included Henry Deutsch himself and Prince Roland Bonaparte.

Number 5 was airborne at 6.41 a.m. With only thirty minutes allowed by the rules, Alberto must return by 7.11 a.m. Conditions were far from perfect with a gusty wind stiffening the fluttering flags. He rounded the Tower in thirteen minutes and was seen to be heading back to St Cloud. But it was obvious that the machine was struggling against the headwind, and it arrived back over the park eleven minutes too late. Before

Santos Dumont could land, the riding wind blew him back over the river. Twice he struggled back over the landing area only to be pushed away by the wind. Quite suddenly the engine stopped in flight. The tiny airship disappeared with the wind over the Bois de Boulogne and was last seen heading for the inevitable trees. Lyle described what happened next:

> A dozen friends sprung to their automobiles and raced away in that direction. Each one dreaded finding Santos-Dumont probably mangled and lifeless. They found him on his feet, with his hands in his pockets looking reflectively up at his airship among the top branches of some chestnut trees in the grounds of Baron Edmund de Rothschild. "I should like to have a glass of beer," he announced, which called forth a nervous laugh of relief.

The house next to the Baron was owned by His Royal Highness the Comte d'Eu. The Comtesse had watched the flight and the subsequent crash from an upper window. Within a matter of minutes a huge hamper of refreshments and champagne arrived on the scene. The airman and his friends soon disposed of it and Alberto hurried over to thank the Comtesse. He found that she was a compatriot, formerly Princess Isabel, daughter of Dom Pedro of Brazil. Before the aeronaut left to recover his machine, the Comtesse gave him a small charm to protect him from accidents. With his track record it was probably a good idea. He had already survived so many mishaps, the odds were lengthening with every flight that he would continue to survive.

Two weeks later he tried again. On this occasion he rounded the Tower in a mere nine minutes. With twenty-one left for the return flight he must surely make it. Santos-Dumont was passing over high buildings when the balloon suddenly lost buoyancy and began to fold. The Brazilian tried to blow air into the envelope with specially constructed pumps driven off the engine, but they failed to help. He was unable to keep the cigar-shaped bag rigid and it doubled on itself like a pocket knife. The propeller began cutting through the wires suspending the lower framework. The petrified airman stopped the engine as the machine jolted against the edge of a hotel roof. He clung for his life as it was dragged across the rooftops before the wooden framework finally came to a stop jammed in a space between two buildings ... six storeys up!

High above the courtyard of the Trocadero Restaurant, Santos-Dumont hung on grimly until firemen lowered a rope from the roof of the adjacent hotel and pulled him to safety. Miraculously the airman was unmarked. When asked by friends what he would do next, the determined young man replied simply, "Why, begin again, of course. One has to have patience."

Patience paid off on 19 October 1901 when the indomitable young Brazilian took off again for the Eiffel Tower in his new design, *Number 6*. He nearly didn't make it when on the return journey the sixty horsepower motor stopped in mid-air. Alberto clambered back along the framework and was able to restart it. With the huge four-metre propeller again turning at 200 revolutions per minute, he was back over St Cloud in twenty-nine minutes and thirty-one seconds. He made it by less than half a minute.

Santos Dumont, in a typically grand gesture, split Duetsch's prize money (about $100 000 by today's values) between his mechanics and deserving charities. He was already wealthy enough for his own needs.

The Brazilian became world-famous. His flight was the sensation of Europe. Empress Eugenie, widow of Napolean Ill, had not attended a social event in the thirty years since the Emperor's death. Yet early in 1902 she came out of seclusion to visit Santos-Dumont at his new airship hangar at Monaco. Such was his standing in France following the Eiffel Tower flight.

Santos-Dumont built another eight airships. All of

France, and especially Paris, followed the adventures of their adopted "son". He became the first airship pilot to "ditch" in the sea when he made a forced landing in Monaco Bay in 1902. A year later he was invited to manoeuvre his new *Number 9* over Longchamps during the military parade at the official celebrations of France's Bastille Day. Was this the world's first aerial flypast?

While he was trying out *Number 9*, Santos-Dumont met and fell in love with a beautiful Cuban girl, Aida de Acosta. His love must have been deep indeed for he taught her to fly his new machine. He followed her flight from Neuilly to Bagatelle when on 29 June 1903 the Cuban girl became the first woman in the world to pilot an airship. It is generally thought that Aida was the one woman in Santos-Dumont's life he would have married. She had everything that appealed to him: beauty, emotion, intelligence and, above all, she loved flying. But somewhere along the line it went wrong. Aida eventually married an American lawyer. Possibly no woman could compete with his all-embracing passion for flight, not even airwoman Aida.

For the next two years Santos-Dumont and his *Number 9* became part of the scene of Paris. He used the tiny airship like a car to travel around the city. He would drift along the Champs Elysees to his favourite restaurant, tie the airship to a convenient lamp-post, and join his adoring friends for a drink. He would fly from St Cloud to his city house, park *Number 9* in the street while he ate breakfast, then return to the airfield. Parisians could always tell when he was visiting his club by the airship tied up outside.

With the news of the Wright brothers' successful flight of a heavier-than-air machine in December 1903, the Brazilian began to consider the new generation of aircraft. Though still building new airships during

1904, he was already working on rough designs for his first aircraft.

He had no set working hours, but amazed his friends with his ability to work continually over long periods, almost without sleep, and at a hectic pace, once he had a project clearly in mind. By 1906 his first aircraft was ready for testing. This was remarkable progress, bearing in mind that no one outside America had yet designed or built a successful aircraft and Santos-Dumont had worked in virtual isolation. Starting from scratch, in two years he had not only designed but also built what was to become Europe's first practical aeroplane.

The craft, a huge tail-first pusher biplane, he called *Number 14 Bis*. The strange name evolved when he made the first flight tests with the aeroplane suspended beneath his final airship *Number 14*. The tests were successful and he was ready for his first attempt at powered flight.

On 13 September 1906 he took Europe into a new era when *14 Bis* made a nine-metre hop witnessed by several members of the French Aero Club. Realising that the twenty-four horsepower Antoinette engine was too puny for the job, Santos-Dumont replaced it with a fifty-horsepower model.It did the trick and the following month he won the Coupe Archdeacon for a flight of 219 metres, during which he accomplished the four phases of flight: rolling, take-off, flight and landing — all phases controlled by the pilot.

Three weeks later he covered a distance of 220 metres in twenty-one seconds to establish the first officially recognised record for height, speed and distance. It was, however, meaningless, as the Wright brothers had already made flights of over forty kilometres and been airborne for thirty-eight minutes. But because their flights had been made in America and were not properly witnessed, they had not been formally recognised.

In 1907 he built another biplane, *Number 15*, which

failed to fly. He then turned his attention to a monoplane design. His biplanes had been big lumbering beasts: *Number 15*, for example, had needed a 100-horsepower engine.

He changed the total concept with his first monoplane, *Number 19*. Almost toy-like, it had a wingspan of only five metres and a two-cylinder 20-horsepower engine. The pilot sat in a seat suspended beneath the wings and between the landing wheels. His diminutive size was now an absolute necessity if he hoped to get the tiny aircraft into the air. He made only three flights in *Number 19*, the longest being 200 metres. After it was damaged during the third flight at Buc in November 1907, Santos-Dumont abandoned the idea.

By the end of 1908 a number of European airmen were on the scene. Farman, Voisin and Blériot were all building aircraft, and flights of close to an hour had been achieved. In England, American-born Cody had just made the nation's first flight of twenty-seven seconds!

In March 1909, after eighteen months of aviation obscurity, Santos-Dumont again made headlines when he introduced the world to a new concept in aircraft. He had revamped his *Number 19* monoplane and called it *Demoiselle* (Dragonfly).

It was an apt name indeed. The tiny machine had a 5.5 metre wingspan and an ability to reach 100 kph — a dazzling performance by 1909 standards. It was built around a framework manufactured from three bamboo poles. The pilot sat on a sheet of canvas stretched between two of them beneath the wing — a sort of air-borne deck chair. It was powered by a two cylinder Daraq engine that developed a surprising thirty-five horsepower.

The *Demoiselle* was to be the Brazilian's crowning design success. One of his earliest flights covered eight kilometres in five minutes, the fastest anyone had travelled through the air.

A few days later he again made the headlines when he became the world's first missing aircraft. He had taken off from St Cyr on a cloudy afternoon and two hours later had not returned. His apprehensive mechanic finally phoned the authorities. The newspaper *Le Matin* sent a reporter to the scene. Surely "le petit Santos had taken a fall . . . perhaps a fatal one", he wrote. Early next morning word was received from the Chateau d'Aion. The *Demoiselle* had landed on the lawn after completing a 20-kilometre flight in 16 minutes. Alberto, the caller continued, was still sleeping soundly, an overnight guest of Comte de Galard.

His new design was the sensation of the Paris Aviation Exhibition of October 1909. Its generous designer announced that he would not take out a patent on the design and made plans available to anyone who wished to build one. Thus the *Demoiselle* became not only the forerunner of the light aircraft loved by private pilots of future aviation eras, but also the world's first home-built aircraft.

Only a year later its fame had spread as far as the United States, where a Demoiselle was flown by France's Roland Garros — later to become aviation's first fighter ace during World War I. It became the favourite of the crowds at the 1910 Aeronautical Tournament held at Belmont Park on New York's Long Island. The nippy monoplane was described by one American as "an unwitting little comedian lending a touch of drollery to a scientific exhibition that was always dead serious and sometimes a little grim".

As it buzzed above the huge crowd, they roared their approval, urging its daring pilot along. They waggishly nicknamed it the "Infuriated Grasshopper". Others referring to its strange fuselage design called it "The Birdcage Parasol".

Santos-Dumont decided to equip the tiny aircraft with a new and more powerful engine but came to grief on the first test flight. Unaccustomed to the increased speed, he overshot his landing run, and trying to bring the *Demoiselle* to a stop short of the airfield fence, he seized the wheels with his hands. It was useless, and the aircraft ended nose down in the palings, with a broken propeller and damaged wings. He was unhurt. Two weeks later, a gust of wind brought the aircraft down on a wing. Again no injuries.

On 4 January 1910 he had his third accident in the new monoplane. The earlier accidents had been relatively minor but this one was a fearful experience. The aircraft was flying at about 150 feet when a wing bracing-wire gave way. The wing folded and the *Demoiselle* plunged earthwards. The aircraft tumbled end over end before hitting the ground.

Alarmed bystanders rushed over to the wreckage. Surely "le petit Santos" had finally gambled once too often. No man could survive such a crash!

Yet again the fates had smiled on the indefatigable Brazilian. He was badly shaken and bruised all over but there was no serious injury. Santos-Dumont later explained that, as the aircraft tumbled down, the maze of bracing and control wires surrounding his seat prevented him from being thrown out. This undoubtedly saved his life. Furthermore, when the *Demoiselle* struck the ground the impact was absorbed by a wing which progressively crumpled before the seat area hit.

Following the accident, Santos-Dumont retired from flying. Over the previous year his health had deteriorated from the early stages of a mystery illness which much later in his life was eventually diagnosed as multiple sclerosis.

During the years leading to the First World War he became a respected consultant in technical and political matters relating to civil and military aviation. He was still to be seen around town dining occasionally at Maxims, or conversing animatedly with friends at his favourite cafe, the Restaurante de La Grande Cascate. He coached two of France's leading pilots, Garros and Audemars, in the finer points of handling the Demoiselles they had constructed, but there is no evidence that he ever again flew publicly.

It was rumoured that before war broke out he made one short flight in private in his beloved monoplane from the Hippodrome Golf Club in Madrid. Possibly he found the physical limitations of his disease had finally put an end to his hopes of ever resuming a flying career.

Not long afterwards the once-extroverted Brazilian sank into a dark mood of melancholy and closeted himself in a house he had built in Petropolis. This house, which he had earlier named "The Enchanted House", became his spiritual refuge. He cut the last ties with Paris high society, and abandoned his friends and all the honours that had been paid to him. Now that he had lost the ability to fly, depression and nostalgia turned him into a recluse.

His depression deepened during the war when he saw aircraft turned into weapons of destruction. An indisputable opponent of war, he naively made a number of anguished appeals against the use of aircraft as weapons. His world was one of anguish and remorse, the revolt of the creator against his once-loved creature, the aeroplane. The thought of having helped conceive such a devastating weapon was more than the emotional South American could bear. He would weep and beat his breast in a gesture of utter despair.

For much of his later life he lived in Brazil. It was a lonely, obscure and unloved old age. He made one pitiful grab at some sort of happiness when in 1926 he turned up at the office of his old friend and fellow flyer, Gabriel Voisin. In an article written thirty years later, following Santos-Dumont's death, Voisin recalled the sad meeting:

My old friend dropped in my office at lssy-Les- Molineaux.

Alberto was disturbed and very shy then. However, his disturbance became understandable when, in the middle of a timid speech, he asked for my daughter's hand. How could I explain to him that it was not possible? Janine was then only seventeen, and my friend was over fifty.

Alberto Santos-Dumont's glorious age of aviation spanned barely thirteen years. Unlike most of his contemporaries it was not eclipsed by a flyer's death in the faltering machines he gave so much to develop. During his last despairing and disease-ridden years, he might have wished his end had come in the skies of France — to have gone out in a blaze of glory, still "le petit Santos", the darling of Paris. Instead, he died in Brazil on 23 July 1932, with his beloved homeland in the midst of civil war. Early that morning, war planes flew over the ageing airman's house near Sao Paolo. It was more than he could stand. Alberto went into the bathroom and hanged himself with his necktie.

France's great aviation pioneer Louis Blériot recalled those heady, never-to-be-forgotten early days when all France had lain at Alberto Santos-Dumont's feet and he was their hero: the father of European aviation. Paying tribute to the brilliant Brazilian, Blériot wrote: "You are the pathfinder. We who come after merely follow."

4

Twelve seconds over Kill Devil Hill

The bright silver dollar shimmered as it spun, briefly catching the rays of the weak winter sun. As it dropped to the sands two brothers rushed to see which side lay up. A simple toss of a coin was to determine which of them would go down in history as humankind's first real pilot.

Bound by a bond so close that they had sworn never to marry, brothers Orville and Wilbur Wright could also be gambling their lives on that glittering coin. But at that breathless moment of anticipation, fear did not enter their minds. Who was to make the first attempt? The young American inventors peered at the upturned silver face.

Fate often deals a strange hand. It did on that cold December day in 1903 on Kill Devil Hill at Kittyhawk, North Carolina. For though Wilbur won the toss, his younger brother Orville was to gain the honour.

Bishop Milton Wright had raised his family in the traditional Presbyterian virtues of honesty, tenacity and hard work. He also kindled and encouraged his sons' interest in the mysteries of flight. Ever since human beings developed the intelligence and skills to communicate, to reason and to build, they had tried to solve the mystery of flight. The birds flew as easily as humans walked. Why should humans not emulate the birds?

Small shreds of evidence concerning ancient history's

would-be airmen had survived the centuries. Artists, scribes or whispered legends had recorded their efforts. Stories from long ago, told around some flickering campfire, or in a castle full of knights, had passed from generation to generation, embroidered by time until truth and embroidery were indistinguishable.

Birds featured in many of the earliest tales of flying that excited the young Orville and Wilbur in their Dayton, Ohio home. King Kai Kawus of ancient Persia was said to have harnessed eagles to his throne to carry him through the air. And legendary aviators Daedalus and Icarus made wings of bird feathers and wax to escape the evil King Minos of Crete. But Icarus flew too close to the sun and crashed in a flurry of melted wax and unstuck feathers.

Human beings were still trying to fly like birds in the sixteenth century when John Damien jumped from the walls of Stirling Castle on what was to be a flight from Scotland to France. Somehow he survived the sickening crash, blaming his failure on the use of chicken feathers rather than those of eagles.

But here and there the occasional brilliant mind realised that flight involved something more than strapping on a facsimile bird wing and jumping off a tower. Clearly, Leonardo da Vinci had realised this when he designed the first helicopter. A rubber-band toy, given four hundred years later to the young Wright brothers by their father, worked on a principle similar to the great Italian inventor's fifteenth century design.

Even as boys the Wright brothers turned their passion into profit by manufacturing kites and selling them to children in the neighbourhood for a small profit. They read every published word they could find on flying. To help pay for their hobby, teenagers Orville and Wilbur built a small printing press on which they published pamphlets and brochures for local shopkeepers, and a local newspaper they called *West Side News*.

Bicycle riding became a nation-wide craze during the early 1890s and Orville and Wilbur became fascinated with the sport. In 1893 they opened a cycle sales and repair shop. In those days bicycles were expensive and were not always well made, and within three years their Wright Cycle Company was manufacturing its own machines. The profits from their $18 Wright "Special" bicycles were ploughed back into aviation experiments centred on producing a controllable glider. They constructed a series of designs ranging from models to full-sized machines.

In 1899 Wilbur wrote to the Smithsonian Institution in Washington inquiring about the latest books and articles on flying. The Institution sent Wilbur a long list and the brothers began in earnest to study the works of other men around the world seeking the same goals. They included Otto Lilienthal, recently killed in Germany testing his latest glider; England's Percy Pilcher, another hang-gliding victim; American gliding pioneer, Octave Chanute; Australian Lawrence Hargrave, inventor of the boxkite; Hiram Maxim, experimenting with steam-powered aircraft; and the Smithsonian's own Doctor Samuel Langley, who had built a successful petrol-engine-powered model aircraft.

Often wading through a mire of conflicting ideas, they examined the theories and experiments of these other seekers. They discarded much of the material, but eventually found a matching pattern of theory and fact. They even turned to the birds, studying the flight of turkey hawks to come up with a method of controlling the wing bank. The intricate design process was like assembling a giant jigsaw puzzle, where only one piece in a hundred actually fitted into the finished picture. The final picture was the design of a biplane glider which was to be the forerunner of the world's first powered aeroplane.

Their dedication to solving the problem of powered flight is illustrated by a letter, dated 13 May 1900,

written in Wilbur's copperplate hand to the ageing
Octave Chanute:

> For some years now I have been afflicted that flight is
> possible to man. My disease has increased in severity and
> I feel that it will soon cost me an increased amount of
> money if not my life. I have been trying to arrange my
> affairs in such a way that I can devote my entire time for
> a few months to experiments in this field. My general ideas
> on the subject are similar to those held by most practical
> experimenters; to wit, that what is chiefly needed is skill
> rather than machinery.

Chanute replied, encouraging and counselling the
brothers. Over the next two years the Wrights built
three man-carrying gliders, each an improvement on
the other. The final machine, *No. 3*, was declared a total
success following testing on the sand-dunes at Kitty
Hawk. The brothers made over 1000 flights in the glider
during a six-week period late in 1902.

They returned home to Dayton convinced that their
machine was suitable to convert to powered flight. The
systems they had devised gave the pilot control about
the three axes. Pitch, roll and yaw had worked well. The
Wright brothers had a practical and controllable aircraft. They were ready for the giant leap forward. All
they needed now to achieve powered flight was to find
a suitable engine and design a propeller.

At this stage only a couple of airships had achieved
any form of controlled flight. The most notable was in
France where Brazilian Alberto Santos-Dumont had
flown his tiny airship across Paris and around the Eiffel
Tower. However, airships relied on gas for their lift
whereas the Wright Brothers' Flyer — like the birds —
would fly by the passage of air over a delicately formed
wing. This was the miraculous lifting force of aerody-
namics.

Discovering that the petrol engines of the day were
too heavy for the power they generated, the Wrights

designed and built their own engine. It developed twelve horsepower and, including the radiator and petrol tank (filled to the brim), weighed a mere ninety kilograms. They then proceeded to design and carve their own propellers.

To test and measure the lift and drag of all the aircraft's components, they built their own wind tunnel, a device that designers of the future would consider mandatory for the testing of all new aircraft designs. The brothers made careful calculations. They deduced that with the extra weight of the engine and two propellers, plus the pilot (neither man exceeded sixty-five kilograms), they had more than doubled the load their glider's wings had to lift.

Using *No. 3* glider as their pattern, they built a new and much larger aircraft which they named the *Flyer*. It had a wingspan of just over twelve metres and, fully loaded, weighed 340 kilograms. This meant that they would have to devise a new sort of take-off system. With their gliders the technique had been simply to run down-slope into the wind with a man supporting each wing-tip until the windspeed was sufficient to lift the glider into the air. Leg-power would no longer be sufficient with the *Flyer*.

Rather than using wheels, they equipped the machine with long wooden landing skids. For take-off the *Flyer* was perched on a wheeled trolley cart which ran along nineteen metres of rails. The aircraft would rest on the cart until, accelerating along the track, it reached flying speed and lifted off.

They returned to the North Carolina coast in November 1903 where it took them three weeks to assemble the aircraft. It was a finicky task to set the wings, biplane elevators and twin rudders at just the right angle. A matter of a degree or two out could spell disaster. A forest of piano wires gave the fragile wood and cloth airframe its strength and rigidity. Each had to be "twanging" taut.

Before attempting any test with the *Flyer* they spent weeks freshening up their flying skills in glider *No.3*. Then a series of frustrating setbacks delayed them. When they first started up the *Flyer*'s engine, it back-fired and wrecked a propeller drive. This was followed by a series of problems with the power transmission system which employed bicycle chains to transmit the engine's power to the twin propellers. Repairs, replacements and adjustments delayed them until December 14, by which time chill winds were blowing across Kill Devil Hill.

The Wrights had been working in isolation away from the prying eyes of the Press and curious spectators who might steal their ideas. They had already taken steps to register their machine with the United States Patent Office. Thus, as Orville and Wilbur tossed a coin to see who would fly, only five trusted men from the nearby Kill Devil Hill Lifesaving Station had been called to the desolate sand dunes to witness the historic moment. Orville recalled catching sight of two small boys, attracted by the strange machine, who made "a hurried departure over the hill for home" when the roaring engine was tested.

One of their five witnesses was equipped with a camera to record the flight and provide positive proof of their achievement. It was a wise precaution in view of the number of cranks and con-men who, in search of publicity or financial backing, had already conned the Press and public into believing that they had actually flown. The Wrights were determined that they would not be accused of charlatanism.

Wilbur won the toss and quickly took his place lying on the lower wing to the left of the engine, his hips fitting into a cradle device. This was attached to wires that allowed the wings to twist in order to bank the

aircraft from side to side. The cradle was also attached
to the rudders for balance. Thus by rolling his lower
body one way or the other he could turn the aircraft. A
small stick at his left hand controlled the elevators
commanding the aircraft to climb or descend. By modern standards it was a primitive and unstable system,
but it had worked on their gliders.

Orville started up the tiny engine with a strap wound
around the flywheel. They waited only briefly for the
motor to warm up and run smoothly because the boxes
enclosing the valves had neither water jackets nor fins
for cooling and tests had shown that the valves became
red hot after a few minutes running. It was primitive by today's standard, but in 1903 it was the best
available.

Wilbur opened up the engine to full power. The spruce
and cloth airframe vibrated as the two propellers spun
up to 300 rpm. Everything was ready. Gritting his teeth,
Wilbur pulled the wire that released the dolly.

The *Flyer* gathered speed so quickly that Orville,
running alongside, had no chance of keeping up. It
gathered flying speed and, just before reaching the end
of the rail, lifted steeply from the trolley. For one magnificent moment it flew, until the nose dropped sharply
and the machine ploughed into the sand, coming to a
shuddering halt just a few metres from the end of the
rail.

Poor Wilbur. Rather than become the first pilot, he
had become the first to succumb to the manoeuvre that
would bring death to generations of fliers. He had
stalled ... but fortunately only a couple of metres off the
ground. Rather than breaking his neck he had merely
snapped a couple of lengths of spruce. The damage was
soon repaired, but the breeze was up and three days
passed before conditions were suitable for another
flight.

Ice covered the rain pools on the dunes on the chilly

morning of December 17. There was a steady winter breeze, just what they needed for a short take-off. Everything seemed right. By 10.30 a.m. the brothers had laid out the take-off track and their friends from the Lifesaving Station had returned. As Wilbur had made the first attempt it was now his younger brother's turn. What followed is best described in Orville's own words:

> After running the motor a few minutes to heat it up, I released the wire that held the machine to the track and the machine started forward into the wind. Wilbur ran at the side of the machine holding the wing to balance it on the track ... Wilbur was able to stay with it until it lifted from the track after a forty-foot run.
>
> One of the lifesaving men snapped the camera for us, taking a picture just as the machine had reached the end of the track and had risen to a height of about two feet.
>
> The course of the flight up and down was exceedingly erratic, partly due to the irregularity of the air, partly to lack of experience in handling the machine. A sudden dart when a little over a hundred feet from the end of the track, or a little over a hundred and twenty feet from where it rose into the air, ended the flight.
>
> This flight lasted only twelve seconds; it was nevertheless the first in the history of the world in which a machine carrying a man had raised itself by its own power into the air in full flight, had sailed forward without a reduction of speed, and had finally landed at a point as high as that from which it started.

That first unpredictable little hop seems insignificant today. Indeed it could have been completed within the economy class cabin of a modern Boeing 747-400 airliner. Nevertheless, it is the starting point from which aviation's progress has been measured. In fact, on that remarkable day, spurred by the competitive nature of humans, the brothers indulged in an informal challenge, making three more flights, each a little farther. On the last, around noon, Wilbur stayed up for fifty-nine seconds, covering a ground distance of 260 metres. However, the true distance through the air was approximately one kilometre, taking the strong head-wind into account.

Like all their aeroplanes, the *Flyer* was extremely unstable in the pitching (nose up or down) plane, caus-ing the frail aircraft to fly a very undulating path. As Orville described it, "The machine would rise suddenly to about ten feet and then just as suddenly dart for the ground."

It was one of these downwards darts that eventually ended their fourth and longest flight of the day. The *Flyer* pitched suddenly and sharply into the sand, snap-ping one of the long struts supporting the elevator. A moment later the capricious wind caught the crippled aircraft and overturned it. The historic little biplane was a wreck. It never flew again. But it mattered little to the ecstatic American brothers. They had flown and soon would build a better machine.

Following lunch (Orville prepared the meal and Wil-bur washed the dishes) they set off to walk the seven kilometres to the Weather Bureau station to telegraph their father. Wilbur, unhurt but possibly a little shaken by the crash that had put an end to his last flight, may have been remembering something he had said earlier. When asked about the dangers inherent in their at-tempts to fly, he had stated eloquently:

> There are only two ways of learning to ride a fractious horse: one is to get on him and learn by actual practice how each motion and trick may be best met; the other is to sit on the fence and watch the beast for a while, and then retire to the house and at leisure figure out the best way of overcoming his jumps and kicks. The latter system is the safer, but the former, on the whole, turns out the larger proportion of good riders. It is very much the same in learning to ride a flying machine; if you are looking for perfect safety you will do well to sit on the fence and watch the birds, but if you really wish to learn you must mount

a machine and become acquainted with its tricks by actual trial.

As the two men walked across the sands they discussed the problems to be overcome before they next mounted their aerial beast. The greatest of these was its virtually uncontrollable pitching. They had an aircraft that would fly; now they must perfect the rider's ability to control their flying steed.

In their usual undemonstrative way the Wright brothers sent a pithy message to the Bishop: "Success. Four flights Thursday morning. All against twenty-one mile wind. Started from level with engine power alone. Average speed through air thirty-one miles. Longest fifty-nine seconds. Inform press. Home Christmas. Orville Wright."

Incredible as it now seems, the triumph of powered flight received little more than passing attention outside the Wright brothers Ohio home town, where a two column headline in the *Dayton Evening Herald* proclaimed, "Dayton boys fly airship".

In America, confused reporting was exacerbated by the secretive brothers' refusal to give out pictures or details of their aircraft. Determined that no one should have the chance of copying, and profiting from, their priceless invention, the Wright brothers did little to correct the situation, other than issue a terse public statement describing their first flights.

Thus, many believed that they were as unsuccessful as other would-be aviators of the day. Some dismissed the brothers as liars. Such claims had been made before and had turned out to be the work of hoaxers or confidence tricksters.

Things did not improve when, in May 1904, reporters were twice invited to witness a flight, only to be informed that poor weather and engine problems had grounded the brothers. As a result the press generally considered the whole business a waste of time — and the world remained mostly ignorant of their achievement. The situation may well have suited the Wright brothers who were keen to improve the performance of their erratic *Flyer II* away from prying eyes.

Over the next two years the Wrights refined their design and by 4 October, 1905 their *Flyer III* flew 38 kilometres in 38 minutes and 3 seconds at an average speed of 60 km/h. Finally satisfied that they now had built a practical and reliable airplane, the brothers were more determined than ever not to reveal their invention to the world without legal protection and some financial rewards for their years of work. Awaiting patents, and unable to obtain orders for machines from the government, the secretive Wrights stopped all flying for two and a half years to prevent industrial spying.

During their self-imposed exile, the first European flights took place. In France, where in 1783 the Montgolfier brothers' hot air balloon had first taken man into the air, the news of the Wright brothers' achievement had spurred intense interest in powered flight.

In May 1904 wealthy Paris attorney Ernest Archdeacon and oil magnate Henry Deutsch de la Meurthe had jointly offered 50 000 francs (US$10 000), a fortune in those days, for the first powered flight around a one-kilometre course. Hearing of the Wright's 38-kilometre flight, a disbelieving Ernest Archdeacon publicly challenged the Americans to bring their airplane to France and collect the Deutsch-Archdeacon prize. Their refusal added weight to the arguments of the sceptics.

The early French experiments paled when compared with the Wrights' achievements. On 12 November, 1906, following several earlier hops, Alberto Santos-Dumont became the toast of Paris when he made Europe's first accredited flight in a freakish boxkite biplane he called *14-bis*. The airman had to stand up to fly his monstrous,

and totally impractical airplane, but nevertheless it
managed to stagger 219 metres across the cavalry field
at Bagatelle.

Unlike the secretive Wrights, Santos-Dumont invited
the press and members of the newly formed Féderation
Aéronautique Internationale to witness the flight. Accordingly, it was the first-ever formally recognised
world record for distance.

Lacking formal confirmation of the Wright brothers'
claims, reaction from the partisan European press was
predictable. An article in the *Illustrated London News*
headlined "The First Flight of a Machine Heavier than
Air" was one of many reports suggesting that Santos-
Dumont had made the first powered flight. The French
newspaper *Figaro* ecstatically declared: "What a triumph ! A month ago Santos flew ten metres. A fortnight
ago he flew seventy. Yesterday he flew still further and
enthusiasm knew no bounds. The air is truly conquered.
Santos has flown. Everybody will fly." *Le Matin* was
more cautious, suggesting that Santos-Dumont was
"the first to fly before witnesses".

Surprisingly, Britain's *Daily Mail* played down the
story. Its owner, Lord Northcliffe, whose growing interest in aviation had already led to his appointing the
world's first aviation journalist, was furious. On reading
his paper's brief and bored report, Northcliffe berated
his editors. The following day the *Daily Mail*'s editorial
reflected Northcliffe's visionary opinions. Devoted to
an assessment of the future impact of aviation, it
concluded:

> The air around London and other cities will be darkened
> by the flight of aeroplanes. New difficulties of every kind
> will arise, not the least being the military problem caused
> by the virtual annihilation of frontiers and the acquisition
> of power to pass readily through the air above the sea. The
> isolation of the United Kingdom may disappear and thus
> the success of M. Santos-Dumont has an international
> significance. They are not merely dreamers who hold that

the time is on hand when air power will be an even more important thing than sea power.

Five days later on 17 November, 1906, to stimulate British interest, Lord Northcliffe announced a prize of £10 000 for the first flight between London and Manchester. However, four years would pass before the first challenge for his staggering prize would be mounted. Indeed, by 1907, only one European machine had managed to stay airborne for a minute.

It was not until January 1908 that Henri Farman, flying a biplane built by Gabriel and Charles Voisin, finally claimed the Deutsch-Archdeacon prize with a modest flight of one minute and twenty-eight seconds. However, it was the beginning of a period of accelerated progress in France and within six months Farman had remained airborne for over twenty minutes and flown nineteen kilometres. Furthermore, other French aircraft builders were beginning to achieve success with their early designs.

Just as it appeared that Europe was catching up, the Wright brothers finally signed commercial agreements in the US and France, and commenced a series of public demonstrations. At Avours, near Le Mans, Wilbur Wright capped a spectacular series of 104 demonstration flights by circling the field until he had covered 125 kilometres. This time their achievements made world headlines. It became a battle of superlatives.

"It is a revelation in aeroplane work. Who can now doubt that the Wrights have done all they claimed? We are as children compared with the Wrights," one exclaimed. A London *Times* report spoke of "triumph ... indescribable enthusiasm ... mastery". Major B.F.S. Baden-Powell, the past-president of Britain's (later Royal) Aeronautical Society, stated: "That Wilbur Wright is in possession of a power which controls the fate of nations is beyond dispute."

On the world stage the Wright brothers had justly

earned world acclaim. However, back home in America they still awaited an approach from government. It finally came late in 1908 when the US Army requested they submit a two-seater for trials at Fort Meyer. Still unconvinced of the suitability of these "new-fangled flying machines", the military were also testing a small airship at the same time.

After a number of successful flights at Fort Meyer, disaster struck on 17 September 1908. Orville and his Army passenger, Lieutenant Thomas Selfridge had completed three successful orbits of the field when a propeller fouled a bracing wire. The aircraft dived into the ground with a fearful crash. Orville was seriously injured and his passenger was killed — the aeroplane's first fatality.

Despite the crash the Army purchased a Wright aircraft for $30 000. The deal included free instruction for two military pilots. Besides fame Orville and Wilbur had finally achieved a modest degree of financial success. However, as others who followed their lead built more advanced types of aircraft, the Wright brothers slipped into the background, trailing behind in the flood of aviation activity their early flights had set off.

In 1912 Wilbur Wright died of typhoid fever. In his diary Bishop Wright wrote: "This morning at 3.15 Wilbur passed away aged forty-five years, one month, and fourteen days. A short life full of consequences. An unfailing intellect, imperturbable temper, great self-reliance and as great modesty, seeing the right clearly, pursuing it steadily, he lived and died."

Orville died in 1948 after a lifetime of service to aviation, a lifetime in which he had witnessed their imperfect little biplane progress to the jet aircraft.

Although aviation progress had quickly overtaken the Wright brothers, it was their achievement at Kitty Hawk, when the rest of the world was still dreaming about flight, that acted as the catalyst to would-be

airmen everywhere. Their dogged persistence made
them great. Refusing to acknowledge an insoluble problem, they had simply kept working at it until they found
an answer. While others merely sat on the fence, the
Wrights rode and tamed their fractious winged horse.
As the famous British academic, Sir Walter Raleigh,
wrote in 1922: "It is not extravagant to say that
17 December 1903, when the Wright brothers made
the first free flight through the air in a power-driven
machine, marks the beginning of a new era in the
history of the world."

5
The dawn of the Air Age

The Grande Semaine d'Aviation de la Champagne — the world's first airshow — was held in the French Cathedral town of Reims in August 1909. Bringing together the best aircraft designers and pilots of the day its impact was recalled by the world's first official aviation correspondent, Harry Harper. Appointed "Air Reporter No. 1" for England's *Daily Mail* in 1906, Harper recalled fifty years later:

> Today, whenever the magic of memory takes me back again to that wonder week of ours at Reims, it becomes clear to me that it was this event, more than any other in the early days, which made the world at large realise that the long promised "air age" was really dawning at last.

During a half-century of aviation reporting, Harper witnessed the aeroplane advance from erratic wood and wire contraptions some likened to "flying verandas", to the supersonic fighters and early airliners of the jet age. However, like many others whose lives spanned the history of powered flight, Harper believed that the airplane truly came of age in 1909 with that first gathering of flying men at Reims.

For some time the newly-formed Aero Clubs of France, England and America had been trying to organise an international gathering of leading aviators to promote the new science. They saw an assembly of each

nation's leading fliers as the ideal way to gain world-
wide public attention.

A month before the airshow, as work progressed on a
specially-constructed airfield and grandstand at Reims,
interest in aviation was given a tremendous boost.
Louis Blériot, one of the entrants for the speed event at
Reims, made a successful crossing of the English Channel. The French airman's 35-kilometre flight, the first
linking two nations separated by water, received unprecedented attention in the world press. Considered
one of the three great epochal flights of aviation progress, it was to rank with Charles Lindbergh's trans-
Atlantic flight in 1927 and Neil Armstrong's 1969 moon
landing.

Around the world over-optimistic journalists reporting on Blériot's flight proclaimed that the age of international air travel was at hand, although in England
and France the more perceptive of them focused on the
future military implications of the aeroplane. In England, so long a safe, secure little island protected from
the French by its navy, London's *Daily Telegraph* editorialised: "No Englishman can learn of the voyage of
Blériot without emoting that the day of Britain's impregnability has passed away. Airpower will become as
vital to us as sea power has ever been." Across the
channel a French newspaper cartoonist depicted the
ghost of Napoleon looking at Blériot's plane and asking,
"Why not a hundred years earlier?"

A month later Blériot and his monoplane were at
Reims, ready to do battle with the world's best. The
Grande Semaine d'Aviation de la Champagne (the
Champagne Region's Great Aviation Week) was financed by the vintners of the region's famed bubbling
product. The organisers realised that competition, besides attracting the crowds, was the key to advance-
ment of aircraft design. Accordingly, they arranged a

series of contests for speed, distance, altitude and passenger carrying.

By the eve of the airshow it seemed as if all Europe had descended on the ancient city. Royalty, heads of state, powerful politicians, military leaders, and the cream of European society were there, attracted by the novel machines and the flamboyant fliers. Hotel suites fetched US$500 for the week (a year's wages for some in those days) and the tiniest room in the humblest pension escalated from US$10 to US$70. Cafes ran out of food, and halls were turned into dormitories. Harry Harper recalled the scene:

> The city had been taken over by flying enthusiasts and their followers. Two thousand American tourists arrived to encourage Glen Curtiss. A special excursion train was run from London and when their steamer ran aground off Calais, three thousand Britons waded ashore with their baggage, rugs and camping equipment. Black market operators made a small fortune dealing in boxes and seats. A Reims theatre mounted a revue entitled In the Air. From Paris came 150 taxis, their drivers charging an exorbitant 30 shillings for the fare from Reims to the Plains of Bethany.

On the first morning more than 100 000 people flocked to the new aerodrome on Bethany Plain. Not since Joan of Arc and her army camped there five centuries earlier had such a crowd gathered. In the extravagently built and decorated grandstands the profligate rubbed shoulders, lunching and sipping champagne as gipsy violinists wandered between the tables. Thousands more promenaded in the sunshine, inspecting the great complex of hangars and grandstands festooned with tricolours and red, white and blue bunting.

Even heavy rain which turned the field into a quagmire and held up flying did not deter the crowd. They hung around and, by late afternoon, were rewarded by the sight of seven aircraft in the air at the same time.

"It was a spectacle never before witnessed in the history of the world," a journalist cabled his New York office.

During the week only twenty-three of the thirty-eight aircraft on display eventually got airborne. At one stage the remains of twelve crashed machines littered the aerodrome testifying to the unreliability of early aeroplanes and the inexperience of many pilots. Those flyer who did get airborne attracted incredible displays of hero worship, particularly some of the dashing young airmen whose show-off antics made them the favourites with the crowd.

The darling of the many women attending Reims was the handsome young Hubert Latham. Born of French and English parents and educated at Oxford University, he had made headlines a month earlier by ditching in mid-Channel in a gallant attempt to beat Blériot to England. At Reims Latham flew around the airfield in pouring rain, nonchalantly rolling and lighting cigarettes in the cockpit of his graceful Antionette monoplane. Young Étienne Bunau-Varilla, who had just received his Voisin biplane as a graduation present from his father, delighted the crowd by tipping his hat each time he passed the grandstand. But none matched the audacity of a Monsieur Ruchonnet. Unable even to drive a car he had purchased his Antoinette only two days before Reims and made his first real flight — just under two kilometres — in front of the gathering. Such were the flying fools of aviation's age of innocence.

Another of the flamboyant fliers attracting attention with his acrobatic displays was Eugéne Lefebvre. On several occasions the French daredevil scattered photographers, skimming low across the field in his Wright Model A Flyer. Harry Harper wrote:

> Incomparably the finest exhibition was given by Eugéne Lefebvre who, after doing three turns of the course, delighted the onlookers by a brilliant performance, showing his absolute perfect command over the machine. He did

circles and figures of eight and three just like an accomplished skater. When he came straight towards the grandstands, suddenly swerving to the right almost over the heads of the people along the rails, the enthusiasm of the astonished throng knew no bounds. To complete the performance he stopped the motor in mid-air, gracefully planed down in a series of swoops, and came gently to earth within a few yards of the grandstand.

Notably absent from the flying were America's Wright brothers. In 1908 the secretive brothers had finally decided to fly in public, and Wilbur had become the toast of Europe following a series of brilliant demonstration flights. Their success had not only silenced the European sceptics, but had brought about a flurry of sales of their biplanes. Six French-owned Wrights were entered at Reims. Nevertheless, Wilbur Wright had stated that their business was building aeroplanes and they were not interested in racing. They were more intent, it seems, or regaining the ground surrendered to France's aeroplane designers.

Since the Wrights had declined to compete, American interest centred on a taciturn, former motorcycle racer named Glenn Curtiss and his *Reims Flyer* biplane. Curtiss was the leading challenger to the Wrights' domination of American aviation and had recently formed his own company to manufacture a biplane he called the *Golden Flyer*. Curtiss saw Reims as the ideal opportunity to demonstrate his aircraft and was confident that a winning performance would guarantee sales. The infuriated Wright brothers considered that Curtiss had "stolen" their invention and, shortly before the airshow, attempted to ground Curtiss with lawsuits alleging patent infringement. The battle would rage for years.

However, as Reims got under way, the intense young speedster (who admitted, "I hate to be beaten") had other things on his mind. He had already set a world motorcycle speed record of 217 km/h in 1907. Now Curtiss was determined to become the world's fastest flyer. He declined to enter the height and distance competitions, waiting instead for the speed event. "I had just one airplane and one motor. If I smashed either of these it would be all over with America's chances in the first International Cup Race," Curtiss later explained.

By the close of the fifth day Latham was in the lead for the distance prize having completed a flight of 150 kilometres. He landed to a 10-minute ovation and, according to London's *Daily Mirror*, the attention of two demonstrative women supporters. "The beautifully-dressed ladies clasped his neck by turns and kissed him frantically," the newspaper reported. It seemed unlikely that anyone would better Latham's 2 hour 13 minute flight, until late in the afternoon when French artist-turned-airman Henri Farman trundled out his boxkite-like biplane and began flying methodically around the course.

Three hours later the sun was down and an evening chill had set in when Farman finally landed, having covered a world-record 180 kilometres. "I am so cold," he told his ecstatic crewmen as they carried him shoulder high to his hangar to thaw out. Farman also won the passenger-carrying competition and took second place in the altitude contest, making him the week's biggest money winner with prize-money totalling 63 000 francs (US$12 000). Latham, who settled for second prize for distance, eventually won the altitude competition when he climbed his Antoinette to 508 feet.

The final event, and highlight, of the week was a speed race for the Coupe Internationale d'Aviation and a 25 000 franc purse (US$4760) donated by ageing American newspaper magnate James Gordon Bennett. Having moved to France after fighting an unsuccessful duel with his fiancée's brother, Bennett owned the *New York Herald* and its French counterpart the *Paris Herald*. A man of extravagant whims, he had spent a fortune nearly forty years earlier sending one of his

journalists, Henry Stanley, into darkest Africa to search
for long-lost missionary Dr David Livingstone. In later
years he had used his wealth to sponsor yacht and
balloon racing, attracted by the whimsy of a sport that
was subject to the vagaries of the wind. Believing that
aviation's latest toy was subject to the same caprice, the
elegant eccentric decided to promote airplane racing.

Race day dawned fine and the biggest crowd of the
week was on hand. Three pilots represented France:
Louis Blériot fresh from his English Channel triumph,
dashing Eugéne Lefebvre in his Wright biplane, and
Hubert Latham in the Antoinette. Britain's inexperienced representative, George Cockburn, a burly rugby
football player flying a lumbering Farman biplane, was
a rank outsider. America's hopes rested with Curtiss.

The competitors were allowed to choose their own
time to challenge for Gordon Bennett's trophy. It was a
race against the clock rather than each other. Each pilot
had to complete two circuits of a ten-kilometre course
marked by black-and-white chequered pylons.

Curtiss made a trial flight and, after fighting to
control his bucking machine in the invisible turbulence
caused by thermal updrafts, vowed never again to fly in
such torrid conditions. That was until he discovered he
had flown the fastest practice lap of the week. Although
he was unsure of the aerodynamic reasons for this
unexpected event, the American had unwittingly stumbled on a technique that would be used by racing pilots
for generations to come. By flying low in thermalling
(updraft) conditions, he required a lower angle of attack
to produce the required lift. This reduced drag and
increased his speed. Quickly refuelling, he took off almost immediately on his official race flight.

Like most fliers of the day Curtiss did not wear a seat
belt, and he grimly wedged himself tightly against the
wooden frame as his *Reims Flyer* was buffeted by the
turbulence. His experience racing motorcycles had

taught the American the importance of tight cornering. He put this knowledge to good use and the crowd gasped as he rounded the pylons, banking steeply and cutting the corners as closely as he dared. Fifteen minutes and fifty seconds after the start he crossed the finish line in a gentle dive. He had averaged 76 km/h, the fastest speed of the week so far.

Cockburn was next away in his bumbling Farman. The game Briton had only learned to fly six weeks earlier and was unable to cope with the conditions. Turning low over the course his wing struck a haystack and the Farman crashed. Fortunately, Cockburn was not seriously injured.

Curtiss sprawled in a deck chair outside his hangar trying to appear unconcerned as Lefebvre tried to better his time and managed only 59 km/h. Next came Hubert Latham. The crowd shreiked "Latham! Latham!" as their idol jauntily acknowledged the sea of waving hands and then climbed aboard the boat-like, varnished wood fuselage of his Antionette. It was soon obvious that his monoplane was too slow, and the crowd groaned when his speed of 67 km/h was announced.

French hopes rested with the final contestant, Louis Blériot in his modified two-seat Blériot XII powered by a big V8 ENV engine. At the completion of the first circuit it appeared as though the Frenchman's modifications had paid off. He had sliced four seconds off the American's lap time. "He's got me beat and that's that," Curtiss was heard to remark.

A great roar went up as Blériot passed the grandstands a second time, crossed the finish line and landed. Standing up in the cockpit he acknowledged the cheering crowd and then rushed to the timekeeper's hut. Moments later Curtiss' manager exploded from the little building and ran towards the American pilot. "You win! You win!" he yelled. Curtiss had taken the race by a mere six seconds!

As the crowd streamed out of the flying ground there was just one topic of conversation — the defeat of Blériot by an unknown American with only ten hours flying to his credit. The more pessimistic of the home crowd saw it as an end to France's brief domination of aviation. But they need not have worried, for French airmen would continue to set the pace for several years to come, and it would be more than a decade before American aviation would again have a significant effect on the world scene.

The seven days of Reims had proved to the world that the aeroplane was a practical machine. More than a hundred successful flights had been made, many exceeding one hour in duration. More than half a million spectators had attended and it set the scene for similar airshows around the world. The importance of Reims was summed up by C.G. Grey, the editor of *The Aeroplane* magazine, in September 1909. He wrote:

> To say that this week marks an epoch in the history of the world is a platitude. Nevertheless, it is worth stating, and for those of us lucky enough to be at Reims during this week there is solid satisfaction in the idea that we were present at the making of history. Perhaps only in a few years to come the competitions of this week may look pathetically small and the distance and speed appear paltry. Nevertheless, they are the first of their kind, and that is sufficient.

As predicted by Grey, new records were set in quick succession. By the close of 1909 Farman had increased his distance mark to 232 kilometres and Latham had almost tripled his altitude record. Curtiss' speed record would remain intact until the 1910 Gordon Bennett race in America, when an improved Blériot monoplane would set a new speed record of 98 km/h.

However, the general belief that many of the pioneering airmen of 1909 were eccentric sportsmen with suicidal tendencies was reinforced shortly after peace and quiet returned to Reims. Just two weeks after the air-show, aviation lost its first aeroplane pilot when Eugéne Lefebvre, whose daredevil low-flying had stunned Reims, was killed testing a new Wright Type A biplane. Two weeks later, France lost another pioneer in a bizarre taxying accident, when Captain Ferdinand Ferber's Voisin biplane dropped into a ditch. The engine fell forward and crushed the unfortunate pilot, starting a great controversy about the safety of "pusher" aircraft which had their engines mounted at the pilot's back.

But to the general public such technicalities meant little as they flooded through the turnstiles at the aviation meets held in England, Germany and Italy in the autumn of 1909. They were there for the excitement and the sheer spectacle, and to cheer their favourites. To the crowds, aviation was a life-and-death spectacle, an aerial entertainment which aroused emotions similar to those felt by the aficionados of the bullfights; man versus machine in an aerial arena. It would take years before they would even start to consider the airplane as a vehicle of transportation.

Nevertheless, the great aviation exposition at Reims had publicly demonstrated just how far aviation had progressed in the six years since the Wright brothers' first flight at Kitty Hawk. Furthermore, to those perceptive enough to look beyond the failure of the lesser lights, and concentrate of the performances of the leading fliers and their aircraft, it was clear that the airplane had come of age as the world's new practical vehicle. David Lloyd George, soon to become Prime Minister of Great Britain, wrote after witnessing the events at Reims:

> Flying machines are no longer dreams, they are an established fact. The possibilities of this new system of locomotion are infinite. I feel, as a Britisher, rather ashamed that we are so completely out of it.

The most poignant words to come from the Grande

Semaine d'Aviation de la Champagne were written by a young Englishwoman named Gertrude Bacon. The heroine of a number of balloon flights with her father, she had raised Edwardian eyebrows by attending Reims unescorted. Before heading home she managed to persuade French pilot Roger Sommer to take her for a flight over the Plains of Bethany. Afterwards she wrote:

> But picture if you can what it meant for the very first time; when all the world of Aviation was young and fresh and untried; when to rise at all was a glorious adventure, and to find oneself flying swiftly in the air, the too-good-to-be-true realisation of a life-long dream. You wonderful record-breakers of today and of the years to come, whose exploits I may only marvel at and envy, I have experienced something that can never be yours and can never be taken away from me — the rapture, the glory and the glamour of "the very beginning".

6
Johnny Moisant:
"Crazy Yankee"

Albert Fileux would never have believed it. Not in his wildest dreams could the Frenchman have imagined jets shuttling between Paris and London. Or airline passengers pampered with arm chairs, movies and champagne. In 1910, when Albert became the first passenger to fly between the two capitals, he shared an open cockpit with an brash American pilot and, for part of the way, a kitten named Paris-London. And the trip took three weeks to complete.

Fileux's pilot, Chicago-born John Bevins Moisant, liked to call himself the "King of the Aviators" even though he had only four flights under his belt when he jammed Fileux into his flimsy Blériot two-seater monoplane and took off from Paris, London-bound. Twenty-two days later the adventurous pair were the toast of Europe.

"Foolhardy ... impossible ... suicidal", leading French pilots exclaimed before the flight. Aviation was in its infancy and pilots rarely exposed passengers to the dangers of their unreliable machines. The progress of flight was still measured in terms of minutes aloft and only the most experienced airmen attempted cross-country flying. Furthermore, Moisant would have to negotiate the English Channel — still considered a kind of aerial Russian roulette, despite daring recent crossings by Louis Blériot and two other pilots.

Characteristically, the American brushed aside

suggestions that he was too inexperienced. Since first attempting to fly, he had displayed a cavalier attitude toward danger that was to mark his aviation career. As he was preparing for that first flight, it was suggested he try a few ground runs before getting airborne. "I am not driving an automobile but am going up in a flying machine," Moisant retorted brusquely. He crashed seconds after take-off. Crawling unharmed from the wreckage, he joked to bystanders, "Well, I had the fun of getting off the ground anyhow."

Daring, brash, flamboyant, a total opportunist, Moisant had come to flying via a succession of jobs — farmer, sugar-planter, banker, revolutionary leader and aircraft designer. His entry into aviation at thirty-six years of age marked the final chapter of what was, in many ways, an improbable, even outrageous, life. Although in America he was best known as the founder of the first professional flying circus, in Central America's brawling republics his fame was more sinister. There, by 1909, he was a gringo to be reckoned with — Johnny Moisant, Yankee revolutionary.

Born in 1873, Moisant was the second eldest of eleven children. His French Canadian parents ran a pastry shop in Chicago's Brighton Park district. In 1892, following the death of his father, John and his older brother, Alfred, headed for California. To finance their venture they borrowed money from their uncle, Raphael Moisant, a Chicago shoemaker. In California the brothers purchased a small farm in Alameda, across the bay from San Francisco.

At that time the governments of Central America were working towards forming a "United States of Central America". Some of the countries involved were in a state of turmoil, as unscrupulous military and political leaders vied for power. Hearing that rich farming land could be picked up for a pittance in American dollars, John and Alfred Moisant moved to Salvador.

It was the beginning of a period that was to make "Johnny" Moisant a legend in the region where a succession of revolutions reached comic opera proportions. In US government circles, however, he would become notorious for filibustering and revolutionary intrigue.

In Salvador the pair acquired an underdeveloped sugar plantation and, joined by their younger brothers George and Edward, set about improving the property. John designed a cheap and simple irrigation system and by sensible farming, and currying favour with influential government officials, the brothers became wealthy and powerful. Within a few years they had expanded their holdings to 20 000 hectares. "Their riches and political power made them practically rulers of their rich little country," wrote Byron R.Newton, an editor on the *New York Herald*.

Their fortunes changed in 1898 when the leader of a Salvadoran separatist movement, General Tomas Regalado, was elected president. The Moisants were not popular with the new regime and, realising that they could expect no favours, John Moisant conceived and financed a plan to overthrow the new president. But Regalado got wind of the plot and confiscated the Moisants' property. The general tortured plantation labourers to obtain evidence, hanging them by their thumbs, and John Moisant was forced to flee to Honduras.

In Honduras he helped finance a plot to overthrow that country's president, on the understanding that the new regime would allow him to open a bank. By 1907, with Salvador under the new leadership of President Figueroa, the Moisants owned the vast Santa Emelia and Santa Ana plantations, controlled three of the most powerful banks in Central America, and had possessions in Mexico, Honduras and Nicaragua.

John Moisant was in Nicaragua when he learnt that President Figueroa's troops had raided the Moisants' Salvadoran ranch house. Edward and George had been

imprisoned — charged with aiding revolutionaries.
Moisant immediately offered his services to Nicaraguan
president, José Zelaya, who was backing the Salvadoran revolutionaries. He was commissioned "Colonel" in the rag-tag revolutionary army. Leading a
hundred Nicaraguan troops and two hundred ill-
trained Salvadoran malcontents, Moisant set sail from
Nicaragua in a gunboat to take the Salvadoran port of
Acajulta.

The town's disorganised garrison quickly surrendered, and Colonel Moisant and his men then marched
on the capital, San Salvador, "borrowing" US$25 000
from a bank as they passed through the town of Sanson-
ate. Though Moisant claimed that the expedition was to
liberate his two imprisoned brothers, it was rumoured
that he planned also to overthrow the Salvadoran government. When they met organised resistance from the
Salvadoran army, Moisant's irregulars fled in panic.
Eluding capture, their soldier-of-fortune leader slipped
back to Nicaragua.

Even though his brothers were eventually released,
Moisant became involved in a second attempt to overthrow Salvador's President Fiqueroa. An embarrassed
United States government put an end to Moisant's
filibustering by sending the cruiser USS *Albany* to
intercept his tiny invasion fleet. Turned back by threats
from the *Albany*'s captain to "blow you out of the water",
Moisant realised he had outlived his welcome in Central
America.

In August 1909 he sailed for France to investigate the
commercial potential of aviation. Apparently he had
convinced Nicaraguan president, Zelaya, that he should
have an airplane and had been given funds to make the
purchase.

"I was interested in flying theoretically long before it
became a practical art," Moisant told a journalist.
"Down South I used to lie on my back and watch the big

buzzards soaring up aloft and wonder how they did it. Now and again I would take the trouble to shoot one and measure its wings and make rough calculations based on its wing area in relation to the weight of its body. I had a firm conviction that man would soon learn to fly, but I was too busy with other affairs to have the time necessary for many experiments, and it wasn't until I went to France and found flying in full swing that I took to the air myself," he explained.

Arriving in France, Moisant rushed to Reims where aviation's first public air show was being held. He was impressed by the flamboyant airmen and intrigued that thousands of spectators paid to watch the great spectacle. Here was a new adventure, and one with seemingly unlimited money-making potential for an airmen with a good business head. The first step was to make his name in the aviation world.

Within three months Moisant had rented a small workshop and built a crude monoplane he called the *Crow*. Impulsive as ever, he believed that becoming a pilot was merely a matter of trial and error. "I went up ninety feet at express speed, and came down faster still," Moisant recalled. "It wasn't the machine's fault, it was mine. I had no experience."

Moisant eventually curbed his impatience long enough to attend Louis Blériot's flying school. Under the watchful eye of his instructor, Alfred Leblanc, he spent a few days "grass cutting" — fast taxying and making little hops in an underpowered, clipped-wing training machine. When eventually allowed aloft, Moisant wobbled erratically three times around the airfield before managing a good landing. His second flight was his licence test, supervised, from the safety of the ground, by Louis Blériot himself.

Moisant purchased a Blériot XI-2 two-seater monoplane powered by a cantankerous 50 horsepower Gnome rotary engine. Armed with a brand new licence

and unlimited nerve, he rushed to Paris to enter the
Circuit de l'Est — a race involving Europe's leading
fliers. The organisers laughed at the "crazy Yankee",
saying he was much too inexperienced to compete in
such a difficult and dangerous event. But Moisant was
determined to cash in on the race publicity and enlisted
the aid of a leading French pilot, Roland Garros.

The new Blériot was at Issy airfield and the Circuit
de l'Est was to commence from Étampes, thirty-five
kilometres away on the opposite side of the city. With
Garros perched behind Moisant's seat shouting directions in his ear, the pair flew across the city to the other
airfield. Moisant later recalled:

> A crowd of 300 000 had assembled, and the police were
> keeping a large space open from which the aviators were
> to start. We dropped plumb down in the midst of the
> aviators as they were about to start. In that way we
> avoided the police and the crowds and accomplished our
> purpose. And while the Frenchmen regarded me as a crazy
> Yankee, the fact that I flew among them with one of their
> own crack aviators perhaps helped my reputation a little."

Next he decided to do something more sensational
than merely tag along behind the race competitors —
his original plan. The flight over Paris had received
publicity in the French press as the first passenger-
carrying trip to cross the city. This gave him an idea
which he confided to Alfred Leblanc.

"*Mais vous etes fou, Monsieur,*" (But you are mad) the
Frenchman exclaimed, wondering if he had heard correctly when the fledgling pilot announced his intention
to fly to London. Blériot threw up his hands in dismay,
saying the 360-kilometres flight was ten times more
dangerous than his Channel crossing. Hubert Latham,
the daring Antoinette monoplane expert, suggested
there were easier ways of committing suicide.

Their concern mounted when they learned that Moisant had no knowledge of the route, was ignorant of the

dangers of flying in bad weather, and had never attempted to use a compass in flight. When he brazenly
announced that he intended to take along his mechanic
Albert Fileux, who had never flown, they decided that
Moisant was a lost cause and gave up in disgust.

Moisant took off from Issy at 5.45 p.m. on 16 August
1910 without even disclosing his plans to poor Fileux.
"When we started from Paris he did not know where I
was taking him. Some newspaper men asked me where
I was off to. I said I was going to try out my machine
and they would probably see me again later in the
evening. I flew from Paris to Amiens, where I arrived at
7.30 o'clock," Moisant recalled.

Next morning the pair set out for Calais. The 115-
kilometre flight was accomplished without incident,
although Moisant had to circle the port three times
before locating the landing ground at Les Barraques.
Moisant found navigating relatively easy. On his map
he had drawn the complete route and the compass
headings to follow. Once in the air, he simply jammed
the compass between his knees then turned the aircraft
until it was on the correct heading. He then picked out
a recognisable feature ahead — a hill or a church — and
flew toward it. Once there he picked another target and
so on. This way he minimised the fluctuating-needle
problems of early aircraft compasses.

A gusty sea breeze blew up as the airmen refuelled at
Calais. Most early fliers avoided flying in wind as turbulence made the unstable aircraft of the day extremely
difficult to control. Many pilots used a lighted match as
a wind indicator. If the breeze was sufficient to blow it
out, they stayed on the ground. But with London and
fame only 145 kilometres away, Moisant pressed on. He
recalled:

> People tried to dissuade me from going, but when I got over
> the Channel the wind was much lighter. I flew about seven
> hundred feet high and had a fairly steady time until I got

over land again. I thought I was over Dover, but later I found it was Deal.

"AIRMAN FLIES ACROSS THE CHANNEL WITH PASSEN-GER... NOVICE'S FIFTH FLIGHT", headlined London's *Daily Mirror*. Journalists located the pair at Tilmanstone as they lunched under the Blériot's wing, sheltering from rain that greeted their arrival in England.

Describing the part played by the passenger — the unsung hero of the whole affair — the *Daily Mirror* reported: " Fileux, who is a burly Parisian, and was clad in blue overalls, stated that he had the utmost confidence in his master, and felt quite at home during his aerial voyage." The report explained how Moisant, lacerated by wind and rain in the Blériot's open cockpit, had felt the cold intensely, noting that his eyes were bloodshot and inflamed. " In order to protect himself he wore over his ordinary suit of clothes a layer of Japanese paper and outside of all, mechanic's overalls."

It was in England that Moisant's considerable luck finally deserted him. As predicted by the French experts, he ran foul of Britain's notorious weather. The airmen spent the night at Tilmanstone sleeping beneath the aircraft's wings. Sometime that evening Moisant acquired a tiny tabby kitten. Some reports say it was given him by a female admirer, others that it was a stray. Whatever the truth, he decided to make the animal his mascot, astutely naming it Paris-London.

Predicably, a rash of stories followed. Nearly all incorrectly stated that the kitten had been on board since the aircraft left Paris. The publicity-hungry airman was not about to ruin a good story with the facts. Thus the delightful myth of the cross-Channel kitten was born. However, it did accompany Moisant on the remainder of the journey and became his inseparable flying companion.

Unfortunately, the tiny mascot, nestled in a button-up pocket of Moisant's baggy overalls, brought little luck. After flying the 264 kilometres from Paris in less than eighteen hours, the rest of the trip — a mere 105 kilometres — would take the hapless flier two and a half weeks, involving seven unplanned landings. The problem was a combination of weather, turbulence and Moisant's inexperience.

On 18 August mechanical problems forced two unscheduled landings, the first in a turnip field and the second in a vegetable garden, where the wooden propeller shattered. Describing the scene as the normally immaculate American surveyed the damage, a journalist wrote: "He was black from head to foot, clothes covered in dirt, his hair matted and his hands and face covered with oil; a diamond ring and tiepin gave an incongruous touch to the whole."

Two days later they advanced only three kilometres before Moisant realised that the wind was too strong for flying. On 22 August they tried again but managed just 30 kilometres before the wind forced them down once more and Moisant damaged the aircraft landing in a farmer's field.

There, just 37 kilometres from their destination, they spent two wind-bound weeks. During the first week Moisant's impatience again overcame his commonsense and he attempted to get airborne in near gale conditions. They barely left the ground before a wind gust dumped the Blériot back onto the field. The propeller was smashed, the wheels buckled, bracing wires snapped and the wings were damaged as the aircraft hit. Somehow Moisant and the faithful Fileaux escaped injury. A crowd of locals cheered as the irrepressible pilot, pointing theatrically at the wreck, shouted, "That machine must get me to London."

The British press loved it all. Daily the papers were jammed with reports; the state of repair, the weather outlook, Moisant's social engagements, even Fileux's admiration of the local "maids of the milk" and taste for

English beer did not escape microscopic attention. Naturally there were a few barbed comments about Moisant's slow progress across the countryside.

"The journey has not been as swift as a bird's," wrote one journalist. "Travelling by steamboat and train the flying man might have been at London three weeks ago," another pointed out. "If Julius Ceaser had attempted to reach Britain by means of an aeroplane, we Britons would still be living in lonely Barbaric happiness," suggested the *Daily Chronicle*.

A letter from the chairman of the Great Central Railway — which ran the service from Dover to London — addressed to John Moisant Esq was published in the *London Penny Illustrated Paper*. It read: "Dear Sir, Persevere. It took us forty years to reach London. You have scarcely been at it a fortnight. Remember Bruce and the spider. Yours encouragingly, Sir A. Henderson, Bart."

On 6 September the wind finally dropped and Moisant took off for London. At 5.23 p.m. the aircraft arrived over London's Crystal Palace show grounds, circled twice then approached to land on the nearby Beckenham cricket field. Moisant misjudged his approach and, clipping a fence, the Blériot ended its odyssey like a great crippled bird — nose down with yet another shattered propeller (the fourth since leaving Paris) and a buckled undercarriage. Both men climbed out, once more unhurt, as a crowd gathered. Uncharacteristically subdued, Moisant stroked Paris-London, as he told reporters:

> I learnt more about flying in the first three miles today than I have over all the rest of the journey. The air above those Kentish valleys was very bothering. I have done what I set out to do and am happy to have at last completed my journey to London, even though I don't know exactly where I landed.

"DOGGED DOES IT," headlined London's *Daily Express*

and, echoing British sentiments, stated: " Few men would have had the pluck to go on trying as he has done. Few men would have had the nerve to face those repeated failures and so to snatch victory from the jaws of defeat. It may be that Mr Moisant's average rate of flight over the journey is not very high. But he has finished ... Bravo!"

In October 1910 Moisant arrived in New York to take part in the Belmont Park International Aviation Meet. With him were a group of young European fliers who, attracted by his enterprise and wealth, had come to America as his guests. "My name is spelt M–O–I–S–A–N–T ... John B ... from Chicago ... I'm not a Frenchman," the rising aviation star told pressmen.

Alfred Moisant, who had agreed to manage his younger brother's new career, had rented an entire floor at the Hotel Astor. There they held court. Determined to steal the limelight from the rest of the aviation world, John Moisant entertained in a style that made even profligate New York society sit up and take notice. His swarthy good looks set many female hearts fluttering, but columnist Kate Karew dashed their marriage hopes in the *New York City American*: "You'd look at him twice dears — I know you would. And you might call him anything from cute to handsome, without going wide of the mark. Yes, and he's a bachelor. Tut, Tut! It's no use! He's wedded to his art."

Twenty four of the world's foremost fliers were at Belmont. The English contingent included elegant Claude Grahame-White who had just completed a triumphant American tour. Moisant's instructor, Alfred Leblanc, Hubert Latham and Count Jaques de Lesseps were among nine Frenchmen out to prove their aviation supremacy. There were sixteen American airmen, including taciturn Glen Curtiss and the "Heavenly Twins" of the Wright brothers' team, Ralph Johnstone and Arch Hoxsey.

Two events attracted world attention: the Gordon Bennett Cup Race, and the Statue of Liberty Race, somewhat exaggeratedly billed by the *New York American* as " the most perilous and spectacular aeroplane race known to the annals of aviation". It carried a winner's purse of US $10 000 donated by an industrialist-millionaire aptly named Thomas Fortune Ryan.

Moisant strutted into Belmont's aviation arena like a glittering gladiator. What he lacked in flying finesse he made up for with his fearless determination. He took part in the preliminary events and almost daily contributed the main feature with a spectacular smash. Somehow he always walked away unscathed, a smile on his face and Paris-London perched on his shoulder. "Hurt? No, not at all. Nothing ever happens to anybody flying," he told newsmen, as he brushed off the dust.

Moisant was the darling of the crowd and he basked in their adulation. He cared little that many of them came only see the crashes — thirty-two fliers had already died during 1910. Worried by Moisant's devil-may-care attitude, Ralph Johnstone cautioned: "Be careful John. There's no point in getting yourself killed. No amount of publicity's worth that."

When the ten days of flying were over, Moisant had wrecked three machines, taken second place in the Gordon Bennett Cup and had won the Statue of Liberty Race (a decision later changed in favour of Claude Grahame-White). Celebrating over dinner at the Hotel Astor, Moisant was approached by Harriet Quimby, women's editor and dramatic critic for *Leslie's Weekly* magazine, who was making her rounds of the theatre crowd. The glamorous journalist had seen Moisant flying at Belmont earlier in the day. "Will you teach me to fly?" she asked. "Anytime you want," Moisant replied.

A year later she became America's first licensed air-woman.

Following Belmont, Moisant announced the formation of a company called Moisant International Aviators. The first full-time professional aerial circus, it employed pilots from France, America and Switzerland and was managed by Alfred Moisant.

From the list of bankers and industrialists on the company's board , and its million dollars in capital, it seems that the lavish parties and the attention-getting flying had paid off. A large administrative force was housed in opulent offices in the new Times Building and John Wanamaker was appointed sales agent.

On 22 November 1910 a specially leased train left New York carrying the Moisant International Aviators. It consisted of three pullman cars for the pilots, executives and mechanics, and four specially equipped wagons housing the aircraft and repair shop. The entire train was emblazoned on the top and sides with the company name. In Richmond, Memphis, Chattanooga, Dallas, Fort Worth, Waco, San Antonio and El Paso the crowds went wild.

Their repertoire included flying over the downtown area, cutting figure-eights, racing against automobiles, and holding speed, altitude and duration contests with one another. Newspapers shrieked praise, calling the barnstorming troupe "a dazzling success". However, thousands of people in each city watched from their roofs rather than paying admission to the fairgrounds.

"We want Moisant ... we want Johnny and Miss Paree [the cat]," the crowds chanted on Christmas Eve, the opening day of their week-long New Orleans performance. Though still the most inexperienced of the aviators, the reckless, showboating Moisant was their hero and the show's star performer. His favourite stunt was shutting off his Blériot's motor and diving down. At Memphis, after diving from 2000 feet, he had misjudged the pull-out and came within a whisker of hitting the ground.

"Moisant's entire style of flying has changed," a worried mechanic told a reporter. "He evidently has been seeing how far he can go without killing himself." Concerned for his safety, members of the troupe implored him to be more careful. But Moisant ignored their pleas It was almost as if he believed that he had as many lives as his tiny mascot.

On the last day of 1910, Moisant was to compete for the US$4 000 Michelin Cup prize, to be awarded to the pilot who stayed in the air the longest. Waving to the huge crowd he climbed away from New Orleans' City Park. An extra fuel tank was strapped to the Blériot's open wooden fuselage and his beloved mascot was snuggled in her special basket.

A few minutes later Moisant arrived at a nearby practice field where the contest was to commence. For some unaccountable reason he needlessly attempted to land downwind. At about thirty feet the aircraft flew into turbulence, pitched nose down and slammed into the ground. Moisant, who refused to use a seat belt, was hurled from the cockpit and landed in a clump of bushes. Bystanders rushed over . This time he did not get up to greet them with his fabled smile. The King of the Aviators was dead. Paris-London had survived the crash , but Moisant had finally used up his own nine lives. *Colliers* magazine wrote his epitaph: "Fear was a stranger to Moisant, and he died with a smile on his lips, his neck broken by a short fall which was the result of a moment's carelessness in landing."

Alfred kept the International Aviators going but, despite the introduction of two women fliers, Moisant's sister Mathilde and Harriet Quimby, their success was never the same following the loss of the star performer. Furthermore, Glen Curtiss' rival barnstorming troupe

now travelled the country. In 1912 the company folded.
Alfred returned to Salvador where his brothers George
and Edward had died of pneumonia. There, while trying
to regain control of their estate, he was murdered,
nobody knows by whom.

The brief but glorious era of the Moisant's International Aviators was over. They had helped spark
America's first love affair with the aeroplane. It was an
affair that blossomed into an enduring romance over the
next quarter-century, warmed by the thousands of barnstorming pilots who followed in John Moisant's slipstream.

Yet as suddenly as the world discovered John Moisant, it forgot him. Less than a week after his fatal crash
the International Aviators opened in Dallas where, after
watching French pilot René Simon perform, the *San
Antonio Express* headlined: "SIMON OUTDOES DARING
AVIATORS IN RECKLESSNESS : HIS FLIGHT AT DALLAS IS
MORE SPECTACULAR THAN ANY MOISANT MADE."

Krupps built the world's first anti-aircraft gun in a vain attempt to stop the balloons leaving Paris.

This 1871 photograph shows the balloon in which Léon Gambetta escaped tethered in the Place St Pierre.

Gambetta says farewell before climbing aboard the balloon *Armand Barbés*. In the background the *Georges Sand* also prepares to lift off.

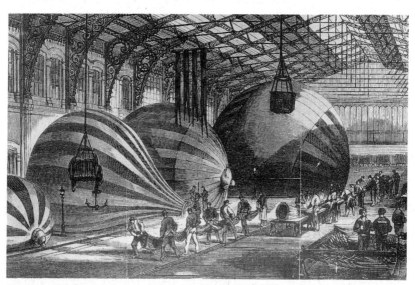

The Gare d'Orléans railway station was put at the disposal of balloon manufacturers Eugene and Jules Godard during the siege of Paris.

Andree's balloon *Oren (Eagle)* being inflated in its special hangar on Danes Island. The photo was taken by G. and H. Hasselblad, official photographers for the expedition.

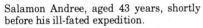

Salamon Andree, aged 43 years, shortly before his ill-fated expedition.

An artist's impression of the Andree expedition leaving Danes Island for the North Pole. The three aeronauts stand on the observation platform above the enclosed gondola which contained their "living quarters". The sails were to increase the balloon's speed.

The *Eagle* stranded forever on the polar icecap. Taken by crewman Strindberg, the photograph was processed from film that lay for thirty-three years beneath the ice.

Andree and Fraenkel pose with a polar bear they shot for food. Remnants of this bear, examined fifty-two years later, solved the mystery of the airmen's death.

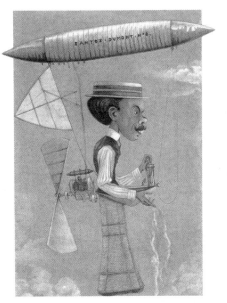

Santos-Dumont's flamboyant experiments were caricatured on the cover of this early edition of *Vanity Fair* magazine.

On 19 October 1901, Santos-Dumont in his airship *Number 6* won the 125,000-franc Deutsch Grand Prix.

Perched on a bicycle saddle (to save weight), Santos-Dumont tests airship *Number 4* while assistants, including a top-hatted passer-by (left), hold mooring lines.

Standing up to fly his *14-bis*, Santos-Dumont makes Europe's first aeroplane flight in 1906. His strange-looking machine was called a "canard" because its design, with the wings at the rear, made it look like a duck in flight.

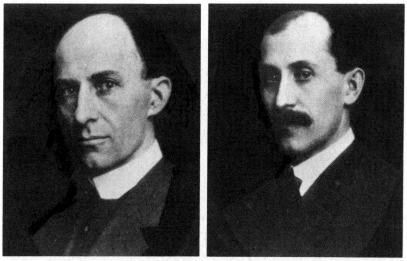

Wilbur (left) and Orville Wright (right) used the profits from their bicycle business to build the world's first successful powered aeroplane.

On 17 December 1903 Wilbur Wright introduces the world to powered flight. His brother Orville watches anxiously as the *Flyer* lifts from its launching rail.

Fresh from his flight across the English Channel, Louis Blériot, here waving his hat to an adoring crowd, was the favourite to win the 1909 Gordon Bennett Cup at Reims.

Born in Paris and educated in England, pilot Hubert Latham was another crowd favourite at Reims. Here he talks with Antionette Gastombide for whom France's elegant Antionette monoplane was named.

GRANDE SEMAINE D'AVIATION DE CHAMPAGNE (Journée du 22 Août)
L'américain Curtiss et son biplan

Phototypie J. Bienaimé, Reims   Librairie L. Michaud, Reims

Photo-postcards of the airmen and aircraft, produced on the first day at Reims, were sold to the crowd. This one shows America's Glenn Curtiss and his victorious *Reims Flyer* biplane.

GRANDE SEMAINE D'AVIATION DE CHAMPAGNE (Première Journée)
Vue d'ensemble des Tribunes

Phototypie J. Bienaimé, Reims   Librairie L. Michaud, Reims

Another Reim's photo-postcard shows Blériot's Model XI monoplane being prepared for flight in front of one of the flag-decked grandstands.

AMBUL

Aviation pioneer Alberto Santos-Dumont (second from right) enjoys an elegant grandstand lunch at Reims.

John Moisant and his flying mascot arrive in New York following the Paris-London flight.

Moisant and Fileaux use a racecourse in Kent to take off in their Blériot XI-2 monoplane.

Down in a farmer's field. This was one of the six forced landings that punctuated Moisant's Paris-London flight. Visible are the trestles Fileaux used to repair the damaged landing gear and replace the broken propeller.

Moisant formed America's first barnstorming aerial circus. Here his brother Alfred (front seat centre) and a local band drum up business and attract local children.

Moisant and the unsuccessful monoplane he built. The American adventurer named it *The Crow*.

Harriet Quimby in her plum-coloured satin flying suit converted from a dress to pantaloons. She poses here with a Blériot monoplane manufactured under licence by the Moisant School of Aviation.

Tall, elegant Harriet Quimby was christened the "Dresden Doll" by New York journalists.

Minutes before Harriet Quimby's cross-Channel flight. Spectators hold the Blériot while Gustav Hamel leans over Harriet Quimby's shoulder to give the engine a final check.

Investigors and Harriet Quimby's mechanic (crouched at right) examine the wreckage of her Blériot monoplane shortly after her fatal plunge into Boston Harbour.

The crew of the Sopwith Wallaby. Captain George Matthews AFC (left) and Sergeant Thomas Kay AFC (right).

Matthews poses with the Sopwith Wallaby at Hounslow aerodrome, near London. For protection against the weather the open cockpits of the Sopwith biplane could be closed in flight and the crew peered out of windows in the side of the fuselage.

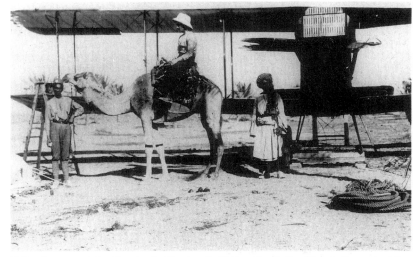

Following a crash-landing in the Persian Gulf, Tom Kay takes a break from repairing the Wallaby and tries his hand at riding a camel.

Matthews and Kay's epic journey ended with this crash in a banana plantation on the island of Bali.

With the world-wide publicity that followed his trans-Atlantic flight Charles Lindbergh became the world's most recognised personality.

Lindbergh's remarkable Ryan NYP monoplane now hangs in the Smithsonian Institution's National Air & Space Museum in Washington DC. The small window in the door at the rear of the wing, and a similar window on the other side, provided the airman's only vision. A periscope above the wing proved useless.

7
Upstaged by the *Titanic*

Shortly before midnight on 16 April 1912 the White Star liner *Titanic* plunged three kilometres to the floor of the Atlantic Ocean. It was a tragedy never to be forgotten by the relatives of the 1500 souls lost in the world's greatest sea disaster. Even today the name *Titanic* can hush the conversation among seafaring people.

The loss of the "unsinkable" liner on her maiden voyage was also a tragedy (but of a different sort) for Miss Harriet Quimby, an ambitious New York journalist turned flyer. She was not on board when the jagged iceberg sliced through the ship's hull. Nor were any of her close friends or relatives. Nevertheless, the *Titanic* disaster all but cost Harriet her place in history. For on the day that the great White Star liner plunged to the bottom of the ocean she became the first woman to fly the English Channel. As the victim of aviation's greatest upstage, the American airwoman missed her chance of achieving the sort of world fame accorded Amelia Earhart a generation later.

Flying was still in its infancy when Harriet Quimby became America's first licensed woman pilot in 1911 and decided to emulate the feat of Louis Blériot. The French airman had become world famous following his epochal 1909 flight across the English Channel. The flight was a feat of incredible courage and had evoked unprecedented international attention. Sensing the future military significance of the aeroplane, the British press emoted: "Britain's impregnability has passed away."

Aeroplanes were still unreliable contraptions, powered by small and often cantankerous engines, and pilots talked in terms of minutes aloft rather than hours. Since Blériot, several other airmen had successfully negotiated the thirty-five kilometres of swirling sea separating England and France. Nevertheless, flying the English was still considered aviation's yardstick of courage and performance. Indeed, flying anywhere was a cross-your-fingers enterprise. The fatality rate was shocking— some one hundred deaths in 1911 alone. Not surprisingly, aeroplanes were considered no fit place for women.

Such was the world of aviation Harriet Quimby had chosen to enter. Nothing in her background seemed to point to a dangerous career in the air. Born in Coldwater, Michigan in 1875, she was the younger daughter of William and Ursula Quimby. Her father, an unsuccessful farmer, had earlier served as a cook in the Union Army.

In 1877 the family joined the rush to California and opened a grocery store in Arroyo Grande, on the coast midway between San Francisco and Los Angeles. The business failed and they moved to San Francisco where the long-suffering Ursula Quimby took control of the family fortunes. She manufactured herbal medicines (which William sold from the back of a wagon) and augmented their income by making prune sacks for a fruit-packing factory.

Energetic and ambitious, Ursula Quimby was determined that her daughters should rise above their humble beginnings and break into society circles. She created an aura of mystery about the family's background and encouraged the girls to suggest that they came from a wealthy farming family. As her daughters blossomed into beautiful young women, tales of a

European education were added. Although educated only at public schools, Harriet and her sister Kittie had the poise and intelligence to carry it off.

It was a time when nice young ladies of good families were expected to make an early marriage and a life devoted to home and husband. Harriet shocked her parents by deciding to become a journalist. In 1902 she joined the staff of the *San Francisco Dramatic Review*. Later she worked as a reporter for the *San Francisco Call* and wrote Sunday features for the *Chronicle*. The glamourous journalist became known about town, and turned heads in the best circles. She became an acknowledged "beauty" — in the age of the Gibson girl — and her portrait hung in the all-male Bohemian Club on Nob Hill until it was destroyed in the Great Earthquake of 1906.

Obviously intent on a career, she apparently did not allow any serious romantic attachments to interfere with her profession. It had been hard enough convincing skeptical editors to take her seriously. Any hint of marriage and children would immediately have terminated her journalistic career.

Harriet Quimby was a "thoroughly modern Millie". An ardent sportswoman, and fascinated by mechanical things, she drove a yellow open runabout and was one of the first journalists to use a typewriter. But some newspapers chose to focus on her fashion sense. "Miss Quimby," an interview in *World Magazine* gushed, "has a low voice and a brilliant smile, and she runs strong to overhung bonnets and antique ornaments such as basilisks, amulet scarabs and the like, so that even in business attire her individuality is very distinctive".

In 1903 she accepted the post of dramatic critic and women's editor for *Leslie's Weekly*, a prestigious New York publication, and the family moved east. Soon she was also writing a steady stream of feature articles and her byline became well-known and highly respected. As one editor put it: " She has about the keenest nose for news I ever met with in a woman."

It was her nose for news that led Harriet Quimby into aviation, when she attended the 1910 Gordon Bennett Cup Race at the Belmont Park Aviation Meeting in search of a story. She was fascinated by the adulation of the crowd for aviators such as France's Alfred Leblanc, and England's Claude Grahame-White and Tom Sopwith who were the matinee idols of New York. Dashing and debonair Grahame-White epitomised the "magnificent men in their flying machines". Society belles paid US$500 for a five-minute flip with the urbane Englishman. "It was g-a-lorious," one bubbled.

Harriet Quimby was particularly inspired by local hero John Moisant — a swashbuckling American pilot who flew with a tabby kitten mascot in his cockpit. Besides taking second place in the Gordon Bennett Cup Race, Moisant was awarded first place in the US$10 000 Statue of Liberty cross country race (a home-town decision which was later overturned when the Féderation Aéronatique Internationale (FAI) awarded the race to Grahame-White).

On the last evening of the Belmont Meeting, while having dinner at the Hotel Astor, Quimby noticed Moisant at a nearby table. She later recalled: "I went directly over to him and told him I wished to learn to fly."

Moisant invited her to join a flying school he was planning to start on Long Island. He was killed in an air crash before she could start training, but the school opened anyway, managed by Moisant's brother Albert, with a Frenchman, André Houpert, as the flight instructor. The school was equipped with Metz-Blériots, built under licence by the Moisants, and powered by 30-horsepower rotary engines.

Undeterred by John Moisant's death, Harriet commenced flying in May 1911. Aware that she was breaking into a totally male-dominated field, Harriet decided to keep her plans a secret — especially from the press. To conceal her obviously female form she designed a special flying outfit. Made of wool-backed, plum-colored satin, it was a long dress which quickly converted into pantaloons. It incorporated a hood which hid her face and hair.

Seeing Harriet taking lessons encouraged Moisant's sister Mathilde to take up flying, and the two women joined the school's five male students. Shortly before her death in 1965 Mathilde Moisant recalled:

> We were all taught the same way. We just had little single-seat machines. The first step was a heavy [under-powered] machine not designed to leave the ground. That was called *Saint Genevive*. She was the patron saint of the fliers in France. After learning to keep straight our next machine was the *Grasshopper* which would go up to five or six feet then come down again. That was to get the feeling of being in the air.

Harriet had been flying for some weeks when she had her first accident. A tire blew out as her Metz-Blériot was taking off. The undercarriage collapsed and the monoplane finished in a crumpled heap. Within minutes reporters were at the scene. To their surprise they found the uninjured pilot inspecting the damage was none other than the women's editor of *Leslie's Weekly*. Next day's papers told the story of an American woman who dared to learn flying. The press nicknamed her the "Dresden Doll Aviatrix".

At that time male chauvinists contended that women couldn't master flying. However, after working with Harriet Quimby, instructor Houpert insisted that an aeroplane was probably safer in the hands of a woman than with most of the men he had taught.

On 31 July, 1911, after thirty-three lessons, Quimby was ready for her licence test. On her first attempt she failed the landing test, which required her to land within 100 feet (30 metres) of a marked point. The following day she landed seven feet nine inches (2.3 metres) from the mark. A *New York Times* journalist covering the event reported that she walked nonchalantly over to the official FAI observer and said, "Well, I guess I get my licence."

Harriet Quimby was the second woman in the world to be granted a licence (the first was Mme Baronne Raymonde de la Roche of France). Two weeks later Mathilde Moisant became America's second licensed female pilot.

With her training having cost $2.50 a minute (then a day's pay for many people), it had been an expensive experience and the journalist turned flyer was determined to make it pay off. Besides, she had always said she wanted to retire at thirty-five and do "some serious writing" — though, to keep that chronological deadline credible, sometime after leaving San Francisco she conveniently dropped ten years from her true age.

Her judgement of aviation as a money-making proposition was astute. Americans had gone aviation mad and were flocking to flying exhibitions. Leading aviators were receiving US$1000 a flight and prize money of US$10 000 was not uncommon. Claude Grahame-White had received US$50 000 just to appear at the 1910 Boston Aviation Meeting.

A month after winning her licence Harriet Quimby thrilled 20 000 spectators, and earned US$1500, with a moonlight flight over Staten Island. A month later she won US$600 for defeating France's Helene Dutrieu in a race at the Richmond County Fair. She shared her flying experiences with the readers of *Leslie's Weekly* in articles such as "How a Woman Learns to Fly" and "The Dangers of Flying and How to Avoid Them".

In December 1911 she toured Mexico as a member of the Moisant International Flyers — America's first flying circus. At the inauguration ceremonies for President

Francisco Madero she became the first woman to fly over Mexico City.

While in Mexico she decided to reach for world fame by attempting a flight across the English Channel. She chose Europe for her attention-getting effort because it had become the centre of world aviation. Even though several other pilots had flown the Channel since Blériot, Quimby shrewdly assessed that it was still a focus of attention — particularly for the first crossing by a woman pilot. She was aware that the notoriety resulting from a successful flight would allow her to increase her "appearance" fee.

She employed a friend of the Wright brothers, balloon designer Leo Stevens, as her business manager. Armed with a letter of introduction to Louis Blériot the pair sailed for Europe on 7 March 1912. In London she sold the European rights to her story to the *Daily Mirror* and then headed to Paris, where she acquired a 50 horsepower Blériot XI monoplane.

Posing as American tourists, Quimby and her manager returned to England and established their headquarters at the Hotel Lord Warden in Dover. As rumors were circulating that an English woman was preparing to make the Channel flight, the Americans placed a shroud of secrecy over their venture. Only Blériot and a few close friends knew of their plans.

Their hopes were dashed on 2 April when newspapers reported that England's Eleanor Trehawke Davies had flown the Channel. She had, but only, as it turned out, as a passenger in a two-seat Blériot piloted by English pilot Gustav Hamel. He was promptly invited to join the American airwoman's team as an adviser.

From the outset Hamel expressed fears for the airwoman's safety and at one stage pleaded to take her place. His incredible plan was to dress in her clothes, secretly leave England, and land on a deserted French beach where she would be waiting to change places.

Quimby wrote: "I adamantly refused his offer, and if he had not been such a dear friend I would have been very angry. I did accept his offer to help me read a compass. That was something new to me."

Delayed a week by stormy weather, Hamel taught the airwoman how to navigate by using a watch and compass. On Sunday, 14 April the wind dropped for a few hours but Quimby steadfastly refused to fly, telling her stunned manager, "I have made it my rule never to fly on a Sunday." The vigil continued until the early hours of 16 April, when there was another break in the weather. Harriet wrote later:

> There was no wind, scarcely a breath of air was stirring. The monoplane was hurried out of the hangar. We knew that we must hasten, for it was almost certain that the wind would rise again within an hour. Mr Hamel jumped into the machine and was off for a short tryout of the engine and to report the atmospheric conditions. He found everything satisfactory and hurried back, making one of those beautiful and easy landings for which he is famous.

By 5.30 a.m. all was ready. It was bitterly cold and daylight had disclosed a bank of fog hanging over the Channel. After a quick discussion, Quimby decided to go ahead. She was well rugged up against the cold. Under her satin flying suit she wore two pairs of silk overalls. Over it she buttoned a woollen overcoat, then a raincoat, and topped the lot with a sealskin shawl.

The world's only known film clip of Quimby reveals the proceedings. Its shows the airwoman powdering her nose before being helped her up into the wicker seat perched high in the Blériot's open cockpit. There was no windscreen to hunch behind and she was at the mercy of wind and weather.

The flickering film shows her mechanic giving a sharp swing to the delicate Chauviere wooden propeller and the little Gnome rotary engine crackling into life. Puffs of oily exhaust smoke whisked back over the six men grimly holding on to the aircraft. Standing on the wing and leaning over Quimby, Hamel listened for the slightest miss that could indicate a fouled spark-plug or faulty ignition. It was running smoothly and Hamel clambered down.

Quimby signalled the ground-crew to let go. The Blériot gathered speed, bumping gently on its bicycle-like wheels. Tail up, a couple of bounces, and she was airborne, and then vanished quickly into the mist. Recalling the next thirty minutes, Quimby wrote:

> From my vantage point my eyes lit at once on Dover Castle. It was half-hidden in a fog bank. I felt trouble was coming, but I made directly for the flagstaff of the castle, as I had promised the waiting *Mirror* photographers and moving picture men I should do.
>
> In an instant I was beyond the cliffs and over the Channel. Far beneath me I saw the *Mirror*'s tug, with its stream of black smoke. It was trying to keep ahead of me but I passed it in a jiffy. Then the thickening fog obscured my view. Calais was out of sight. I could not see ahead of me at all nor could I see the water below. There was only one thing for me to do and that was to keep my eyes fixed on the compass.

By all the rules of good airmanship she should have turned back. Cloud-flying was unknown in those days and the Blériot was notoriously unstable and had no blind-flying instruments. She had no way of keeping control other than the "seat of her pants" — the tricks of the trade of the early flyers who relied on wind noise in the wires, engine note, the feel of the slipstream, and a finely tuned sense of balance.

Either by good luck or an uncanny natural ability she was able to keep the monoplane on an even keel and, with the aid of a hand compass jammed between her knees, headed in the right general direction.

Occasionally she glanced at a small bronze East Indian idol she carried for good luck. Quimby had rescued it from the editor's desk in the *Daily Mirror* offices.

It had once belonged to a French airman who swore it had brought bad luck. Once a week the *Daily Mirror* held public ritual executions of bad-luck talismans and the Frenchman's idol had been slated for the next funeral pyre. Now named "Ganesha", it was Quimby's only company as she battled through the fog.

Despite the layers of clothing it was bitterly cold. Silently the airwoman thanked Hamel for his thoughtful last act of tying a huge hot water bottle to her waist. As the minutes ticked by she approached mid-Channel, every nerve strained to sense the slightest change in the aircraft's attitude.

The concentration was exhausting and minutes passed like hours. Should she lose control, or her engine fail, the chances of surviving a crash-landing in the fog-shrouded Channel were remote indeed. She wrote:

> My hands were covered with long, Scotch woollen gloves, which gave me good protection from the cold and fog. But the machine was wet and my face so covered with dampness that I had to push my goggles up on my forehead. I could not see through them.

At one stage as she descended, the Blériot's Gnome engine appeared to flood and began backfiring. "I figured on pancaking down to strike the water with the plane in a floating position," she wrote. "To my great relief the gasoline quickly burned away and my engine resumed an even purr."

Describing the final moments of the flight, she recalled: "Glancing at my watch I knew that France must be in sight if only I could get below the fog and see it. So I dropped down till I was only about half my previous height. The sunlight struck on my face and my eyes lit upon the white and sandy shores of France. I felt happy but I could not find Calais."

She had missed Calais by fifty kilometres and eventually landed on a beach at Hardelot. But it really didn't matter. She had crossed the English Channel. Within minutes people came running from all directions. They rushed up and began shaking her hand and patting her shoulders. The ecstatic airwoman was hoisted shoulder high and carried into town.

"They were chattering in French, of which I comprehended sufficient to discover that they knew I had crossed the Channel. They were congratulating themselves that the first woman to cross in an aeroplane had landed on their fishing beach," Quimby recalled.

It was little short of a miracle that Harriet succeeded with her flight, considering the fog, her lack of experience, and her machine's lack of blind-flying instruments. Moreover, she was flying a new type of Blériot for the first time , and had never used a compass before.

Nevertheless, as she relaxed in her hotel that night, Harriet Quimby was confident she had finally "arrived" on the world aviation scene. She could picture the next day's headlines: AMERICAN AIRWOMAN CONQUERS CHANNEL. Tomorrow she would be the most famous airwoman in the world.

Poor Harriet Quimby. She could not have picked a less propitious day for her flight. When the story of her courageous achievement arrived at the desks of the news editors of the world, it was swamped beneath a mountain of copy detailing the tragedy of the *Titanic*. Her front-page story became a few forlorn paragraphs tucked away in the bowels of the papers. Her achievement went almost unnoticed, until the shock of the *Titanic* disaster eventually died down and she did receive some publicity in America.

The reaction of the *New York Times* was tempered by its disapproving attitude of the strident calls being made by the growing women's suffrage movement in 1912. Pointing out that the flight had already been accomplished by a man, the paper churlishly editorialised: " The feminists should be careful about exulting over Miss Quimby's exploit. They should not call it a

great achievement, lest by so doing they invite the
dreadful humiliating qualification, great for a woman."

Harriet Quimby arrived back in New York on 12 May
1912, only a week after 15 000 women had demonstrated on Fifth Avenue in support of women's suffrage.
The suffragettes, it seems, had little time for Quimby,
especially after she rejected their suggestion that she
name her new Blériot *The Pankhurst* or *The Cat* (after
the celebrated suffragettes Emmeline Pankhurst and
Carrie Chapman Catt). They were even more incensed
when she joked in *World Magazine*: "If I had to choose
one, *Cat* would be more appropriate. Really you would
be surprised how purely feminine a monoplane can be
when it wants to."

On 1 July a huge crowd turned out at Squantam Field
for the week-long 1912 Boston Aviation Meeting. They
came to see America's brash new barnstormers such as
daredevil Lincoln Beachey, nerveless Charlie
"Spareparts" Hamilton, California's dapper Farnum T.
Fish, the first airmail pilot Earle Ovington, New England's air ace Hank Terrill, and Harriet Quimby —
billed as the Queen of the Channel.

By mid-afternoon the meet was in full swing.
Jammed in the stands overlooking Dorchester Bay, the
crowds were entertained by races, spot-landing competitions, flour bombing, aerobatics and, for the rich and
daring, the thrill of joy-flighting.

Quimby was busy. She had purchased a new 70-
horsepower two-seat Blériot, disregarding its reputation as the trickiest aircraft the French designer had
produced. Several European flyers had already met
their death in the type, which was reputed to have a
critical centre-of-gravity balance problem when a passenger was on board.

The airwoman carried a number of passengers and,
between flights, posed for photographers, cutting a
glamorous figure in her plum-colored outfit. Still seek-

ing world acclaim, Quimby had announced her intention of attacking a speed record of 93 km/h set at Boston the previous year by Claude Grahame-White.

Late on the first afternoon Quimby decided to make a trial flight around Grahame-White's record course. She took airshow manager William P. Willard along for the ride. The flight lasted about twenty minutes and the crowd waited eagerly to compare her time with the record. Leo Stevens described her return.

> The speck grew larger until the dragonfly outline of the Blériot again shaped itself against the blue sky. We could see that Miss Quimby was coming down, flying at a speed of about 85 mph. At about 2500 feet altitude she passed over the field. Suddenly something happened. The Blériot seemed to dip, nose pointed downward, tail thrust upward.
>
> The next instant we saw a body (Willard) hurl itself upward out of the machine, apparently leaping 50 feet in the air, describe an arc, then come plunging downward well ahead of the monoplane. Instantly Miss Quimby righted the machine. But a moment later the Blériot again dipped, stood in a perpendicular position with its nose down and tail up, then turned completely over. Then Miss Quimby, flung from her seat, dropped, her body whirling over and over.

The crowd hushed, then screams raced through the stands. Many covered their eyes but most, unable to look away, watched horrified until the two bodies disappeared in a spray of water a hundred yards from the shore. "My God, they're killed," someone shouted. Women fainted. Willard's son led the rush to the water's edge. Stevens collapsed. The bodies were quickly brought to shore where a doctor pronounced that the flyers were dead. Both had broken backs.

True to tradition, the show went on. But for the rest of the week the pilots wore black armbands and each aircraft streamed black crepe in honor of their dead comrades.

A special service was held for Harriet Quimby in New

York City on 4 July 1912. Among the large gathering
were representitives of the New York Aero Club, the
Italian Aero Club and the Aeronautical Society of America. "Her name is added to the long list of those who have
freely given their lives in order that the world might be
greater and grander," said the minister. She was buried
the following day. The *San Francisco Call* said: "Her
mentor was the soaring albatross."

Many wild theories were put forward about the cause
of the accident. America's great aircraft designer Glen
Martin probably came closest to the facts when he
attributed it to the aircraft's inherent instability and
overcontrolling, which was compounded by excessive
descent speed. He also pointed out that had Harriet and
Willard been strapped in the accident would not have
occurred.

That was the tragedy of the whole affair. It need never
have happened. No matter what triggered the Blériot's
pitch down, if the pair worn seat belts, Willard would
not have been tossed overboard, which put the machine
totally out of balance, and Quimby would not have been
flung to an appalling death. But in 1912 seat belts were
not popular and many aircraft did not have them. Most
crashes occurred on landing, and many pilots — particularly in monoplanes — preferred to jump at the last
moment rather than risk being crushed by the engine.

Harriet Quimby was one of the long list of casualties
of aviation's age of innocence. That optimistic, hit and
miss, try it and see, childhood of flying. Her star burned
brightly for only a short time yet she proved that women
possessed the intelligence, ability and courage to fly.
She opened the door for the airwomen who followed. In
an article she wrote for *Good Housekeeping*, published
after her death, she predicted:

I think the aeroplane should open a fruitful occupation for
women. I see no reason they cannot realize handsome
incomes by carrying passengers between adjacent towns,

from delivering parcels, taking photographs or conducting schools of flying. Any of these things it is now possible to do.

Just as fate had played an ironic twist at Harriet Quimby's moment of glory, her death was bizarre. Had she been able to report on her own tragedy she might, with a wry smile, have started:

Harriet Quimby, the rising aviation star who was denied top billing by the SS *Titanic* in the world's greatest upstage, today played her final performance ..."

8
The flight of the Sopwith Wallaby

1919 was a year of high aviation adventure. Besides marking the start of a flurry of early airlines, it encompassed two of the great milestone flights of aviation history: the crossing of the Atlantic by Alcock and Brown, and the epic England–Australia flight of the Vickers Vimy G-EAOU ("God 'Elp All Of Us") by Ross and Keith Smith and their crew.

A lesser known, but equally daring flight took place during 1919. Like the Vimy G-EAOU epic, it also occurred during the England–Australia challenge and involved a single engine Sopwith Wallaby biplane crewed by Australian Flying Corps airmen Captain George Matthews and Sergeant Thomas Kay.

In one of aviation's most magnificent failures Matthews and Kay got to within a day's flight of Australia before ill-fortune brought their flight to an end in a banana plantation in Bali. Their long-forgotten story was the stuff of a true Biggles adventure.

Born in South Australia in 1883, George Matthews was a navigation officer with the Howard Smith shipping line when the First World War erupted. He joined up and served at Gallipoli with the Australian Light Horse before transferring to the Australian Flying Corps in 1916. Following a stint flying fighters in France, Matthews became a flight instructor specialising in aerial navigation. His flight mechanic (and assistant pilot), Thomas Kay was born at Spring Mount,

Victoria in 1886. He worked as an engineer in Ballarat before joining the Australian Flying Corps as a mechanic. Following the armistice, Kay worked for Rolls Royce in England and qualified for his pilot's licence.

Matthews and Kay were among the first to respond to the remarkable challenge issued in Australia on 19 March 1919 which stated: "With a view to stimulating aerial activity, the Commonwealth Government has decided to offer £10,000 for the first successful flight to Australia from Great Britain, in a machine manned by Australians."

The idea was the brainchild of Prime Minister W.H."Billy" Hughes who had already used aircraft to commute from London while attending peace talks in Paris. Aware of the remarkable publicity already being generated by a £10 000 British prize for the first nonstop Atlantic flight, Hughes was determined to promote Australia, and its aviation future, with a similar award. "It would be a great advertisement for Australia and would concentrate the eyes of the world upon us," Hughes told government colleagues.

The sheer distance between London and Darwin — 17 600 kilometres — was so daunting that Hughes and his organisers set tough experience requirements for competing crews. Ironically they refused to allow the entry of two of Australia's greatest pioneer fliers of the future, Charles Kingsford Smith and Bert Hinkler. They dismissed Hinkler's plan to fly solo as too dangerous, and judged a team including Kingsford Smith as too inexperienced.

By October 1919, Alcock and Brown had conquered the Atlantic, and the public's attention turned to the six teams that were preparing to make the flight to Australia. According to the rules, they were allowed to set their own starting date. However, once started the flight had to be completed within thirty days.

Matthews and Kay were the first away. On 20 October

1919 they announced that, weather permitting, they
were setting out on the long haul to Australia the
following day. At 8.30 the next morning they arrived at
Hounslow Aerodrome, near London, to find mechanics
busy tuning the 360 horsepower Rolls Royce Eagle
engine of their Sopwith Wallaby biplane.

The big, two-seat Wallaby — based on Sopwith's BI
bomber — was a modified copy of the Sopwith Atlantic
that Australian test pilot Harry Hawker had used in a
unsuccessful attempt to fly the Atlantic just five months
earlier. Hawker and his navigator had been miraculously rescued by a passing ship after being forced down
in mid-Atlantic by an over-heating engine.

A crowd of journalists hung around a notice board
announcing: "Machine: Sopwith; Destination: Australia; Starting Time : When Fog Clears." Seeing the
airmen approach the Wallaby plane they rushed over to
get pictures and interviews. Asked if he was confident
of reaching Australia, Matthews replied: " No, but I am
hopeful. It is impossible to be confident in the face of
such a task, but I am satisfied that nobody could have
a better machine for the attempt."

Kay explained how, besides looking after the engine,
he would also share the flying load with Matthews,
using the specially installed set of dual controls in the
rear cockpit. "The human factor is reliable," he ob-
served, adding shrewdly: "the only unknown quantity
is the engine's power of endurance under varying
[climatic] conditions. The conditions of this flight are
such that a preliminary test was impossible."

The pair loaded their in-flight rations (chocolate,
tinned food and flasks of hot cocoa) into the cockpits
then pulled fur-lined leather flying suits over their
Australian Flying Corps uniforms. Watching their
preparations, an eagle-eyed reporter asked why the
Sopwith was not equipped with a collapsible boat like
the one carried aboard Harry Hawker's Sopwith

Atlantic. "That would merely prolong the agony," replied Matthews.

It was mid-morning before the fog cleared sufficiently for the airmen to make a start. Finally they took off at 11.44 a.m., circled the aerodrome for 25 minutes, then headed south east for France. As the Wallaby climbed slowly it was joined by a Sopwith Triplane fighter piloted by Harry Hawker.

A few days earlier Hawker, in his capacity as chief test pilot of the Sopwith Aeroplane Company, had completed the Wallaby's final flight tests. After determining that the Wallaby had a maximum speed of 193 km/hr and a cruising speed of around 160 km/hr, he suggested to Matthews they should soon overtake the slower Caudron biplane already being flown along the route by French pilot Étienne Poulet who was attempting to blaze the trail to Australia and the Far East. Although the Frenchman was not an official competitor in the contest and not entitled to the prize-money, the Australians were concerned lest a "foreigner" steal their glory.

When the Wallaby crossed the coast and headed out over the English Channel, Hawker waved good luck and turned back. Ahead of Matthews and Kay lay a bank of fog. As they neared France the fog became denser and the airmen were forced to land at Marquise (near Calais), barely 160 kilometres from their starting point.

The following morning they carried on to Cologne in Germany where Matthews received a cable from Prime Minister Hughes. It read:

> Wish you and Sergeant Kay every success in your great adventure. Every one of your fellow citizens hopes that an Australian aviator will be the first to fly from England to Australia and so achieve what will easily be a world's record in aerial navigation. Want you to take no unnecessary risks, to plug on day after day doing your best, but nothing foolhardy. If you cannot make Australia in 30 days never mind. The main thing is that an Australian should

get here first. If you do that you need not worry. Good luck.
Hughes.

Hughes subsequently sent similar messages to other
competitors. Clearly he was concerned for the safety of
the crews who had answered his government's challenge and was worried that the thirty-day limit might
be unrealistic. In retrospect there seems little doubt
that if no crew made the flight within thirty days, the
prize-money would be awarded to the first to arrive —
just so long as it was not the Frenchman!

In Cologne Matthews had arranged to pick up a set
of maps covering an alternative route he had chosen
across Germany and Austria. The airmen hoped to
shave their flight time by taking a slightly shorter, but
more northerly, route across Europe than the one rec-
ommended by the British Air Ministry. It was a decision
the Wallaby's crew were to regret, for it would take them
into the teeth of unusually early, and severe, winter
weather.

They got their first real taste of winter in Cologne
where they were grounded by snow. After several days
on the ground Matthews was appalled by a story he
noticed in a British newspaper. It was the first of many
inaccurate reports that were to plague all of the
England–Australia fliers. Matthews recalled:

> I borrowed a London 'daily' from a British naval officer
> stationed on the Danube. From it I learned that we had
> crashed at Cologne and broken some of Kay's ribs, besides
> injuring his ankle so seriously that he had washed out for
> the flight; also that the Royal Air Force in the city were
> fixing us up with spares and spoon-feeding us generally. As
> a matter of fact our landing in Cologne was quite inten-
> tional. We landed there to obtain aerial maps unprocurable
> in England and neither Kay nor the Wallaby suffered so
> much as a scratch.

Matthews and Kay were snowbound in Cologne for
7-10 days (depending on which report one believes —

even the airmen's records are hazy). They eventually managed to hop another 150 kilometres to Mayence where bitter winter conditions kept them grounded until the end of November. At Mayence the frustrated airmen made three fruitless attempts to continue their flight. Each time they got airborne but had to turn back. Matthews explained: Our handicaps were snow, fog and rain. In other words the weather was against us. The fog was so thick that we simply lost track of everything, and it would have been sheer madness to attempt to get over the lofty mountains or through the dense clouds.

They eventually got through to Vienna on 29 November where they were again delayed by bad weather, this time for almost a week. After leaving Vienna for Belgrade on 4 December their run of ill luck continued when heavy rain and fog forced them to land in a pig paddock 160 kilometres from Belgrade.

Yugoslavia was still in a state of turmoil following World War I with revolutionaries and patriots vying for power in this politically volatile part of Europe. Thus it was not surprising that the two uniformed Australian airmen were not welcomed by the party of Yugoslav troops that soon surrounded them and at gunpoint demanded their papers. Matthews recalled: "After one glance at our German maps (from Cologne) they promptly arrested us as militant Bolsheviks. They secured possession of our passports and identification papers."

Matthews and Kay were imprisoned for four days in a 3-metre square room. Fed only bread and pig's fat and unable to reason with their captors it seemed that they were destined for the firing squad. The two airmen eventually decided that they must escape at the first opportunity. It came the next morning when their guard was sleeping off the effects of a night's heavy drinking. "We grabbed our papers and bolted for the aeroplane," Matthews recalled.

The weather was still appalling but they preferred to risk the fog rather then a firing squad. Fortunately the engine started immediately, although the noise aroused their captors. As they roared into the air a volley of bullets whistled around the escaping airmen. In his log Kay recalled their escape from the "pig paddock" with the terse entry: "4-12-1919. Reved up engine (cold) hard to start. Reved up splendid and ran perfect to Novisad. Landed on good aerodrome at 1230."

The Wallaby's fuel supply was low when they eventually landed at Novisad Aerodrome near Belgrade. French troops still occupied the town. Matthews wrote: "They gave us a cordial welcome but when we asked for petrol we were met with a look of blank consternation." A train ride to Belgrade to meet with the Commanding Officer did not help. There was no spare petrol anywhere in the area. Matthews and Kay were grounded again.

In Belgrade they learned that much had happened to the other race competitors in the seven weeks since the Wallaby had left England. Four other aircraft had set out for Australia: the Alliance Endeavour crewed by Captain Roger Douglas and Lieutenant Leslie Ross; the Blackburn Kangaroo crewed by Lieutenant Valdemar Rendle, Captain (later Sir) Hubert Wilkins, Lieutenant David Williams, and Lieutenant Garnsey St Clair Potts; the Martinsyde A1 crewed by Captain Cedric Howell and Lieutenant George Fraser; and the Vickers Vimy crewed by Captain Ross Smith, Lieutenant Keith Smith, Sergeant Walter Shiers and Sergeant James Bennett.

Of the four machines, only the Vickers Vimy was still flying. The Alliance Endeavour had crashed only minutes after take-off killing its crew; the Martinsyde had come down at night in the Mediterranean off Corfu island and Howell and Fraser had drowned; and the Blackburn Kangaroo had been forced to retire following an engine failure and emergency landing on the island of Crete.

Even though Matthews and Kay were now well behind the Vimy there was still every chance that the Smith brothers could falter, giving the Wallaby the chance to regain the lead. It all depended on them obtaining some petrol. After three weeks of sheer frustration Matthews and Kay managed to cadge enough fuel to reach Bucharest from a passing French flier. From Bucharest they headed on towards Istanbul.

The airmen felt bitterly cold during this part of the flight despite the Wallaby's adjustable seats and sliding glass windows which enabled the two open cockpits to be converted to an enclosed cabin during bad weather. Flying at 13 000 feet they logged an air temperature of "46 degrees (Fahrenheit) below freezing point".

In the afternoon as they approached Adrianople a seized fuel pump caused a forced landing in what appeared to be a nice grass field. Matthews wrote: "As soon as the machine touched ground it sank to the axles in a quagmire. Sergeant Kay repaired the fault but we only got away by Kay hanging on to the tail and making a flying jump for the fuselage at take-off."

Landing in Istanbul late on 23 December the airmen heard the news that the Vickers Vimy had reached Darwin in just under twenty-eight days to take the £10,000 prize. Sportingly they immediately cabled their congratulations. There was never any discussion about giving up. They had come too far and been through too much. Theirs would be the second aircraft to reach Australia — and the first powered by a single engine.

Following Christmas, while methodically checking the engine prior to the over-desert section of the flight, Kay discovered a leak in the water jacket. After spending ten days vainly scouring the town for welding equipment, he was forced to use the airmen's last resort — Wrigleys Chewing Gum. Chewing a great wad he mixed it with powdered asbestos and plastered the gummy mixture over the hole. For added strength Kay tightly bound the area with copper wire. "Run engine and found everything OK", reported the resourceful mechanic.

On 14 January 1920 Matthews and Kay set out across the desert on the long 2700-kilometre haul to Baghdad. Reflecting on the flight so far, Matthews said: "Although it took us three months to get clear of Europe our actual flying time during that period was not more than twenty hours and the delays were not due to any defect in our engine, petrol or lubricating system. Our sole handicaps were those of rain, snow and fog."

They covered the 800 kilometres to Aleppo, Syria in six hours, landing in heavy rain on a bogged airfield. A week later "cheered by the first good weather of the trip" they covered the 730 kilometres to Baghdad in just over four hours. Here, using Royal Air Force facilities, Kay was able to carry out a major engine overhaul before they set out on the next leg to Bushire which — for once — they reached without incident.

The next day they departed at 6.45 a.m. on a daunting 1900-kilometre non-stop flight to Karachi. This was considered by most England–Australia pilots as the horror stretch of the whole flight. Thirty minutes after the Wallaby departed, authorities at Bushire received an urgent cable from Bandar Abbas, midway along the route to Karachi, advising the airmen that a massive sandstorm was in "full blast" over the Persian Gulf and on no account to leave Bushire. As the Wallaby carried no radio there was no way to warn Matthews and Kay of the storm.

It struck when they had travelled about 500 kilometres. Matthews wrote: "We encountered the storm and found it up to specifications. Blinded, our mouths, ears and nostrils choked with sand, tossed like a ship in a monsoon, and having a visibility of barely 50 yards, we battled against the elements."

Fearing that they would lose control and crash, the airmen attempted an emergency landing on the beach near the settlement of Bustaneh. Battling the turbulence they struck the steeply shelving sand in a nose-down attitude, shattering the propeller and landing gear and damaging the nose section of the fuselage. One of the landing wheels seemed to have disappeared until Kay noticed it floating away in the Persian Gulf. Plunging into the surf, fully clothed, he brought off a "particularly neat save".

Leaving Kay to guard the Sopwith, Matthews trekked along the beach to Bandar Abbas, where the British Consul provided a relief party, supplies and a launch to take them back to the crash site. Plagued by the storm, the return journey took four days. Kay, who had been provided with food and drink by a passing Parsee doctor, could not resist giving his companion a friendly serve when the party finally arrived back at the wreck.

"You're some skipper, I *don't* think. You break half my ribs in Cologne. The other half in Vienna. Now you go joyriding around Persia in a launch leaving me with no rations but a tin of Castrol [oil] — I am off to Ballarat by the next train," Kay joked.

The Sopwith was man-handled into a nearby stand of date palms by a party of convicts from the local jail. Then for two weeks Kay worked his magic using iron fence posts, bits of wood and lots of ingenuity. Finally he spliced the broken wheel axle with an old iron bar and fitted the spare propeller which they had carried since leaving London.

Unfortunately, the spare propeller had been warped by three months strapped to the side of the Wallaby's fuselage where it was exposed to the elements. When Kay tested the Sopwith's engine the propeller caused a vibration which the airmen feared would eventually cause mechanical damage. However, with no likelihood of finding a replacement until they reached India they decided to carry on.

They reached Jask, near Bandar Abbas, on 23 February 1920, where the wheel axle again gave way and damaged the lower port wing. Kay recalled another nightmare repair job: "We were in the blazing desert sun so we dragged it three miles to the shelter of an Englishman's verandah and there repaired it again. [Ten days later] It was then dragged three miles back to the aerodrome and from there we reached Karachi in a non-stop flight."

In Karachi Matthews and Kay met up with another Australian team heading for Darwin. Lieutenants Ray Parer and John McIntosh had left England on 8 January 1920 in a beat-up war-surplus de Havilland DH9 bomber. Even though the Vimy has already won the prize-money the adventurous pair were determined to fly home to Australia and set up an aerial taxi business.

"I was genuinely amazed that they should have got through to Karachi in such a machine," declared Matthews on meeting Parer and McIntosh and inspecting their battered old aeroplane.

Hoping to keep an eye out for each other the four men agreed to continue the flight home together and headed off in loose formation towards Delhi on 11 March. En route Parer was forced to land to take on more fuel and eventually caught up again at Delhi.

In Calcutta Matthews and Kay continued their fruitless search for a new propeller. It seemed there was little chance of finding a replacement until they reached Australia. Short of waiting months for one to arrive by sea their only worthwhile alternative was to continue on, carefully nursing the engine to minimise vibration.

The Australians met up with two Italians in Calcutta who were taking part in another monumental flight — from Rome to Tokyo. For mutual safety during the crossing of the jungle ahead it was arranged that all four machines fly together to Bangkok (via Rangoon). However at the last minute the DH9 developed engine problems and Parer and McIntosh remained behind for repairs.

On the flight to Bangkok Matthews and Kay were forced to decrease engine power to 1500 revolutions to reduce vibration. This caused their cruise speed to drop from 160 km/hr to 120 km/hr and they soon fell behind the Italian pair. (The Italians eventually arrived safely in Tokyo.)

In Bangkok the Australians were delayed for several days when Kay was struck down with dengue fever. They eventually set off for Singapore on 7 April. The flight, which included a fuel stop at Signora, took over twelve hours and was punctuated by a rough running engine.

"After two hours engine missing badly and revs dropped by 200" Kay wrote in his engine log, noting that at Signora he had cleaned the engine's spark plugs, replaced the brushes in the magneto and adjusted the tappets and valve clearances. Kay's log notes that subsequently the engine "ran perfect to Singapore".

Shortly before leaving Singapore on 12 April, Matthews stated: "I shall proceed to Java today at the same rate of speed and hope to reach Darwin on Tuesday 20 April."

The Wallaby's flight down the Indonesian archipelago started well. The first stop at Kalijati on the island of Java was on schedule. However, during the flight from Singapore both Matthews and Kay had noticed a distinct change in the note of the engine. Next morning, while conducting a routine check of the gauze strainer in the oil system, Kay discovered the reason. The strainer was coated with brass and steel filings. One of the engine's ball races had disintegrated! It was a testament to the strength of the Rolls Royce Eagle engine that it had kept running.

Unable to obtain a proper Rolls Royce spare, Kay was forced to adapt an automobile ball race to do the job. Two days later, following a thorough ground test, he declared the engine again fit for flight and they headed on towards Bali.

Six hours later, approaching the airfield at Grokgak, near Singaraja, the main administrative centre of Bali, the epic flight came to a sudden and unexpected end.

They were low, and manoeuvring for a landing, when the Sopwith came down short of the field in a banana plantation. The plane was severely damaged and Kay sustained broken ribs. Their incredible battle against the odds was over.

No reports of the day give a specific reason for the crash although there are implications that the Wallaby lost speed and stalled. A suggestion that they suddenly lost power due to a failure of the propeller, or its shaft, comes in the *Official History of Australia in the War of 1914-1918*, where Matthews reports: "We started cheerily on the penultimate stage of the journey to Australia. Sourabaya was reached safely, but soon afterwards the warped propeller caused trouble, and in a forced landing at Bali the wings were smashed."

Trying to look beyond the time caused by long delays on the ground, Matthews put the flight into its true perspective when he wrote: "Our flight, from start to finish, occupied nearly six months. However our flying time for the 10,000 miles from Hounslow to Java was 110 hours — an average of approximately 100 mph."

Praising his "mechanic and pal" Kay, whose skills he credited for bringing them so close to Australia, Matthews continued: "I could not have secured a better and more reliable companion for the arduous adventure. It seems a grievous pity that a man with his expert knowledge should be allowed to drift back into ordinary civil occupation. Australia must develop commercial aviation to an extent which will retain men such as Kay in the jobs for which they were practically born."

Matthews and Kay returned to Australia on the steamer *Roggeveen*, arriving in Sydney on 11 June 1920. In the hold were the remains of the Wallaby, which was eventually rebuilt and put into commercial service. Six weeks later Parer and McIntosh limped into Darwin in their battered de Havilland biplane — the second airmen to reach Australia.

Tom Kay went on to become a civil engineer and eventually a sales representative for the Shell Company of Australia.

Matthews became a commercial pilot and in 1923 he joined the newly formed airline QANTAS, on the Charleville–Cloncurry run. In 1930 he formed Matthews Aviation Company, operating a small seaplane between Melbourne and Tasmania.

It seems as though Tom Matthews never lost his sense of adventure nor his faith in the Sopwith Wallaby. An Australian Department of Defence letter dated 12 June 1922 indicates that he was planning to use the rebuilt biplane in an attempt to complete the first flight around the world. This flight never eventuated, possibly because a team of US Army Air Corps pilots made the flight soon after.

9
Fifty-eight hours without sleep

The two men were hunched over a large globe in the reading room of the San Diego Public Library. They had driven up to the building moments earlier and dashed into the room. A bemused librarian watched as the tall gangling fellow produced a length of string, and held one end with his thumb on the dot that identified New York City. His companion ran the string around the globe's painted surface, across the pale blue of the Atlantic Ocean until he located it over Paris. Then he pulled the string tight and marked its length. The pair then measured it against the map's scale.

"Three thousand, six hundred miles," said one. "Then I'd better design her for a range of four thousand miles," the other replied.

An unknown pilot, Charles Lindbergh, and an unsung aeronautical engineer, Donald Hall, were about to set the aviation world back on its heels. It was 1927 and no pilot had yet flown alone across the Atlantic. In the next sixty days Hall was to design and build an aircraft that would make his young companion the most famous flier of his time.

The story of "Slim" Lindbergh's immortal Atlantic crossing encompasses more than just the 33-hour flight. It also involves the sixty days during which he and the brilliant Hall turned a dream into a silver high-winged Ryan monoplane they named the *Spirit of St Louis*.

Lindbergh was born in Detroit on 4 February 1902.

He spent his childhood on a small farm where he acquired a love for mechanical things. At the age of eleven he drove and maintained his father's Model T Ford. When he was eighteen he enrolled in an engineering course at the University of Wisconsin but after two years left to embark on a new career — flying.

By 1926 he had achieved that goal. He had been a wing-walker, parachutist, barnstormer, Army Air Service Reserve pilot and was then Chief Pilot of the tiny Robertson Aircraft Corporation. The company operated a mail service between St Louis and Chicago using old de Havilland 4 biplanes which had seen better days in World War I. It was tough work and involved flying at night, often in very rough weather. If the weather became impossible or fuel ran out, the pilots' parachute was usually the only way to reach safety. Lindbergh had survived two such jumps, one in fog and one in a nocturnal snow storm. The fatality rate among the mail pilots who criss-crossed America was shocking, yet this was tolerated. You got the mail through somehow or it could mean no job tomorrow, with the contract awarded to some other company.

It was during a long, lonely, night mail-haul that Lindbergh first dreamed of an Atlantic flight, after a prize of $25 000 had been offered by a New York hotel magnate. The young airman considered that the weather conditions over the Atlantic could be no worse than those he constantly battled on the night mail-runs. It was merely a matter of finding an aircraft with the range and reliability to make the flight. All he would have to do was point it in the right direction and not fall asleep.

Once Lindbergh had reasoned that he could make the crossing there was no stopping him. He was not deterred by a stream of newspaper stories of dead, injured and missing pilots, on abortive trans-Atlantic flights. Supremely confident that with his mail-flying

experience he had unique qualifications, the young airman set about finding the "right" aircraft.

An Italian immigrant named Bellanca had designed
a monoplane that was reputed to have an incredible
load-carrying performance. This would be ideal for lifting the hundreds of litres of fuel that the flight would
consume. It was priced around $15 000.

Lindbergh approached a group of St Louis businessmen: he had saved $2000, would they put up the rest?
Nine of them were so impressed with his cool determination that they agreed to back the flight. "Just find the
right aeroplane and leave the finance to us," they told
the ecstatic young airman.

Lindbergh took the next train to New York and met
Giuseppe Bellanca. Recently in financial difficulties,
Bellanca had taken on a new partner, Charles Levine.
Though the Italian was ready to sell his new aircraft to
the airman, Levine was only prepared to sell it to the St
Louis group and reserved the right to provide another,
more famous, pilot for the Atlantic flight. Lindbergh
refused these terms and, utterly discouraged, took the
train back home.

All along he had believed that Bellanca's *Columbia*
was the only aircraft capable of making the Atlantic
flight. Now he had to set his sights lower and approach
other manufacturers.

Travel Air were not interested in letting an unknown
airman attempt such a flight in their aircraft, nor would
Fokker sell him a single-engined model. Both companies had too much to lose in bad publicity if he
failed. And few believed that Lindbergh could possibly
succeed.

Lindbergh was getting desperate when he remembered an earlier offer from a little-known company on
the west coast. Ryan Airlines had offered to build a
special aircraft for $10 000. But the problem was time:
already several pilots had announced their intentions

of challenging for the $25 000 prize. Could Ryan come up with an aircraft by early May, the date he had planned to make his attempt? It was only two months away and to the best of his knowledge Ryan had not even prepared preliminary drawings.

He arrived at the small company's San Diego offices on 23 February 1927. Claude Ryan was not there and Lindbergh was surprised to hear that he had sold his interest a few weeks earlier. However, his former partner, B.F. Mahoney, introduced the pilot to the company's only designer, Donald Hall. Lindbergh was delighted to find that Hall had given the project some thought and had planned to modify a standard Ryan M-2 monoplane for the flight. But the more he talked with Lindbergh the more it seemed that, even with massive changes, the M-2 was not the machine for the job. Following their mid-conference rush to the local library, when Lindbergh confessed to not knowing the actual distance he would need to cover, Hall bravely declared that a totally new aircraft was the only answer.

When Mahoney had guaranteed a price and a sixty-day delivery he had been thinking in terms of a modified standard aircraft. In view of the designer's revised concept, Lindbergh asked if Ryan could still honour that offer.

The young and enthusiastic new president reaffirmed his offer. He was impressed with Lindbergh's dedication and efficient manner. His mail-flight background showed that, unlike many of the flying fools whose predictable failures did little for the cause of aviation, here was a pilot with not only the right attitude but also the right qualifications. Mahoney was committing his organisation to a sixty-day nightmare for little or no profit. But he realised that a successful flight by his aircraft could open the door to a very lucrative future. He liked the odds and took a gamble, fully aware that if Lindbergh went missing, the company could go broke.

For the next two months Ryan Airlines worked around the clock. Once Hall had drawn up his plans he found that few of the standard M-2's off-the-shelf parts were of any use. Only the wing ribs and the tail surfaces matched the new design and everything else had to be built from scratch. To carry the enormous weight of extra fuel, the wings were to span three metres more than the standard aircraft. A greatly strengthened undercarriage system was built to support twice the normal weight.

A completely new fuselage was designed to house the massive fuel tanks. It was necessary to put the huge main fuel tank under the wing near the centre of gravity. As this was the area normally occupied by the cabin, the pilot's cockpit was enclosed in the fuselage behind the tank. Lindbergh would thus have no forward vision and could only look out of the small windows on either side. It was like driving a car with the windshield blanked off. To see ahead the pilot would have to stick his head out into the chilling slipstream.

Among the Ryan employees was an ex-submariner who came up with the idea of fitting a small periscope to allow forward vision. Although incorporated into the design, it was used very little during the aircraft's life.

Lindbergh and Hall spent every waking moment at the factory. Besides witnessing the birth of his aircraft, the airman spent hours on end studying charts and working out his navigation detail. He had virtually no formal training in the theory of dead reckoning and pure navigation, as his mail flying had always been over land, using ground features.

Exactly sixty days after the agreement had been drawn up, the new Ryan NYP (New York–Paris) was wheeled from the hangar. Lindbergh carried out a series of test flights that he and Hall had carefully planned.

The aircraft performed perfectly, exceeding Lindbergh's design requirements.

In honour of the businessmen who had backed him, Lindbergh named the Ryan *Spirit of St Louis*. Empty it weighed 977 kilograms. Designed to carry a fuel load of 1912 litres, it could actually carry slightly more, and with the pilot on board, the aircraft weighed 2334 kilograms. In effect, the *Spirit*'s useful load was a remarkable one-and-a-half times its empty weight. The 223-horsepower Wright Whirlwind engine gave it a maximum speed of 199 km/h, though for best range Lindbergh would cruise much more slowly. Its still-air range was an astonishing 6720 kilometres and fully laden it would get off the ground in about 800 metres.

Hall's design was a masterpiece of pure performance. It had been conceived with just one objective: to fly the Atlantic. Ryan had produced more than just a flying fuel tank. The company had given Lindbergh a superbly designed and executed machine that would do the job. It was now up to the young airman to justify the 4700 hours of design and construction that the exhausted staff at Ryan had dedicated to the *Spirit of St Louis*.

He flew to New York in two fast stages, refuelling at St Louis on the way.

In recent weeks several would-be contenders had made disaster headlines. Noel Davis and Stanton Wooster were killed on take-off in the Keystone. Frenchman René Fonck's aircraft was seriously damaged, as was Admiral Richard Byrd's Fokker. Lindbergh's original choice, the Bellanca *Columbia*, had damaged its undercarriage while preparing for the Atlantic.

There was a flurry of activity as Lindbergh arrived at New York. The *Columbia* was already there, repaired and awaiting last minute adjustments before pushing off across the Atlantic. Byrd was coming in, flying a new Fokker, and had announced his intention to set off as soon as possible. Then fog dropped in over the Atlantic.

Three aircraft sat at Roosevelt Field waiting for the weather to clear. A long and frustrating week passed as tension mounted and nerves were on edge. The crews were mobbed by thousands of spectators who turned up every day hoping to see one or all of the aircraft depart. The airmen's mood was not helped by the news that no trace had been found of Frenchman Charles Nungesser and his crewman Francois Coli, missing in the Atlantic since 8 May. Their aircraft *White Bird* had vanished approaching the coast of America.

On 19 May Lindbergh checked the midday forecasts for the next day's Atlantic weather. The prospects were as grim as ever and like the others he decided there would be no chance of departing. On his way to the theatre that night he decided to phone the weather bureau just on the off-chance. He was stunned to hear that sudden and unexpected clear weather was on the way. Conditions over the Atlantic should improve next day. He cancelled his theatre visit and quietly planned to leave at dawn.

Unable to sleep, Lindbergh drove to the airport before first light. He was relieved to see no signs of activity around the camps of his Atlantic rivals. With the tanks filled to brimming, the heavily loaded Ryan was wheeled out into the dawn light. The airfield was still water-logged from days of pouring rain and the wheels bit deeply into the muddy grass.

With the aircraft positioned at the extreme end of the longest take-off strip, there were 1525 metres of grass runway available. It should have been ample. But as Lindbergh signalled for the chocks to be removed and opened to full throttle, the *Spirit of St Louis* hardly moved in the cloying mud.

The spectators ran forward and pushed on the wing struts until the monoplane gathered speed and out-paced them. Nevertheless it was a tension-filled take-off for pilot and spectators. The mud and patches of water so robbed the Ryan of acceleration that Lindbergh needed twice the normal distance to become airborne. The *Spirit of St Louis* eventually bounced into the air with only metres of runway left, barely clearing the telephone wires at the edge of the airfield.

Holding just 250 feet above Long Island, the airman set heading for Europe. En route to Cape Cod the rain stopped and Lindbergh picked up a tail wind. The perilous take-off was behind him, but ahead now lay a long battle against exhaustion, and a fight against sleep that would test Lindbergh beyond the limits of endurance.

The first 400 kilometres of the flight were above open sea to Nova Scotia — his first over-water flight. Three hours out he was already feeling the effects of the cramped little cockpit. What was worse he was drowsy, and the effects of the sleepless night before were beginning to catch up on him. Lindbergh took his first sip of water.

Approaching the ragged Nova Scotian coast he flew into a violent storm. The Ryan bucked and shuddered in the turbulence and Lindbergh worried constantly about the flexing wings of the still heavily overloaded aircraft. To lessen the shock he reduced speed as much as possible. Flashes of lightning illuminated the forests and rocky coastline of Nova Scotia as he passed over them and headed out into the Atlantic. Fortunately the storm abated as he left the coast behind.

His next leg would overfly land briefly near St John's, Newfoundland, but from then on it would be open ocean until he reached Europe.

Once clear of the storm Lindbergh was again affected by the urge to sleep. To fight off drowsiness he shook his head, stamped his feet and flexed his muscles. "The worst part about fighting sleep is that the harder you fight, the more you strengthen your enemy, and the more you weaken your resistance to him," he wrote later.

Still flying at about 250 feet to pick up the lifting benefits of ground effect and the best of the tail wind, Lindbergh's battle against sleep was helped by an ice field. As he flew over the dazzling expanse of ice, the intense brightness snapped him awake.

Just under twelve hours out of New York he crossed St John's. In the gathering dusk he pointed the *Spirit of St Louis* out into the Atlantic. By reading the waves he estimated a fifty-km/h tail wind. As darkness arrived he saw icebergs and in the fading light noticed fog building up below. The fog thickened over the next few hours and Lindbergh slowly climbed to 9000 feet to stay in the clear.

In complete darkness the Ryan droned on. The moon had not yet risen. Being inherently unstable, the aircraft required almost constant attention to hold height and heading. Thus Lindbergh could not relax his hands and feet from the controls for more than a few seconds at a time. However, the aircraft's inability to fly "hands-off" was, in an indirect way, of help in his battle against sleep. There was no way he could risk catnapping for brief periods as pilots of very stable aircraft often did. The young American knew that just a few seconds of dozing could mean death.

In the two hours before the moon rose he encountered another problem. Flashing his torch outside he noticed ice was forming on the airframe. He was in cloud. To stay there would be suicide, because the extra weight, and loss of lift, as the ice increased would soon force him down. Lindbergh immediately turned the aircraft around and searched for clear air. The *Spirit of St Louis* finally came out into the clear and Lindbergh turned east again, weaving his way between pillars of cloud that now became visible and less menacing as the moon rose.

But with the icing problem gone he was again overtaken by the compelling urge to sleep. Opening a window he diverted a blast of chilling air on to his face, but it provided only momentary relief. It became a life and death battle, as Lindbergh explained: "I let my eyelids fall shut for five seconds; then raise them against tons of weight. Protesting, they won't open wide until I force them with my thumb, and lift the muscles of my forehead to help keep them in place."

Six hours out of St John's the Ryan flew into the grey dawn, but light brought no relief. "The uncontrollable desire to sleep falls over me in quilted layers. This is the hour against which I have tried to steel myself. I know it's the beginning of my greatest test — the third morning since I slept," he records.

Twenty hours out of New York Lindbergh decided to descend below the clouds to re-establish visual contact with the sea. At 2000 feet he broke out below the overcast and saw by the wave direction that he still had a tail wind. Descending momentarily to fifty feet he was able to see spray blowing from the wave caps, indicating a wind force of at least eighty kph. He realised the hopelessness of survival if he was forced down on the water.

Lindbergh was worried that the numerous alterations of heading he had made to avoid the ice and storm clouds may have put the Ryan well off track. And with cloud and fog obscuring the sea for much of the flight so far, he was not really sure how much variation there had been in wind direction. With his senses and reasoning power dulled by lack of sleep, the airman eventually ignored the problem of accuracy. As long as he reached somewhere on the coastline of Europe it would be sufficient.

He was flying above a bank of low cloud when the nose suddenly dropped, a wing went down, and the Ryan was diving towards the water. Lindbergh positioned the controls to level his machine only to find he was now in a steep climbing turn. He was unable to control the aircraft.

"I had been asleep with open eyes," he later recalled. Shocked into waking, he slowly and methodically brought the Ryan back under control. He focused his dwindling reserves of concentration on the plane's primitive flight instruments until he had settled back into level flight. But it was like flying in a dream and his conscious mind was barely awake.

Twenty-one hours out he sighted a coastline with hills and trees clearly visible. Lindbergh shook his head in disbelief. He was in mid-Atlantic. He must be so far off-course that the aircraft had hit Greenland. It was the only explanation. How else could there be land so soon? As he reached the island, it disappeared. The mid-sea mirage had been a figment of the pilot's strained imagination. He wrote in his log: "I'm on the borderline of life and a greater realm beyond, as though caught in the field of gravitation between two planets, acted on by forces I cannot control."

He recorded that vague ghostly forms with human voices joined him in the cockpit, but it appears that at this stage Lindbergh was too tired to be greatly concerned by the extraordinary phenomena. "I'm capable only of holding the plane aloft and laxly pointing towards a heading I set some hours ago. No extra energy remains. I'm as strengthless as the vapour limbs of the spirits to whom I listen."

As the overpowering desire to sleep flooded over him, Lindbergh resorted to punching his face as hard as he could, hoping the pain would alert him. He felt nothing. "The alternative is death and failure," he repeated incessantly.

He was holding his face in the slipstream when a tiny dot on the ocean caught his attention. It was a small fishing boat. Suddenly he was wide awake. Closing the throttle he circled at low level. "Which way to Ireland?"

he shouted out the window. There was no response, but it scarcely mattered for the airman knew that land could not be far off.

Shortly after, he saw a purple ribbon on the horizon. lt must be land. Only half-believing he flew on, fearing another mirage, for by his reckoning he was two and a half hours ahead of schedule. A few minutes later he crossed a rugged coastline. He was now alert and refreshed as excitement pumped adrenalin through his system. Checking his map Lindbergh could hardly believe his deductions. The rocky coastline was undoubtedly Ireland's Dingle Bay. He was only five kilometres off his intended point of landfall! After 3000 kilometres of ocean such a minute error was astonishing.

Thoughts of sleep had vanished as he crossed over to England. Above Cornwall he ate his first meal — a dry meat sandwich and a sip of water. The six-hour flight to Paris was no effort. He had won his battle against sleep. He was again wide awake and functioning as though the previous fifty-two sleepless hours had never existed.

It was dark as the *Spirit of St Louis* circled the Eiffel Tower before turning towards Le Bourget Airport. There he made his first night-landing in the "blind" Ryan. It was a minor miracle that he touched down safely.

As Lindbergh finally switched off the magnificent Wright engine that had run without missing a beat for thirty-three and a half hours, it seemed as if the whole of Paris was rushing across the brightly lit airfield to greet him. By next morning he was the world's most famous airman, "Lindy — The Lone Eagle".

To the American people he became a national hero, their greatest airman of all time. But to the world his flight had even greater significance, because it inspired a surge of optimism in the reliability of aircraft. Air transport was gaining respectability, and the idea of great international airlines was passing out of the stage of being just crazy dreams.

The Bellanca monoplane *Columbia* made a successful crossing of the Atlantic two weeks later, although its time was ten hours longer than Lindbergh's. Nevertheless, it proved the airman's original contention that the Italian's machine was capable of making the crossing.

Donald Hall, the brilliant designer of the *Spirit of St Louis*, and the men who built her are the forgotten heroes of America's greatest flight. They gave Lindbergh the machine to do the job.

The miracle of Lindbergh's flight was not merely the flying skill he displayed in reaching Paris, for any number of airmen had that skill. What placed the shy, quiet young man far ahead of his peers was his determination. And nowhere was that better illustrated than in his struggle against sleep. His Atlantic crossing must go down as one of the epic endurance feats of human history. Lindbergh went without sleep from the time he made that chance phone call to the weather bureau until he landed in Paris fifty-eight hours later.

The magnitude of the experience inspired the young pilot to write, as he sighted Ireland: "This is earth again, the earth where I've lived and now will live once more ... I've been to eternity and back. I know how the dead would feel to live again."

10

"Martin Jensen, where the hell have you been!"

On the evening of 21 May 1927, when Charles Lindbergh, landed in Paris after conquering the Atlantic, all the world celebrated. The commander of Paris' Le Bourget Airport wrote eloquently in his diary: "Your exploit is eternal, Lindbergh, but the fever of that night of waiting is not. Who will ever give it us back? ... The victor, the air athlete, the scaler of the ocean ..."

To a world mesmerised by Lindbergh's achievement, anything now seemed possible. One of the most remarkable results of his flight was the unprecedented worldwide media attention given to the unknown young flyer. This was a catalyst to the fertile minds of the Honolulu newspapermen Riley Allen and Joe Farrington.

A half a world away, in the offices of Honolulu's *Star Bulletin*, the two began planning to recapture that frenzy of media fever. Comparing Lindbergh's Atlantic crossing with the 3840-kilometre hop (2400 miles) between the Unites States mainland and Hawaii, they realised that a trans-Pacific challenge to Hawaii was now feasible. They could think of no better way to focus world attention on their group of islands which was starting to promote tourism and the export of its luscious pineapples. Tragically, their brainchild was to bring about a disastrous air race which almost negated the gains of Lindbergh's flight.

Two days after Lindbergh's triumphant landing in Paris, a cable was tapped out from the offices of the *Star*

Bulletin. Addressed to James D. Dole, a Hawaiian businessman visiting San Francisco, it read:

> In view of Lindbergh's Atlantic flight the Pacific remains one great area for conquest aviation. This moment ripe for someone offer suitable prize non-stop flight Hawaii. From angle advertising islands and yourself we believe an exceptional opportunity your offer twenty-five thousand dollar prize for this achievement. Particularly in view your national pineapple advertising featuring your name we believe you now to do this. Prize should be known as Dole Prize. This will put your name in every newspaper in the world besides great credit Territory pineapple industry. We are prepared to cooperate every possible way. Await anxiously favourable reply on which we would like first announcement. Appreciate early reply by wire. Not publishing anything until hearing from you. Riley Allen. Joe Farrington. Star Bulletin.

Though never before seriously interested in aviation, Hawaiian pineapple magnate James Dole had also been fired by Lindbergh's flight and by the public and press reaction it generated. Never one to miss a good business opportunity, he acted quickly. Two days later, as the world continued to heap praise on Lindbergh, a special edition of the *Star Bulletin* announced:

> James D.Dole, believing that Charles A.Lindbergh's extraordinary feat in crossing the Atlantic is the forerunner of eventual trans-Pacific air transportation, offers US $25,000 for the first flier and US$10,000 to the second flier to cross from the North America Continent to Honolulu in a non-stop flight within one year after the beginning August 12, 1927.

Though shorter than Lindbergh's flight, Dole's challenge involved an extra 704 kilometres of open sea, making it the longest over-water flight to date. Whereas New York hotelier Raymond Orteig had dangled a US$25 000 carrot for Lindbergh's Atlantic crossing, James Dole decided to go one better and offer an extra US$10 000 for the runner-up.

The fact that Dole had so readily agreed to sponsor the competition said much about the instantaneous reaction to Lindbergh's achievement. Prior to his flight, all but a handful of America's hard-nosed businessmen had steered clear of investing in aviation. In 1927 aeroplanes were considered a dangerous form of transportation. But now that Lindbergh had demonstrated that aviation technology was rapidly maturing, some were already visualising the dawn of transoceanic air services.

Besides a flood of advertising and movie contracts, the young flyer received several more imaginative proposals. Philadelphia merchant Ellis A. Gimbel pledged US$100 000 for any company that would employ him to operate a Philadelphia–Paris air service, while industrialist Harry F. Guggenheim offered to sponsor Lindbergh to tour the nation promoting commercial aviation.

In Lindbergh Dole saw an opportunity not only to promote his pineapples but also to provide his beloved Hawaiian Islands with a better postal service. The Boston-born businessman had moved to Hawaii following a holiday in 1900 after graduating from Harvard. His cousin Sanford B. Dole was the territory's first governor. James Dole had eventually formed the Hawaiian Pineapple Company to develop the commercial opportunities of the succulent fruit. In the early 1920s, like other business colleagues, he had watched the development of airmail services on the mainland and dreamed of them extending to Hawaii. However, few dared to suggest such a service publicly, particularly after the debacle in 1925 when three US Navy flying boats failed to complete a California-Hawaii flight.

An Honolulu-based joy flight service started by barnstormer Charlie Stoffer in his biplane "Charley's Crate" had come to an end in 1924 when he sailed for the mainland and a job as a Hollywood stunt pilot. Following an abortive attempt in 1926 to form an inter-island airline, Hawaii's only commercial service was being operated by a recently arrived pilot named Martin Jensen. Flying a 5-place Ryan, the Honolulu-based joy-flight pilot also made occasional charters carrying businessmen, newspapers and urgent mail between the major islands.

Travel and mail services to the American mainland were still inhibited by the long sea voyage. Such was the problem that faced James Dole with pineapple plantations on the islands and his market on the mainland. In a second *Star Bulletin* press release on 26 May, the following day, Dole explained:

> The flight of Captain Lindbergh is an evidence of the startling progress being made in aeronautics. It seemed obvious that a flight from the mainland (to Hawaii) should be the next in order to have the future of aviation brought nearer to the present. Consider the help given Honolulu's progress by the cable, the radio, the automobile and the truck. What would we be without them today? The continued progress in aviation may mean within a few years mail delivered in Honolulu 20 hours from the mainland. It may mean that in the case of emergency the businessman or visitor can make the journey in a day.

Sounding a word of caution, Dole also stated: "No precautions can be too great to satisfy all who are sincerely interested in the permanent development of aviation. It is natural for all of us in Hawaii as well as followers of aviation the world over to hope that this contest be doubly successful. First that it may cost no brave man either life or limb and second that the continent and Hawaii may be linked by air."

Believing that Lindbergh was the focal point to maximise race publicity, and the flyer most likely to succeed, Dole concluded: "I should be glad to see Captain Lindbergh the man first to make this flight successfully, and be able to greet him at the airport in Honolulu."

Dole's hopes were to be dashed. Lindbergh failed to

respond and instead would come a brave but ill-prepared band of fliers attempting to match the Atlantic hero on an even more daring trans-Oceanic flight. Lindbergh had made it look almost easy as, with the world press riding at his shoulder, he had casually conquered the Atlantic. Possibly he had made it look too easy for the ten impressionable fliers who would soon die for Dole's glittering prize.

The challenge was officially named the North America–Honolulu, Hawaii Trans-Pacific Flight. This would later be shortened to become the Pacific Air Race and in the press, thanks to Dole's public relations efforts, it would be more commonly called the Dole Race or Dole Derby. Once the news hit the mainland newspapers there was no shortage of entrants. In 1927 America's commercial pilots led a hand-to-mouth existence and the prize-money (about half a million dollars in today's values) represented a fortune. Scores responded — stunt fliers, World War One aces, barnstormers and hopeful young "Waldo Peppers" — swashbuckling optimists high on courage and low on suitable experience.

Understandably, those seriously involved with America's struggling aviation businesses feared the Dole Challenge might be a giant step backward in their efforts to promote air travel. No airline of any real consequence had yet appeared in America, whereas most European nations already had at least one major airline. Juan Trippe was still trying to form Pan American Airways and the other major carriers would not appear until the 1930s.

Though Boeing was capable of producing excellent passenger aircraft, and in fact operated a small regional air service, the American public still travelled by land. Would-be airline builders had to compete with excellent railways, and the highways built for Henry Ford's ubiquitous Model T. Few Americans were interested in the high cost and discomfort of flying. And the frequent newspaper reports of plane crashes did not help public confidence — seven Atlantic hopefuls had died in the two months prior to Lindbergh's flight!

To the average American the airplane still meant barnstormers, wing-walkers, Hollywood stunts, suicidal mail pilots and $5 joy flights in tumbledown biplanes. Many of Dole's entrants fitted that image. If aircraft were ever to be considered as people-carriers rather than merely mail-carriers, American aviation needed a period to consolidate. It needed time for the public to forget the tragic headlines and absorb Lindbergh's success and its promise for the future. Instead it seemed destined to get a death-or-glory race.

From the beginning Dole vainly attempted to ensure that his challenge would not turn into a game of aerial Russian roulette. In an effort to fulfil his wish that it "cost no brave man either life or limb", he enlisted the National Aeronautical Association (NAA) to help organise the race. The NAA was the American branch of the Féderation Aéronautique Internationale — the recognised world governing body for all aviation competition.

It soon became clear that most entrants were planning to leave at the first possible moment of the twelve-month period of the Dole challenge. Realising the event now had all the makings of a race, the committee changed the rules and drew lots, and allocated pilots starting positions. As contestants would have to fly through the night, the start was set for noon on 12 August 1927 — the day of the full moon. Fortuitously, it was also the twenty-ninth anniversary of Hawaii's annexation as a US territory.

The rush to get away first also precluded the entry of the more professional contenders who would have needed more time to obtain purpose-designed aircraft with adequate range and equipment. Instead, most entrants were seat-of-the-pants fliers, lacking even the basics of the instrument flying skills which Lindbergh had gained as an airmail pilot. Nor did their aircraft compare with his specially built Ryan monoplane. Except for a few hastily thrown together back-yard specials, they planned to use over-tanked standard aircraft that were not designed to lift safely the massive fuel loads the flight required.

Over-water navigation posed another problem for pilots who still found their way by pinpointing landmarks. And, whereas Lindbergh had the whole of Europe to make landfall, their island target would require bulls-eye accuracy. Just a couple of degree's compass error would be enough for the fliers to miss the island by 160 kilometres and the unpredictable winds could blow them even further off course. As one entrant, stunt pilot Art Goebel, succinctly put it: "There are but two goals. The Hawaiian Islands or the bottom of the Pacific Ocean." With such long-odds, only fifteen daredevils eventually paid the US$100 entry fee. Most of them clearly lacked adequate flying experience.

The NAA's race committee included Major Clarence M. Young, head of the Enforcement Division of the government's year-old Aeronautics Branch of the Department of Commerce. Flexing the bureau's infant muscles, the committee introduced rules regarding crews and aircraft performance. With the benefit of hindsight, they were grossly inadequate. However, to the cavalier fliers of the day they seemed exceedingly restrictive. Young appointed Lieutenant Ben Wyatt USN, a pilot who specialised in aerial navigation, to weed out inexperienced crews, and arranged for bureau inspectors to check the aircraft. He decreed that each plane must carry an experienced navigator, who had to pass a written examination and flight test given by Lieutenant Wyatt. Furthermore, all competing aircraft would be required to demonstrate that they could carry sufficient fuel for the flight plus a 15 per cent safety margin.

Six weeks before the event the Dole racers were upstaged when the tri-motored US Army Fokker C-2 *Bird of Paradise* flew from Oakland to Hawaii. A few days later civilian airmen Ernest Smith and Emory Bronte made the flight in a single-engine Travel Air monoplane, crash-landing out of fuel on rugged Molokai island. However, as neither crew qualified for the prize Dole decided his race should go ahead. With the glory gone, it now became a gamble for cold, hard cash!

By early in August, ten of the entrants waited at Oakland's brand new Bay Farm Island airfield to be checked by race officials. They were besieged by journalists who dissected the event daily in America's newspapers. The fliers' life stories, their hopes (and fears), aircraft and equipment details, the route, weather predictions and navigation techniques filled page upon page. The race had become America's favourite topic. In offices and speakeasies, barber-shops and hotel lobbies everyone was talking "Dole Derby". When short on hard news, reporters fed the insatiable public with girl-meets-flyer stories. Socialites chatted with pilots. Wives, daughters and the "girls they'll leave behind" were splashed across the pages. Model agencies had a field day providing the press photographers with pretty girls:

"O-o-oh *Lieu*-tenant Goddard, what pretty black stripes you've got painted on your airplane. Why don't you paint some curly ones too," said model Merle Hanna, posing for the camera in front of Norman Goddard's monoplane *El Encanto* (*The Enchanted*). "I beg your pardon, young lady, but those lines are not decorations, they are a drift indicator," the former Royal Flying Corps pilot answered. "But I don't get your *drift*, Lieutenant," cooed Miss Hanna. Such were the offerings of one West Coast paper.

Not to be outdone, a rival newspaper found its girl-meets-flyer story when, complete with leis, hula

dancers and guitars, the Hawaiian contingent celebrated the naming of its lone entry: "Substituting salt
water taken from the beach at Waikiki for champagne,
Miss Ruby Smith, Oakland bathing beauty, yesterday
christened Martin Jensen's monoplane *The Aloha*.
While a Hawaiian stringed band played native airs, the
girl stood on the wings, sprinkling the water on Jensen,
Captain Paul Schulter the navigator, and the plane," it
reported.

However the real female news item was a "mad-on-
flying school ma'm":

"WILL BRAVE DEATH IN HAWAIIAN AIR RACE" headlined
Oakland's Post Enquirer, stating that Mildred Doran, a
22 year-old Flint, Michigan school teacher, was "radio
operator and consulting navigator" in the Buhl Airsedan *Miss Doran*. Her father worked for the aircraft's
owner, William Malloska — millionaire owner of Lincoln Petroleum Products and operator of Flint's airport.

The air-crazy Mildred Doran flew daily as a passenger in one of the aircraft Malloska operated. She had
conceived the idea of becoming the first woman to fly
the Pacific early in 1927 and Malloska, undoubtedly
sensing the promotional value, had placed an order for
the Buhl on the day Lindbergh flew the Atlantic. When
the Dole prize was announced, it had seemed a perfect
opportunity and they entered the biplane, naming it
after the dark-haired young woman who one reporter
described as "the prettiest little pigeon on wings".

When asked by a reporter of the San Francisco *Bulletin* about the dangers of the flight, she explained
naively: "No, truly, truly, I'm not in the least bit worried
or anxious. This flight is the dream of my life! And as
for taking chances — well, life is a chance, isn't it?"

Her pilot was John Augy Pedlar, a close friend who
was employed by Malloska. An affable barnstormer and
former wing-walker, whose lack of experience was
matched by his lack of nerves, Pedlar epitomised the

flying-circus image. He limped, chewed gum incessantly, and flew in gaudy knickerbockers and a straw hat. Alarmed by the pair's lack of navigational experience, Lieutenant Wyatt quickly intervened and appointed a naval navigator, Lieutenant Vilas Knope, to the *Miss Doran*'s crew. As the Buhl was not radio-equipped, Mildred Doran's role was relegated to that of passenger, although her sponsor insisted she was the aircraft's "captain".

Randolph Hearst's San Francisco *Examiner* gave extensive coverage to its own entry and pre-race favourite, the prototype Lockheed Vega, *Golden Eagle*, to be piloted by debonair New York stockbroker Jack Frost — an Army Air Service veteran who was looking for a way back into aviation. Another highly fancied contestant was Hollywood stunt pilot Arthur C. Goebel in the Travel Air monoplane *Woolaroc*. A second Travel Air, the *Oklahoma*, was piloted by Ben Griffin, an unusually quiet and conservative flyer by 1927 standards.

Other contestants who had arrived at Oakland were former Lafayette Escadrille pilot Major Livingstone Irving in the Breese monoplane *Pabco Pacific Flyer*, World War One fighter ace Bill Erwin in his Swallow monoplane *Dallas Spirit*, and Charles Pankhurst in the Air King biplane *Miss Peoria*. The Air King was entered by its manufacturer, the National Airways System, owned by S.F.Tannus, who hoped to promote his grandly titled but little-known organisation. Another biplane, the International *Miss Hollydale*, was flown by barnstormer and Hollywood stunt pilot Frank Clarke.

On 10 August the start was postponed as the race committee considered that no aircraft or crew was ready to leave. Mechanics were still working feverishly on last-minute modifications. Organisers were still trying to recruit extra navigators capable of passing Wyatt's relatively simple test.

On the same day, the Dole drama had begun to unfold

when an aircraft crashed minutes after taking off from San Diego to join the race. Its two naval crew, Lieutenants George Covell and Richard Waggener were incinerated when their boxy Tremaine Special monoplane flew into a cliff. There had been reports that the Tremaine was tricky to fly, a problem exacerbated by the fact that the crew were located behind a massive fuel tank and, like Lindbergh's in his *Spirit of St Louis*, had no forward vision. Despite all James Dole's careful planning, the race had already claimed its first victims. Worse was to come.

On 12 August at Vail Field near Los Angeles another last-minute entry, the Bryant monoplane *Angel of Los Angeles*, took off on its first test flight. It was a revolutionary design, well ahead of its time, in which pilot and navigator sat side-by-side in a short pod-like fuselage which also housed two Bristol Lucifer sleeve-type radial engines. The Lucifers were mounted in tandem, one pushing and the other pulling — a design layout similar to that used by Cessna more than thirty years later.

Only two days earlier the pilot, British war ace Arthur Rogers, and architect and part-time designer Lee Bryant had given up hope that their machine would be completed in time, but they had been given a reprieve when the start had been postponed. Rogers climbed steadily after lifting off from Vail Field. Just past the airfield boundary the Bryant appeared to stall, dropped a wing, and spun out of control. At the last moment Rogers parachuted from his twin-engined special but was too close to the ground to survive.

The following day the Fisk International tri-plane *Pride of Los Angeles* left Los Angeles for Oakland. A strange-looking machine advertised as a 22-seat airliner, the Fisk had been flying in the Los Angeles area for some time. It had been purchased for the race as a publicity stunt by cowboy movie star Hoot Gibson. There was a mad scramble to have it re-engined and the passenger area crammed with fuel tanks in time for the start. It was reported that Gibson had trouble finding an experienced crew prepared to risk their lives in the aerial white elephant, and had even approached Australia's Charles Kingsford Smith who was in America to prepare for a trans-Pacific attempt.

However, behind Kingsford Smith's carefree facade was a careful and meticulous pilot and he retorted: "I doubt if the damn thing will ever get off the ground." Kingsford Smith had talked with preparing competitors at Oakland and was appalled at the overloads some were planning to carry, and their general lack of planning and navigational experience.

The *Pride of Los Angeles* was flown by former military-pilot-turned-lawyer, Jim Giffin, on the delivery flight to Oakland. He was one of two pilots among a crew of three nominated for the race. The crew sat side-by-side in an open cockpit just forward of the tail and had terrible forward visibility. This may have had something to do with Giffin's decision to overshoot, moments before touching down at Oakland. Believing he was baulked by another aircraft, Giffin opened the throttles to go around. The right engine responded but the left engine backfired then stopped as the lumbering triplane staggered low across the mud flats of San Francisco Bay. The Fisk clipped the water and came apart in a sheet of spray. Miraculously, all three crewmen survived unharmed.

The pre-race toll stood at three dead and three aircraft destroyed as three more contestants pulled out. San Francisco's Robert Fowler was unable to find a suitable airplane and Captain Fred Giles of Brisbane, Australia failed to arrive in his Hess Bluebird biplane *Detroit Messenger*. Finally, on 15 August, the day before the start, Frank Clark and his navigator Charlie Babb took off in *Miss Hollydale* and headed out across the Golden Gate. Many thought that the Hollywood flyer had jumped the gun and was making a glory-seeking dash for Hawaii. However, Clark had wisely decided that his International biplane was not suitable for the race and had returned to Los Angeles.

"THEY'RE OFF TODAY", the San Francisco *Examiner* headlined on August 16. The front page had a special banner depicting aircraft streaming from Oakland to Honolulu. A photo montage of the pilots carried the caption: "The crack pilots who will try to bat the Hawaiian home run". Diagrams showed the positions of merchant ships and seven navy destroyers along the route, and illustrated the new-fangled radio beam which had helped guide the Army's *Bird of Paradise* and would assist those racers who had had the foresight, and the money, to install radio receivers.

During the night huge rollers had compacted Oakland's sparsely-grassed runway and water wagons had laid the dust. No one really knew how much of the strip the pilots would need to become airborne, as the trial flights had been conducted with their special fuel tanks only half filled. Some further measure of safety might be provided by the extra 600 metres of roughly levelled "over-run"at the far end of the airfield.

Engines were given a final test run before tanks were topped to brimming. Fuel loads varied between 5015 and 6815 litres, giving all race aircraft massive overloads and limiting their cruising speeds to well below 160 km/h for most of the race. Like Lindbergh, all the contestants had chosen 200-horsepower Wright Whirlwind J-5 engines. The superb new nine cylinder, air-cooled radial was light, economical and reliable (by 1927 standards). It was reputed to run for at least forty hours without requiring repairs — a paltry performance today, but a superb technical achievement at the time. Undoubtedly it was the best choice for the flight to Hawaii.

Less than an hour before the start the Air King *Miss*

Peoria was disqualified following tests that indicated it
would run out of fuel 360 kilometres short of Hawaii.
The owner, Tannus, was furious and loudly abused the
committee, the Department of Commerce aviation rep-
resentatives and the other contestants. However *Miss
Peoria*'s crew, Charles Parkhurst and Ralph Lowes,
were relieved. They had encountered a succession of
problems crossing the country from Illinois in the hastily modified airplane.

Only eight starters now remained and their crews
watched anxiously as ambulances, fire engines and
crash trucks were parked at intervals along the length
of the field. Some looked drawn and nervous. Goebel
was reported as being close to tears. Police and marines
manned rope barricades holding back a crowd estimated at 50 000. Cameramen and reporters recorded
the last hectic moments — the final weather briefings,
the last-minute compass checks, the good-bye em-
braces. Each pilot solemnly received a Bible, the crews
squeezed into their tank-cluttered cabins, and local
aeroplanes wheeled overhead as they waited to escort
their favourites to the coast.

Bulletin reporter Robert Willson's race-start assign-
ment was to follow the "flying schoolma'am". As her
crew were making final preparations to her red, white
and blue painted biplane, Mildred Doran waited in a
small tent surrounded by a mountain of good-luck bou-
quets. In the days leading up to the race her presence
had already given the *Miss Doran* more publicity than
all the other entrants combined. Now, at the start of the
race she was the centre of media attention. Willson
wrote: "The comely little school teacher, attired in an
olive drab costume, golf stockings and a helmet, stepped
into the plane named for her, smiling and waving at the
crowd. J 'Auggie' Pedlar, wearing his weather-beaten
straw hat, and Lieutenant Vilas Knope, the navigator,
looked grim as though they seem to realise the re-

sponsibility their pretty passenger placed on their shoulders."

A few minutes before noon, Major Ed Howard took his position at the starting point and committee men checked the telephone circuits strung along the fringes of the take-off run. On Howard's command the Travel Air *Oklahoma* was pushed up to the starting line, its tail almost touching the fence of the airport boundary.

On the dot of 12 noon, the starter's flag dropped and Ben Griffin had first spin in the deadly roulette. Men pushed his *Oklahoma* to help it accelerate, falling away as it picked up speed. With only half the strip used, the monoplane was airborne. It had survived the first round.

Norman Goddard was next in *El Encanto*. He was not so lucky. Despite having the letters HBH emblazoned on its tail, which he swore stood for "Hell Bent for Honolulu", the Englishman's lurching monoplane lifted only a few feet before dragging a wingtip and ground-looping in an explosion of dust. The tail came up, the aircraft rolled on its side and the left wing and tailplane were demolished.

The only things "enchanted" about the Goddard Special were the lives of its two crew, for miraculously there was no explosion, and they scrambled from the wreck uninjured. Surveying the remains, the pair began a heated argument about who had been in control and caused the accident. The navigator, Lieutenant Ken Hawkins, later said: "I would rather have crashed in mid-ocean than have had this happen."

At 12.09 p.m. Livingston Irving's *Pabco Pacific Flyer* started its run. Following Goddard's accident the crowd was now strangely quiet. The former Lafayette Escadrille pilot was Oakland's sole entry. Seven times his Breese monoplane skipped off the ground, each time flopping back in a cloud of dust. After the last bounce, Irving closed the throttle and ended his run just yards from where the over-run dropped into San Francisco Bay. His tail skid was broken. "Damn plane just wouldn't fly. Tow her back guys and we'll give her another go," Irving yelled to his ground crew.

During the twenty minutes it took to tow the *Pabco Pacific Flyer* clear of the airstrip, Jack Frost and navigator Gordon Scott waited patiently at the starting line with the *Golden Eagle*. Throughout the whole morning's proceedings Frost and Scott were the most relaxed and confident of the race crews. This may well have been because they knew that Lockheed's superb Vega had performed brilliantly during a number of long trial flights. Furthermore, in its quest to produce its own race-winning headlines, the Hearst organisation had spared no expense with their entry.

Their Vega was not only lavishly equipped with the latest instruments and equipment but, in case of emergency, could dump its heavy fuel load and jettison its landing gear to increase range, or to safely ditch in the ocean. The fuselage also contained carbon-dioxide charged bags designed to keep the wooden skinned monoplane afloat for at least thirty days.

When finally given the command to take-off, Frost and the *Golden Eagle* made it look easy, and they had reached 200 feet by the time they passed the airfield boundary. Minutes later he was waggling his wings to employees gathered on the roof of downtown offices of the San Francisco *Examiner*.

As Pedlar's *Miss Doran* was pushed to the line, those nearby could see the pilot adjusting the tilt of his straw hat and furiously chewing on his gum. The plane's namesake, curls peeping out beneath her helmet, waved from the window of her cabin. The Buhl was the most overloaded of the Dole racers. Besides 5715 litres of fuel, it also carried the weight of a superfluous passenger and her specially panelled cabin, adapted to provide the young woman with a private dressing room! However, the 31 square metres of lifting surface provided by the Buhl's biplane wings were equal to the task. The crowd was ecstatic when the *Miss Doran*, though using most of the take-off run, lifted safely "carrying a flower of American womanhood towards Hawaii."

As the *Aloha* took off past the crowds, there was no doubt about its Hawaiian links. Sporting the most exotic paint job of the race, it was finished in sunshine yellow, had a scarlet lei painted around its nose and on its sides carried the Great Seal of Hawaii. Pilot Martin Jensen climbed just enough to clear the roofs of San Francisco as he chased *Miss Doran* out across the Golden Gate.

The crowd began to relax as yet another airplane took off safely. This time it was Art Goebel and his navigator/radio operator Lieutenant Bill Davis in the Travel Air *Woolaroc*. They were followed by "Lone Star Bill" Erwin in his race-built Swallow *Dallas Spirit*. Among the cheering crowd was his 20 year-old wife Connie, who had originally been nominated to navigate on the flight, before the committee decided she was too young and inexperienced. In her place Erwin now carried a naval veteran, Alvin Eichwaldt.

The crowd hung on as Irving's mechanics worked on the Pabco *Pacific Flyer*. The tail skid was repaired and, finding no fault in the engine, the crew were preparing to top up the tanks, when their attention was diverted by the sound of an approaching aircraft. The drama was not over. Three aircraft were returning to the field — *Miss Doran* and *Oklahoma* with engine problems, and *Dallas Spirit* with its fuselage fabric peeling away.

Police rushed to clear the landing area as Griffin arrived over the field with smoke streaming from the *Oklahoma*'s engine. Despite the fuel overload Griffin landed safely. Mechanics soon confirmed his worst fears — that he had "cooked the engine" and was out of the race. Griffin had been warned previously by a Wright

Aeronautical Company field engineer that the fuel he was using was likely to cause his Wright Whirlwind to overheat.

Pedlar arrived overhead with the *Miss Doran*'s engine missing badly. Dumping fuel he landed safely. Erwin in the *Dallas Spirit* was unable to dump fuel, and his control problems were exacerbated by the drag from long streamers of fabric that flapped around the Swallow's tail. Making a long, flat, powered approach he executed a superb landing. An inspection showed that slipstream had lifted the fabric around the navigator's drift sight-hatch and had peeled it back from the side and bottom of the fuselage. Hearing that it would take at least half a day to repair, the disappointed Erwin withdrew from the race.

Meanwhile, the *Pabco Pacific Flyer* had been repaired and the crowd held its breath as Irving made his second attempt to take-off. After several bounces Irving showed his inexperience by desperately hauling the Breese off the ground. In response, the overloaded machine mushed into the air, clawing for height on the verge of the stall. After clawing to about 50 feet it flopped to the ground and disappeared in the now all-too-familiar cloud of dust. The crowd roared when the crew emerged unhurt and Irving's long-suffering wife, Madelaine, and their five-year-old daughter rushed to the crash site to embrace the frustrated flyer.

The strain was telling on Mildred Doran who was in tears and understandably was having second thoughts. Some of the crowd called out to her not to go. Pedlar seemed too busy supervising mechanics changing the Buhl's spark plugs to take much notice as navigator Knope tried to talk her into staying behind. However, it seems that, after being the driving force behind the whole project, she feared humiliation more than the vast Pacific. Journalist Louise Landis later reported in the San Francisco *Bulletin*: "She started the second time knowing full well there was real danger ahead. In fact I know she was scared to death when she entered the little cabin of that plane on the last trip. But no one was going to call her a quitter. She wouldn't stay behind."

When word came that the airplane was ready for another try, the white faced school teacher walked quietly back to her cabin. Minutes later her aircraft was a speck out over the bay. Almost two hours behind the leaders, *Miss Doran* was the last to leave. Next morning's headlines were predictable:

"DISASTER HAUNTS THE DOLE FLIERS" ... "ONLY FOUR AWAY OUT OF 15 ENTRIES". One paper reported a "publicity-mad promoter leaving a trail of carnage". Throughout the night newspaper switchboards had been jammed with anxious callers asking, "What's the latest news?" There had been little to report, as only the *Woolaroc* was equipped with two-way radio. Ships along the route reported vague "sightings" and a series of radio messages from the *Woolaroc*. Goebel had climbed above the solid layer of low cloud to 6000 feet where navigator Davis had a sky full of stars for his celestial navigation. "300 miles out" ... "517 miles out" ... "750 miles out" ... "1485 miles out" ... Terse morse-keyed reports marked their progress.

The *Aloha* had last been seen scuttling low over the Farrallon Islands, forty-eight kilometres off San Francisco. The Hawaiian pilot had planned to stay low all the way, partly not to waste precious fuel climbing his headily laden airplane, but more importantly for the sake of accurate navigation. His crew mate, Paul Schulter, was a merchant seaman and had no flying experience. He was accustomed to reading a sextant from the deck of a ship and using the actual horizon while taking bearings on the sun, moon and stars. To do so while flying high required a number of intricate corrections to be made and Schulter was not confident of his ability to get accurate readings under such circumstances. Though it meant the added hazard of low flying over water, the pair had considered it the lesser of two evils, for without accurate navigation they would never find the islands. As the *Aloha* carried no radio, reception range was not a factor.

The Farrallon Islands gave the race crews their only opportunity to visually fix their position on the long over-water crossing. Like the others, Schulter had pin-pointed their exact position, checked the time and rapidly calculated their drift and ground speed since passing over the Golden Gate twenty-three minutes earlier. From his position behind the cabin fuel tank, he had to pass messages to Jensen along a string pulley line. He pegged a note on the line and sent it forward between the narrow gap through which he could just glimpse the pilot. Jensen pulled it down, scanned the instructions, and altered heading. Now there was nothing but open water to Hawaii, and any further changes would be based on astro navigation or indications of drift from the sea's surface.

Besides navigating, Schulter had the job of operating the hand pump of the *Aloha*'s auxiliary fuel system. Short of funds, Jensen had initially planned to top up the aircraft's fuel system in flight from a stack of five-gallon fuel cans. However, when forced by the committee to equip the Breese with a proper long-range tank, he had installed a last-minute, minimum-cost system that included no fuel gauges. The only way to ensure that the aircraft's main tank was not running dry was for Schulter to frequently top it up until fuel was seen to overflow through a vent hole. This not only wasted precious fuel but was also a serious fire hazard, compounded by Schulter's insistence on chain-smoking.

All afternoon, as Schulter smoked and pumped, Jensen clung to that heading. An unbroken layer of low cloud prevented Schulter from "shooting" the sun. The cloud still persisted at twilight — the best time to take a star shot with the horizon still clearly visible — and by 8 p.m. the pair were enveloped in darkness.

Somewhere close by, the *Woolaroc* cruised about 4000 feet above the *Aloha*. Art Goebel could afford the luxury of flying above cloud since Davis was an experienced aerial navigator and had the added advantage of also being a qualified pilot. Unlike Schulter, Davis did not worry about being denied a sight of the earth's horizon while using his sextant. Furthermore, the *Woolaroc*'s radio allowed him to tune in on the San Francisco and Maui radio beams.

For the first four hours of flight Goebel had steered 250 degrees, the first of eight headings Davis had pre-computed to follow the Great Circle course to Hawaii. Their aircraft was equipped with three magnetic compasses, besides an electrically driven Earth Inductor Compass which was not subject to the oscillations and errors of ordinary compasses. Davis also had a Pioneer Drift Sight and a supply of smoke bombs with which he could determine how much the wind was affecting the aircraft's track.

An hour out, Davis had tuned in the radio and had heard the steady "on course" signal in his earphones. As darkness fell, the reassuring hum of the San Francisco beacon faded. They climbed to 6000 feet, where Davis resorted to taking regular sextant shots on Polaris though the open hatch alongside his position near the rear door. Every four hours he passed Goebel a new Great Circle heading on the "string telephone".

Throughout the night Davis transmitted position reports and passed messages via the ships along the route. One addressed to his mother in Atlanta, Georgia stating "All's Well", reached the Davis home an hour and a half later. Starting from the *Woolaroc*'s morse key, the signal went by ship's radio, shore radio,telegraph, and finally telephone to the far side of the continent.

Shortly after sunrise the cloud began to break and Davis was able to drop smoke bomb's to check their drift. The predicted north-east wind had swung to the south and he sent a message forward telling Goebel to alter heading to port. A note came back suggesting Davis had made a mistake, but the navigator insisted that there had been a big change in the wind, adding that it had boosted the *Woolaroc*'s ground speed to 160 km/h.

Goebel altered course and Davis radioed their position," latitude 24.35 north, longitude 150.43 west". As this put them only 720 kilometres from Honolulu Davis tuned in the Maui beacon. They should soon be in range and the navigator prayed it would confirm his calculations. Their position report was picked up by the S.S. *City of Los Angeles* and relayed to Hawaii. Two hours later, as they came in range, Hawaii's Wahaiwa radio station picked up another message from Davis estimating that they would arrive at Honolulu's Wheeler Field in two and a half hours.

The information was passed to the thousands who were already waiting at the airfield. Most Honoluluans had been given the day off to attend the celebrations and within an hour the crowd had swelled to 30 000. A three-kilometre traffic jam trailed back along the road to Honolulu. Stunting army planes, dancing girls and bands kept the impatient crowd entertained. As James Dole and Hawaiian Governor Wallace G. Farrington joined the throng waiting at the airfield, Dole told waiting reporters: "Hawaii is on the lips of the world today and in the minds of countless millions of people."

Hawaii had gone aviation mad. Besides a stream of stories about the race preparations, newspapers had been filled with aviation advertisements, and Honolulu stores were offering free toy aeroplanes to their customers. The elegant new Royal Hawaiian Hotel had been chosen as race headquarters and was preparing to host all the arriving fliers. Besides a lavish reception, a luau-style dinner dance was planned for the following night.

About an hour out, the *Woolaroc*'s radio signals ceased, and there was growing concern until Davis came back on air after discovering and repairing a broken connection. Shortly after, he finally picked up the Maui radio beam. They were on course and about 120 kilometres from the finish. The *Woolaroc* passed Diamond Head shortly before one o'clock local time. The delirious crowd watched as an exuberant Davis began firing off all the aircraft's distress flares and smoke bombs. Waiting army planes moved in to escort the *Woolaroc* to Wheeler Field. The two airmen had not realised that they were in the lead until a grinning army pilot held up one finger to signify they were the first to arrive. The race was theirs.

At 12.24 p.m. local time the *Woolaroc* touched down. The Travel Air had taken 26 hours, 17 minutes, and 33 seconds to fly from Oakland to Honolulu. It is said that Davis's first words on jumping from the aircraft were: "How are the rest of the boys ?"and that he appeared distressed when told there had been no word of the other starters. One of the first to reach them was a despairing Marguerite Jensen who rushed up, pleading for news of her husband. Pale and close to tears she listened as Goebel said he had not sighted the *Aloha*, before briefly collapsing alongside the airplane.

The crowd surged forward as the airmen were garlanded in leis. James Dole wrung their hands, then asked anxiously if they had seen anything of the other competitors. The two fliers shook their heads. The celebrations continued but Davis and Goebel were distracted. Like everyone else they had one eye on the horizon. The exhausted airmen were eventually driven to the Royal Hawaiian Hotel to rest.

While the crowd waited anxiously for signs of other aircraft, Jensen and Schulter in the *Aloha* were north of the islands and short of fuel. Since nightfall the previous day they had been living a nightmare. Realising the dangers of flying at night with no moon or stars to illuminate the ocean, Jensen had decided to climb above the cloud. He also hoped that Schulter could "shoot" the stars and fix their position: "I was able to climb to about 4000 feet. It was still a dense fog [cloud]. Here I experienced vertigo when I was unable to get above it," Jensen recalled years later, telling how he completely lost control. One moment they were climbing wings level, then a few seconds later the aircraft was spiralling to the left.

In those days pilots called it "the graveyard spiral" — a dreaded manoeuvre, where the harder one tried to pull out, the tighter the turn and the faster the rate of descent became. Jensen's years of stunting at airshows across America finally paid off when he somehow managed to convert the spiral into a spin. He had come out of a spin so often for the crowds that he could do it with his eyes closed. Just using "the seat of his pants", he knew exactly when to push the stick forward, kick on the opposite rudder, centralise and climb out of the ensuing dive.

Three times this happened and when, the third time, the altimeter showed they had recovered just a few hundred feet from the water, Jensen decided to remain low again. Somehow they survived the night, with Jensen concentrating on the quivering needles of the altimeter and his crude turn and bank indicator. Jensen recalled a miraculous encounter with the Pacific when the *Aloha* skipped on a wave-top like a giant stone:

The altimeter registered 100 feet above sea level which I had held for some hours. Perhaps the density in mid Pacific was different and caused an error for no doubt I must have been actually no more than 5 or 10 feet above the water. I hit the top of a wave and the spray ripped a long slit in the stabiliser fabric. The fact that I never once during the flight took my hands off the throttle or stick saved us. I had instant control and climbed immediately to 500 feet.

At dawn Jensen was still at 500 feet and continuing to steer 248 degrees — the heading he had been given over the Farrallons. When their estimated flight time expired without a trace of land, Schulter sent a note forward to Jensen suggesting they circle for two and a half hours until noon. He was not confident of getting an accurate reading until the sun was highest. The frustrated pilot had no options left. Now concerned purely with survival, Jensen throttled back to conserve fuel.

At noon Schulter's sextant showed they were circling 304 kilometres north of Honolulu. Clearly they had been thrown way off course by the wind change that Davis in the *Woolaroc* had detected. They had emptied the auxiliary tank and, with no gauges, had no idea of how much fuel remained in the wing tanks.

Two hours later some of the crowd were leaving when the *Aloha* landed with just 15 litres or twenty minutes of fuel remaining. "Martin Jensen where the hell have you been?" wailed his distraught wife, clutching the exhausted airmen. "Peg, I never saw so much damn water in my life," Jensen answered. Apologising to Dole for not winning, Jensen explained that they would have won if he had he been able to afford a radio to home in on the Maui navigation beam. Had Jensen not had to circle for two and a half hours waiting for Schulter to shoot the sun, they could have beaten the *Woolaroc* by a half hour.

An hour later, it became clear that the *Golden Eagle* and the *Miss Doran* were down in the Pacific. By then their fuel would have been exhausted. Next morning a massive sea search was mounted. Army, Navy and civilian planes took off from the islands. Martin Jensen dragged his weary body back into the *Aloha* and searched for five hours. From San Diego the aircraft carrier *Langley* took her twenty-eight aircraft far out to sea to scour the mainland end of the route. The *Langley* was skippered by Captain John Towers, who had commanded the NC-3 flying boat on its abortive attempt to cross the Atlantic Ocean in 1919.

Convincing evidence that flares were seen burning high up on the slopes of Mount Mauna Loa led to an extensive search being made of the volcanic peaks of Hawaii Island. The brother of the *Golden Eagle*'s navigator, Gordon Scott, spent much of the following year searching the island. He was frequently assisted by Martin Jensen who by then was flying the *Aloha* on passenger flights for Lewis Hawaiian Tours. Although no trace was found, there are many who still believe that the *Golden Eagle* crashed near the peak and that wreckage will one day be discovered littered in a rocky crevice.

The official search was called off after ten days, but not before an army search plane crashed into the sea, killing its two crewmen. They were not the only searchers to lose their lives. The Dole affair was to suffer a final tragedy. On 18 August "Lone Star" Bill Erwin announced that he and his navigator, Alvin Eichwaldt, intended to search along the route in the repaired *Dallas Spirit*.

Following his forced withdrawal from the race, pilot Erwin had been criticised by his Texan backers for pulling out and was urged to try again. Furthermore, Erwin had initially been keen to use the Dole flight as part a flight between Dallas and Hong Kong. Dallas businessman William E. Easterwood had offered US$25 000 for such a flight. It seems that, besides searching for the lost fliers, Erwin still had plans of continuing on from Hawaii in an effort to claim the Easterwood Prize. With criticism already being levelled at the running of the Dole affair, officials of its organising committee were among the many who tried to dissuade Erwin. He refused to listen and announced to the press that he would, "zig-zag over and if necessary zig-zag back".

Erwin equipped the Swallow with a radio acquired from the wrecked *Pabco Pacific Flyer* and set out from Oakland at 2.15 p.m. of 19 August. For some hours all went well. The men were obviously still in high spirits at 5.45 p.m. when they radioed, "Just saw a rum-runner to the south and had a hell of a time keeping Ike in. Signed Bill." But six hours out, soon after nightfall, things started to go wrong. After several garbled messages, navigator Eichwaldt radioed: "SOS — we are in a tail spin. We came out of it OK but we're sure scared. It was a close call. I thought it was all over but came out of it. The light on the instrument board (panel) went out and it was so dark that Bill couldn't see the wings." It seems that Erwin had succumbed to the problems of vertigo that had plagued Martin Jensen. Moreover, the Texan's troubles were exacerbated by the loss of his instrument lighting.

Ten minutes later a second pitiful signal was picked up. It started, "We are in anr [another?] ... SOS." The transmission ended abruptly as the aircraft presumably spun into the sea. Given Jensen's experience, Erwin's similar loss of control at night signposted the probable fate of the other lost fliers. Radio operators on the mainland later reported that over the last few minutes of flight the *Dallas Spirit*'s transmissions rose and fell in pitch. This, they explained, was caused by the wind-driven generator slowing down then speeding up as the aircraft first lost then rapidly increased speed as Erwin battled to maintain control. As Eichwaldt's final message came over the air, the transmission note whined higher and higher until, at 9.04 p.m., it ended in a last pitiful wail when the *Dallas Spirit* crashed into the sea.

Following the loss of the *Dallas Spirit* the San Francisco *Examiner* wrote on its front page: " 'Lone

Star' Bill Erwin and his daring mate Alvin 'Ike' Eichwaldt today stand with that heroic quintet of Dole Racers in the shadowy wings of the Pacific's great ampitheater while a worldwide audience thus far clamours in vain to recall them to the stage."

However, soon the newspapers were reporting mounting criticism and public revulsion at the loss of life: "DOLE'S RACE TO DEATH" … "AVIATION ASININITY" … "WAS IT WORTH THE PRICE — 10 LIVES" … Headlines and articles slammed the organisers. "Such an orgy of reckless sacrifice must never be permitted again in this country," the Philadelphia *Enquirer* asserted. Much of the criticism was unfairly levelled at the unfortunate James Dole, suggesting he personally had "enticed inexperienced and ill-prepared pilots to their death in home-made crates". It ignored the fact that the race committee had set the standards and run the race. Not to mention the cavalier approach of many of the so-called professional pilots themselves.

Standard Oil aviation executive G.O. Norville echoed the feelings of many of the aviation community in a letter to National Aeronautical Association president, Porter Adams. He suggested that planners had been blinded by Lindbergh's success and had ignored basic safety matters. Seeking more positive regulation in the future, Norville wrote: "The progress of aviation has been retarded to such an extent that it will take at least two years of conscientious effort to place it again in the position it held on August 1, 1927."

In defence of James Dole, the *Honolulu Advertiser* in its editorial of 28 August 1927 intoned: "The lessons taught by the tragedies attending the Dole flight will have a moral effect on those who would now follow the others across the Pacific. Preparation, navigation, radio connection, a 100 per cent expedition will be the result. Successful accomplishment of a new undertaking brings to light unheard of difficulties, and a way is pointed to solving the problems. Tragedy in pioneering breeds caution, and too much caution in hazardous undertakings is never possible."

By the end of the year, when the immediate furore had died a little, the Aeronautical Chamber of Commerce of America summed it all up in its prestigious *Aircraft Year Book*, which stated:

> The event was marked by unnecessary crashes and loss of life, due in part to a scramble to win prize money, in some instances without proper preparations and without regard for the fitness of equipment. When it is recalled with what care Lindbergh, Chamberlin, Bryd, Maitland and a succession of trans-oceanic fliers went about their preparations, and to what constant testing their flying equipment was subjected, a statement made by Martin Jensen, winner of second place in the race, throws an interesting light on the rush and hurry attending the start of this hazardous undertaking. Jensen wrote: "Five days before the start of the race not even the fuselage was on my plane, but in those five days I worked night and day, making preparation, always against great odds." The storm of criticism against ill-considered ocean flights, under conditions of insufficient preparation, and possibly inadequate equipment, will have a steadying effect, it is believed, in all future attempts in this field.

11
The loss of the airship
Italia

For over half a century a small gold medallion and a large oak cross, bearing the tricolour of Italy, have lain buried beneath the snows of the North Pole. They were dropped there from a height of 500 feet by General Umberto Nobile, commander of the airship *Italia*, as it circled the pole at 1.30 a.m. on 24 May 1928.

As the medallion of the "Virgin of Fire" and the cross entrusted to Nobile by Pope Pius Xl fell from the cabin of the silver dirigible, with them went the good fortune that had attended Nobile's aviation career. For the *Italia*, the pride of fascist Italy, was doomed never to leave the polar ice cap, and Nobile was destined to be persecuted, demoted and exiled by dictator Benito Mussolini and his henchmen.

Deeply patriotic, Nobile had built the *Italia* to bring glory to his country by exploring the Arctic and conducting the first out-and-back flight to the North Pole. Nobile had established himself as one of the world's leading designers and manufacturers of lighter-than-air dirigibles. Born in 1885, he had been turned down for military service during the First World War after being found unfit for active service.

Instead, the slight, agile young engineer concentrated his efforts on airships, and soon after the war's end had developed the giant Aeronautical Construction Company. This was the era of the Zeppelin, which seemed to provide the solution to safe aerial transportation. With Germany rapidly establishing a lead in the construction of the great dirigibles, Nobile had finally been claimed by the Italian army for his technical expertise and he quickly rose to the rank of General.

Throughout the early 1920s Nobile avoided the growing political cancer of fascism that overran Italy's military and civilian circles. Fascist attempts to discredit Nobile and take over his factory had failed. Among his strongest enemies was General Italo Balbo, Mussolini's ambitious Secretary of Air and one of the founders of Italian fascism. Believing that Italy's aviation future lay with aeroplanes (and with himself), Balbo plotted against Nobile and his airships and secretly turned Mussolini against them. Nobile was oblivious to his imminent fall from favour.

In 1925 Nobile's career reached its pinnacle. He teamed with Norwegian explorer Roald Amundsen and American millionaire Lincoln Ellsworth to cross the North Pole in the airship *Norge*, a machine designed, built and commanded by the Italian. Completing one of history's great flights, the *Norge* crossed a third of the world. Its 12 500-kilometre route took the airship from the Mediterranean to the Pacific, via the North Pole, in a flight time of 171 hours.

As leader of the expedition Amundsen claimed credit for the remarkable flight. However, Nobile seemed to get all the recognition — which was not surprising as the Italian had designed and commanded the airship. Widely interviewed by the world press, Nobile tactlessly, perhaps, gave insufficient acknowledgment to Amundsen's role. The situation was exacerbated by Mussolini, who shamelessly used the great flight to publicise his new fascist state. To do so the dictator manipulated the politically naive Nobile and forced a wedge of hate between the unwitting General and Amundsen. In the end the Norwegian bitterly blamed Nobile for appearing to take all the glory.

By 1927 Nobile had planned a new airship expedition, a flight to the North Pole and back to the starting point. This was a feat not yet achieved by any aircraft. It would include a series of flights over uncharted areas of the ice cap. His fascist enemies welcomed the magnitude of the expedition, in the secret belief he would never return. They hoped it would prove to be an expeditious way of removing yet another popular and powerful opponent of their beliefs. Discussing the risks in a public address Nobile stated:

> We have absolute confidence in the preparation of this expedition. All that could be foreseen has been foreseen. Even the possibility of failure or catastrophe. We are quite aware that our venture is difficult and dangerous. Even more so than that of 1926 [the *Norge* flight]. But it is this difficulty and danger that attracts us. Had it been safe and easy, other people would already have preceded us.

In April 1928 his new airship *Italia*, an improved sister ship of the *Norge*, left Milan for the expedition's base at Kings Bay, Spitzbergen. She carried aloft a crew of twenty, 2500 kilograms of equipment, 2000 kilograms of ballast, 4200 kilograms of petrol, 300 kilograms of oil and Nobile's pet terrier, Titana.

Following delays in Norway caused by bad weather the airship finally reached Kings Bay on 6 May. There Nobile was to get his first taste of the token assistance he was to receive from the Italian government. The government supply ship *Città di Milano*, which had been assigned as base ship for the expedition, was awaiting them. Her captain, however, refused to assign any of his crew to assist in the man-consuming docking and mooring of the airship, until he received "orders from Rome". Well aware that it would take several days, he suggested that the airship circle around until orders arrived.

Fifty Norwegian seamen and local miners finally came to Nobile's aid and the *Italia* was secured to her mooring mast. She hovered quietly within sight of the battered shed that had hangared the balloon used by the 1897 Salamon Andree expedition. A Swedish expedition that had disappeared on a flight to the North Pole.

Nobile made two exploratory flights, charting 50 000 square kilometres of the ice cap, before setting out on the ill-fated polar flight on 23 May 1928. On board were sixteen men and adequate equipment to survive a lengthy period on the ice, should they be forced down. Included in the crew were several observers: Finn Malmgren, a Swedish professor of meteorology; Dr Francis Behounek, a Czechoslovakian professor studying atmospheric electricity; Dr Aldo Pontremoli, professor of physics at the University of Milan; and Ugo Lago, a young journalist from Syracuse.

The flight to the Pole proved deceptively easy when it was aided by good weather and a tailwind that at times reached 45 km/h. However, it was the unforecast strength of the tailwind that concerned Nobile, who knew that it would turn into a headwind on the return flight. Then, unless the wind abated, it was unlikely their petrol supply would keep the three 250-horsepower Mayerbeck engines running for long enough to get back to Spitzbergen.

The alternative was to overfly the Pole and keep heading on to Canada. But there was heavy weather ahead and it was an equally uninviting option. Caught between a rock and a hard place, Nobile circled the Pole and waited for a final weather forecast from his meteorologist, Finn Malmgren. Based on a radioed weather report from Tromso in Norway, he predicted that the winds would die away early on the return journey. Their best chance, Malgren advised, was to return as planned to King's Bay. On this recommendation, Nobile made the final and fateful decision. After circling the Pole for two hours, the *Italia* headed southwards into the teeth of the wind and swirling mist — towards disaster.

Twenty-four hours after setting course they should have been home, but they were only half- way there! Though capable of over 100 km/h the airship's speed over the ground had been less than 45 km/h. Rather than dying away, the polar storm was increasing in intensity. The semi-rigid dirigible lunged and warped in the wind, and the crew had great difficulty in controlling the canvas and steel monster.

It was too late to turn back and head with the wind for Canada. They were past the point of no return. Weather reports coming in by radio still suggested that the *Italia* was nearing the edge of the storm. A new and more dangerous enemy attacked the bucking airship as ice began to form on the gas bag, control surfaces and engine propellers.

They were flying at 750 feet when the airship's elevator control suddenly jammed in a nose-down position and the *Italia* plunged towards the ice. Nobile immediately ordered the engines stopped, which stopped the descent and allowed the airship to rise like a free balloon above the mist into bright sunlight. While the crew worked to repair the controls, the navigators took vital sunshots which fixed their position at 288 kilometres north-east of Kings Bay.

However, while the balloon hovered in brilliant sunlight the relative warmth caused its gas cells to expand and blow off precious gas. So when they finally freed the controls and descended again below the cloud (to prevent further loss of gas), the *Italia* was dangerouly "heavy" — the term used by airshipmen to denote the lack of lift resulting from a shortage of gas.

Only thirty minutes later, at 10.30 a.m. on 25 May, General Nobile was the first to notice signs of an unusual list towards the tail. They were cruising at 900 feet above the ice with all controls set for level flight, yet they were descending tail-down at a rate of three feet a second.

Nobile called for full power and up-elevator to stop the descent. It had no effect other than to further raise the angle of the nose. With a twenty degree nose-up attitude, the *Italia* was still heading down towards the ice. Realising that a crash was imminent, Nobile ordered the engines stopped to prevent fire and the ballast chain dropped. Thirty years later Nobile had not forgotten the terror of that moment. He wrote:

> My recollection of those last terrible instants is very vivid in my memory. I had scarcely had time to reach the spot near the two rudders, between Malmgren and Zappi, when I saw Malmgren fling up the wheel, turning his startled eyes on me. Instinctively I grasped the helm, wondering if it were possible to guide the ship onto the snow field and so lessen the shock ... Too late! There was the pack, a few yards below and terribly uneven. The masses of ice grew larger, came nearer and nearer. A moment later we crashed.

The rear engine gondola struck first. Motorman Vincenzo Pomella threw up his hands to protect his face as the tiny cabin was dashed against the ice and disintegrated. The airship pitched forward and the main cabin hit next. Its lightweight steel and canvas structure was ripped from the main body and split apart, spilling its occupants and equipment out onto the ice. Nobile recalled:

> There was a fearful impact. Something hit me on the head then I was caught and crushed. Clearly, and without pain, I felt some of my limbs snap. Some falling object knocked me down head foremost. Instinctively I shut my eyes and with perfect lucidity and coolness formulated the thought: "It's all over!" I almost pronounced the words in my mind.

Relieved of the weight of rear engine and cabin, the *Italia* bounced off the ice and rose again quickly. Still on board were six men including journalist Lago and Dr

Pontremoli, asleep in their cabin inside the main hull.
By the time the six had realised what had happened and
reached the gaping hole left with the destruction of the
cabin, it was too late. They peered down at their friends
lying amongst the litter of wreckage on the ice. There
was no way of controlling the crippled airship which
now rose quickly like a free balloon. They were too high
to jump for it. They were doomed.

On the ice, those who were conscious saw one man
overcome his terror sufficiently to act. Chief Engineer
Ettore Arduino was throwing everything he could lay
his hands on down to his ice-bound companions:
precious tins of fuel, food and a prepacked survival bag.
His quick and unselfish action undoubtedly saved their
lives. Within minutes the *Italia*, blown by the wind, had
drifted aimlessly out of sight amid the clouds, never to
be seen again.

Nine men lay among the wreckage. Two were seriously injured; Chief Technician Natale Cecioni had broken both legs, and Nobile had a broken leg, arm and
fractured ribs. Two others had painful shoulder and rib
injuries. One other survivor that had reached the ice
safely was Nobile's pet terrier *Titana*.

Among the equipment that littered the ice they found
a three-metre-square tent and a sleeping bag, into
which Nobile and Cecioni were placed and made as
comfortable as possible. Every piece of wreckage might
have some use, so everything was gathered. One of the
first items found was the expedition's field radio, which
appeared to be in working condition. It was immediately
passed to Guiseppe Biagi, the ship's radio operator, who
was in need of something to take his mind off the awful
shock he had received a few minutes earlier while
searching the area for useable equipment.

Some distance from the main wreckage Biagi had
seen a man sitting on a block of ice. On investigation,
Biagi came upon motorman Pomella who had been in

the rear gondola when the *Italia* struck the ice. Pomella had his back to the radio operator and was bent forward apparently intent on replacing a shoe near his foot. He did not answer when Biagi called to him and when touched gently on the shoulder he toppled slowly forward onto the ice. It was then the horrified radio operator saw that one side of his face had received a crushing blow. Pomella was dead.

Three hours after reaching the ice Biagi had the radio working and began sending out emergency calls, "SOS Italia. Nobile. SOS Italia. Nobile". However, although he could hear other distant radio transmissions, no one answered his calls.

Initially in shock and considerable pain, Nobile was convinced that he was only hours away from death. But helped by the warmth in the tent, he eventually came out of shock and again took command of the situation.

After searching the litter of wreckage and the surrounding ice the men gathered 127 kilograms of concentrated food — mainly pemmican, chocolate and powdered milk. Eating normally, this represented about three weeks supplies, but Nobile reckoned that, if they cut individual rations to 300 grams per day, they could hold out for six weeks. They also had a revolver, ammunition, a signal pistol, several tins of petrol and matches. Luckily, when the cabin had disintegrated, all the navigation equipment had spilled out and the survivors had two sextants, maps and logs.

All were well dressed for the cold and had snow boots and sunglasses. However, their only protection from the cold was the tent, a sleeping bag and a blanket. Nobile recalled:

Being meant for four people it was too small for the nine of us. Cecioni and I alone took up more than a third, seeing we had to keep our legs stretched and motionless. Seven people had to fit in the remaining space, besides the wireless batteries, which I had advised them to bring inside to preserve them from the action of extreme cold which would diminish their efficiency. On the other hand there were advantages in being crowded up like this, since at any rate it made the cold much more bearable.

Through occasional breaks in the cloud the survivors took shots of the sun and were able to fix their exact position, which they broadcast with the emergency calls. Hour after hour, day after day, Biagi sent out calls to the *Città di Milano*. But no one answered because no one was really listening. Their frustration grew as they heard the ship's radio operator sending scores of the crew's personal messages to friends and relatives, and speculative stories by journalists, back to Italy.

It became clear that the ship's operators were not even bothering to listen for their distress calls. Worse, every few hours the ship's operator would send a routine call to the *Italia* indicating that they believed the airship was down and that he was listening for a distress call. Later he advised that base knew the survivors' position was near the twentieth meridian (completely inaccurate) and he ended, "Trust in us. We are organising help."

In fact at this stage, several days after the crash, the Italian government had still made no move to commence a search for the missing expedition, even though the *Città di Milano* had received a message from the *Italia* just before the accident, advising that the airship was encountering severe head winds and giving its position. The procrastination of the ship's captain, Guiseppe Romagna, probably reflected his knowledge that his government had little interest in finding Nobile and his men. Indeed, in Italy it was already presumed that they were dead. In contrast, the Swedes, the Russians, the French, the Finns and even the British had all made moves to begin searching for the lost airship.

In Oslo a testimonial dinner was being held to honour an Australian, Sir Hubert Wilkins, and his pilot, Captain Ben Eielson, who had recently crossed the North

Pole in their Lockheed Vega aircraft. Among the guests was Roald Amundsen. When word reached the guests that Nobile was missing, 58-year-old Amundsen put aside his bitter feelings for his former colleague and announced he would lead a search.

The French Air Force quickly made a seaplane and crew available to him and the Norwegian whaling vessels *Hobby* and *Braganza* commenced searching north of Spitzbergen. The Russians sent two icebreakers to the area, and Swedish and Russian aircraft were despatched to Spitzbergen. The attention of the whole world centred on the search and yet the *Città di Milano* still bobbed at anchor in the safety of the harbour at Kings Bay "awaiting orders".

A friend of the missing airman, Milan merchant Arturo Mercanti, attempted to induce the Italian government to mount a search but was everywhere confronted by bureaucratic red tape. He finally blew the case wide open by threatening to personally finance a search and to tell the world press that the Italian government was not solvent enough to spend a few lire to save Nobile and his men. Only then did Mussolini act. He sent one aircraft commanded by Major Umberto Maddalena to Kings Bay!

For over a week the survivors waited and listened. They had dyed the tent a red-ochre colour with some sea marker to make it more visible from the air. Thus it was to become known internationally as "The Red Tent". Their morale lifted on the fifth day when they shot a polar bear, which provided them with over 100kilograms of fresh meat. However, their spirits fell again soon after when they heard a journalist broadcasting from their base ship a theory that the *Italia* had probably struck a mountain and exploded with the loss of all aboard. The next day they heard a report that the President of the Italian Senate had commended the crew of the *Italia* for sacrificing themselves in the name of science. In the eyes of Italy they had been given up for dead!

Several of the group decided that their only hope now lay in a small party setting off for base camp to bring help. As the pack ice was drifting southwards at that time of the year, they believed they could cross the 300 kilometres to Spitzbergen in two to three weeks. At first Nobile resisted the idea because he did not wish to split the group, but was eventually persuaded. Two Naval officers, Commanders Zappi and Mariano, and meteorologist Finn Malmgren set off across the ice carrying sixty kilograms of food and the lone blanket for protection.

On 6 June, after twelve days at the radio, Biagi was listening to a regular news report broadcast from Rome when he suddenly exclaimed, "They've heard us." Clamping his headphones tighter, he copied down the vital report, then turned and read it to his companions: "The Soviet Embassy has advised the Italian Government that an SOS from the *Italia* has been picked up by a young Soviet farmer, Nicholas Schmidt, at Archangel on the evening of 3 June."

Later that day they received a call from the *Città di Milano* which was relayed via a radio station in San Paolo, Italy. All of a sudden it seems the ship could receive the Red Tent's calls. Strange coincidence. Or was it? At that moment it seemed not to matter. Rescue was imminent ... or so they thought.

Nobile ordered a special feast of double rations. He wrote: "We celebrated the event by distributing to everyone 5 pieces of sugar, 10 malted milk tablets and 2 ounces of chocolate. We had never treated ourselves so generously. Laughter and chatter filled the tent. 'We still have to go through some hard trials. It's not over yet!' I warned them."

For the next two weeks the weakening survivors waited in vain for rescue. Several times they heard and saw searching aircraft in the distance. Their camp was obviously invisible from the air unless an aircraft came directly overhead. Finally, an air radio link was organised and on 20 June Italian pilot Maddalena was talked over the camp and dropped life-sustaining supplies. Two days later another aircraft found them and bombarded them with food and clothing. Neither aircraft was able to find a suitable landing place anywhere near the camp.

Meanwhile, the Russian icebreaker *Krassin* was gradually heading through the icepack towards the Red Tent. It was a painfully slow process. And a tiny three-man dog-sled team had set off from Spitzbergen, led by Captain Sora, an Italian army ski instructor, accompanied by a Dane and a Dutchman. Sora had defied the orders of the captain of the *Città di Milano*, who had threatened him with a court martial. The army officer's seemingly futile gamble was his personal gesture of reproach for the official Italian lack of action and the lack of interest in Nobile's predicament. Captain Sora's gesture almost cost him his life.

On 19 June, as Sora and his companions set off across the ice, a Latham 47 seaplane was heading out over the Barents Sea for the search area. On board was Amundsen, the "White Eagle of Norway" as he was called, and five French airmen. The Latham was seen crossing the coast, and then just disappeared forever. Subsequent inquiries suggested that its water-cooled engines were not suitable for sub-freezing conditions and may have overheated.

Five days later a Swedish pilot, Lieutenant Lundborg, located the Red Tent and was able to land his tiny ski-equipped plane on a stretch of ice nearby. He could carry only one passenger, and he advised General Nobile that he had orders to fly him out. Nobile wanted to be the last to leave and insisted that the injured Cecioni be the first to be airlifted out. Lundborg retorted that his orders were from Rome and he must take the General first. He argued that Nobile was needed to help organise the search for the three men who had left on foot, and also the six still missing in the *Italia*. Only then did the injured Nobile agree. With his dog in his arms he was carried to and stowed in the tiny Fokker.

Accusations were quickly levelled at Nobile for forsaking his men and taking the first chance at safety. Considering the orders passed to Nobile by his Swedish rescuer, this was unfair. Also, at the time it was planned that the others would be brought out in the same way in a matter of hours. Unfortunately for everyone, the daring Swede wrecked his aircraft on the second attempt and had himself to be rescued. The remaining survivors were to face another two and a half weeks on the icecap.

To his dismay and amazement Nobile was put under virtual house arrest back on board the *Città di Milano*. Still immobilised by his injuries, he needed assistance if he were to help organise a combined search. Such assistance was not given. He suggested to the ship's captain, Romagna, that the radio operators should "listen more perseveringly" for messages from Biagi at the Red Tent and he tried to find out why the ship's radio operators had not heard Biagi's SOS calls for twelve days and had seemed to spend most of their time exchanging family messages for the ship's company. Nobile was shocked by Romagna's preposterous excuses. "My dear General. If logic is to count for anything we were perfectly right in imagining that it was impossible for you to transmit and so it was a waste of time to listen for you," came the Captain's incredible answer.

When Nobile insisted on an explanation of Romagna's "logic", the Captain disclosed that when the *Città di Milano* suddenly ceased receiving transmissions from the *Italia* (minutes before it crashed) he had been convinced that the airship's radio operator, Biagi, had been killed when the airship went down. Romagna had even figured out how it had happened.

We thought he had leaned out of the port hole and at that moment the screw of the wireless (the generator's airscrew) had come loose and cut off his head," he told the astonished Nobile. It appears that the conviction of Biagi's death was so firmly rooted in Romagna's mind that it pervaded his crew, who also held out no hope of receiving a radio message from the *Italia*. Indeed, Nobile later learned that a junior radio operator had in fact heard part of one of Biagi's emergency messages on 29 May — four days after the crash — but when he had reported it to the Chief Radio Operator was told not to talk "nonsense".

No wonder Nobile believed that there was a conspiracy to discredit him and that his enemies in Italy would have been quite happy for the survivors not to have been found. Furthermore, even after they were located, the Italian authorities were among the first to infer cowardice.

On 11 July the *Krassin* was heading at walking pace through thick ice when two figures were seen in the distance. Commanders Zappi and Mariano had finally found help. Mariano was near death but Zappi was surprisingly fit. They reported that their companion Malmgren had given up and died much earlier. Later, there were to be suggestions that the two men had deserted their Scandinavian companion, and even vague suggestions of cannibalism were levelled in various quarters. All of these suspicions were part of an official campaign to blame Nobile for the whole *Italia* disaster. Adding to the whole drama, a Russian search plane went missing before the *Krassin* eventually reached the Red Tent at 9 p.m. on 12 July 1928.

The battered icebreaker worked her way to within 150 metres of the camp before stopping. The survivors had hardly settled on board before messages came flooding in by ship's radio. The first one addressed to radio operator Biagi read: "Wish to advise that Municipality of Rome has issued order to seize household effects since you failed to pay tax on your dog." Some welcome home!

On her return voyage the Krassin rescued the downed Russian airmen. Shortly after, Finnish and Swedish aviators picked up the gallant Captain Sora and his companions. They had been stranded and were starving. Their sledge and dogs had disappeared through a crack in the ice days earlier.

Before returning to Italy, Nobile pleaded with his government to be allowed to lead an expedition to search for the missing six crewmen and the remains of the *Italia*. His request was denied and he was ordered to Rome. Other nations continued a low-key search, without success. On 23 September the *Krassin* anchored off Cape Neale while crewmen erected a portable shelter and stocked it with provisions in case survivors reached there. Then she slowly steamed away. The search was over.

Back in Italy, Nobile was given a tumultuous welcome by the Italian public — over a quarter of a million people greeted his arrival in Rome. In contrast, he was cold-shouldered by the official establishment which set up a commission to investigate the incident. On it sat many of the General's political enemies: buzzards circling their prey. Outside Italy it was reported that the whole thing was a mere formality. The fascists had finally found a way to topple the hero from his pedestal. Seven months later Nobile was officially blamed for the loss of the *Italia*, and the failure of his mission was judged to be a crime.

In September 1928 a float from Amundsen's Latham seaplane was washed up near Tromso, Norway, ending forever speculation that the Norwegian explorer was awaiting rescue somewhere on the Arctic ice. For him, it seemed, death had come quickly.

But not so for his one-time companion on the *Norge* who it seemed would be forever condemned to the tortured, living death of an outcast in the country he loved so passionately.

It was more than Nobile could stand and he eventually emigrated to the Soviet Union where he designed several airships for the Russians. In 1939 he accepted a post at an American aeronautical college in Chicago. With the fall of Fascism following the Second World War, Nobile returned to Italy and cleared his name. With his reputation restored, and finally recognised for his polar achievements, he was offered a teaching position at the Aeronautical Institute of the University of Naples.

In 1958, when the United Stated nuclear submarine *Nautilus* made its epic journey under the North Pole, its captain wrote to Nobile: "From your courageous flight over the polar ice pack in 1928 it was established that there was no land between Alaska and Spitzbergen. Without this knowledge, found by you and confirmed by the aerial expeditions that followed you, we would not have known enough to undertake our voyage."

The fate of the six men who disappeared into the swirling polar mists aboard the hulk of the *Italia* remains a mystery. The answer lies with the wreckage of the airship and the bodies of the six, entombed forever in the sub-freezing ice and snow of the Polar cap. One day they may be discovered by future explorers of the inhospitable wilderness at the top of the world.

12
King of the Pacific

Prime Minister W.M. "Billy" Hughes played a key role in the early days of Australian aviation. Not only did he promote the aeroplane as a transport solution for this vast and isolated country but, unwittingly, he helped shape the career of Australia's great pioneer, Charles Kingsford Smith.

In March 1919, while in Paris for peace talks following the end of World War I, Prime Minister Hughes persuaded his government to offer £10 000 ($20 000) for the first Australians to fly from England to Australia. Hughes had used one of Britain's first airline services to commute between London and Paris and had quickly grasped the potential of air travel. Furthermore, a similar cash offer by a British newspaper for a trans-Atlantic flight was attacting world-wide attention, and Hughes felt that Australia could benefit from similar publicity.

Many Australian military airmen still in England awaiting demobilisation applied to make the flight. One of them was Lieutenant Charles Kingsford Smith MC. The 22-year-old Australian Flying Corps fighter pilot had already decided to turn his skills into a civilian career and saw the England–Australia challenge as the ideal opportunity to make his name.

Kingsford Smith, "Smithy" to his mates, teamed up with two other Australian Flying Corps pilots to crew a war-surplus Blackburn Kangaroo bomber. However, excitement turned to outrage when the team was told they could not compete unless they employed an expert navigator or undertook further training themselves.

Hughes' race advisers — a special committee of the Royal Aero Club — considered the trio too inexperienced. Hughes explained to the press: "We feel we are responsible for the safety of these young fellows, and could not allow them to start on a voyage half-way around the world without any knowledge of navigation."

Bitterly disappointed, Kingsford Smith resigned from the Kangaroo's team. The whole sad affair had received wide coverage in the Australian newspapers, which added further to Kingsford Smith's belief that he had lost face. While his team mates looked for a qualified navigator, he decided to visit a brother in Oakland, California. Before sailing he told them: "I don't know when or exactly how yet, but I'm going to make that bloody Hughes sit up and take notice of me ... and I'm going to fly to Australia."

By the time Kingsford Smith reached California a Vickers Vimy bomber flown by Adelaide airmen Ross and Keith Smith had won Hughes' prize. His disqualification still preyed on the young airman's mind and he felt honour-bound to prove himself. In a letter to his mother Kingsford Smith disclosed that he was already planning another way to fly home. For him the future lay across the Pacific. He wrote:

> I am once again full of optimism after the last few black weeks I've had with this darn Australian flight falling through ... However dears there's lots of fight left in me, and I have every intention of coming home to you by air, but from this country. You know there is another prize offered for the job [trans-Pacific] amounting to $50 000 and I think I can get people over here sufficiently interested to back me ... Of course I am keeping it right out of the newspapers. No second fiasco for me, thanks."

The US$50 000 trans-Pacific offer was made by

Hollywood film producer Thomas H.Ince and, from the outset, Kingsford Smith suspected it was a cheap publicity stunt. "Somehow I smell a nigger in the woodpile," he remarked.

Kingsford Smith estimated the flight would cost US$22 000, the major item being US$16 500 for a converted war-surplus Vickers Vimy bomber similar to the machines that had flown the Atlantic and won the England–Australia challenge.

The sheer distance did not deter Kingsford Smith. He was confident of overcoming the fear that airmen of the day had of over-water flight. He had already experienced and survived his first dramatic meeting with the great ocean, twelve years earlier at Sydney's Bondi Beach.

"Boy saved from drowning", read the headlines. A fearless ten year-old Smithy and a swimming companion, foolishly ignoring the dangerous riptide, had been swept out to sea. When he was eventually brought back to the beach rescuers thought he had drowned. It took thirty minutes of artificial respiration and a "miracle" to bring the youngster "back from the dead".

Searching California for a backer, Kingsford Smith approached the Los Angeles Chamber of Commerce, but its members were not interested. Nor could America's Manufacturers Aircraft Association assist. However, when Vickers cabled Kingsford Smith, stating bluntly, "Cannot supply Vickers machine," the AMAA asked its members to help find a suitable aircraft .

The first response came from Donald W. Douglas, then virtually unknown. The young designer offered to build a suitable aircraft. Another letter suggested that the Australian purchase a government-surplus US Navy F-5L flying boat for US$12 400. "Buy it from the Navy," the letterhead exhorted. The problem was Kingsford Smith didn't have the money.

With his meagre savings gone, he found work as a

stunt pilot for Universal Studios and barnstorming with the Moffett-Starkey Aero Circus. He was still searching desperately for backers when a fellow stunt pilot, Omar Locklear, was killed during a film stunt. The nationwide publicity surrounding the fireball death of Hollywood's best-known stunt pilot virtually ended any hope of finding backers around Los Angeles. Kingsford Smith wrote home: "Omar's death, which had been front-paged in the newspapers, did nothing to help people have confidence in planes."

The last straw came when the air-circus manager ran off without paying his pilots. Flat broke, Kingsford Smith finally gave up. Swallowing his pride, he worked painting signs until he had enough cash for the cheapest berth on the S.S. *Tahiti*, which sailed for Australia in December 1920.

Seven years later, after establishing his flying credentials with Australia's infant aviation industry, Kingsford Smith returned to America, still determined to be the first person to fly the Pacific. Just five days earlier, accompanied by his business partner Charles Ulm, he had completed a record-breaking 12 000 kilometres flight around Australia. The flight in a single-engined Bristol Tourer was to promote interest in a trans-Pacific flight and had attracted a £3500 guarantee from the New South Wales government.

On the voyage to California Kingsford Smith and Ulm were accompanied by another partner, Keith Anderson. In 1923 Anderson and Kingsford Smith had been pilots with a struggling West Australian air service, and later had started an outback trucking company. When that failed, the pair had formed their own tiny air service and had been joined by Ulm early in 1927.

When the Australian reached San Francisco, aviation was on everyone's lips. Only months before, Charles Lindbergh had flown the Atlantic, and now the town was busy with preparations for the Dole Derby, which offered US$25 000 for the first plane to reach Hawaii. Within days Kingsford Smith was invited to pilot a dubious-looking Dole racer. He refused, which was just as well, for only two aircraft completed the ill-starred and ten lives were lost.

Kingsford Smith eventually purchased the Fokker F.VII3m *Detroiter* from the American-based Australian explorer, Hubert Wilkins, who had used it during his 1926 Wilkins-Detroit Arctic Expedition. Kingsford Smith paid US$15 000 for the *Detroiter* minus its motors. The problem of finding the money to buy three new Wright Whirlwind J-5 engines was solved by a chance meeting with Australian retail magnate Sidney Myer. Hearing of their dilemma, Myer wrote a cheque for US$7500 to cover their cost.

Over the following months the trio went $4000 into debt equipping their Fokker — now renamed the *Southern Cross*. With the bad press resulting from the disastrous Dole Derby they could find nobody who was interested in backing their flight. When funds promised from Australia failed to materialise, the project seemed doomed and Anderson returned home, promising to come back if the flight came off.

Worse was to come when a new government was elected in New South Wales and the incoming Premier stated that he wanted nothing to do with "cheap stunts". Shortly after, Kingsford Smith received a cable directing him and his crew to abandon the flight and return home. Infuriated at such official arrogance, Kingsford Smith tore up the Premier's ultimatum, declaring: "Who gave this man the right to order free Australian citizens around? He can go to hell. We're not snotty-nosed schoolboys."

There was a brief ray of hope when an oil company offered to sponsor them if the *Southern Cross* could set a new world endurance record. Following two close but fruitless attempts the offer was withdrawn and the pair seemed doomed to sell the Fokker and return home.

A few weeks later Los Angeles banker Allan Chaffey introduced Kingsford Smith and Ulm to millionaire philanthropist G. Alan Hancock. Sensing that the down-and-out Australians needed a little relaxation, Hancock invited them to join him on a ten-day cruise on his yacht.

Four days into the voyage the remarkable American put an end to their financial worries. Purchasing the *Southern Cross* for the US$16 000 the airmen now needed to get out of debt, he immediately loaned the plane back to them for the trans-Pacific flight. Hancock also lent them money to cover their flight expenses.

Ulm now concentrated on planning the flight while Kingsford Smith took the *Southern Cross* to the Douglas factory for final modifications. He then flew it to Oakland where the last instruments and radios were fitted for the flight. He left nothing to chance. Besides the navigator's master aperiodic compass and a Pioneer earth inductor compass, he also equipped the aircraft with two steering compasses. It also carried two drift meters, sextants, long- and short-wave radios and the latest blind-flying instruments.

Two Americans were chosen to make up the crew: Captain Harry Lyon, a highly-qualified merchant marine navigator from Maine, and James Warner, an experienced radio operator from Kansas City.

Kingsford Smith now began to display the meticulous professional pilot hidden by his happy-go-lucky public image. He spent hours aloft training the crew. And he spent hours refining the accuracy of his blind flying, by using only the Fokker's turn-and-bank and rate-of-climb indicators. Normally he would also have the altimeter, airspeed and compass to help.

To increase their stamina he and Ulm worked on a "training course", which involved alternating between driving a car, doing exercises, flying the plane, more exercises, more driving and so on. The period was gradually extended until the pair were able to stay active for forty hours.

On 31 May 1928, after ten months in the United States they were ready for the great adventure. The last of the 5400 litres of fuel was pumped into the tanks, and moments before they climbed on board someone handed Kingsford Smith a small Australian flag. He told reporters: "Nothing has been left to chance. We are fully prepared, and if we fail, we will have not the slightest regret." Shouting "Cheerio", Kingsford Smith climbed aboard the *Southern Cross* to attempt the longest ocean flight ever undertaken.

Minutes later they were airborne and heading out over San Francisco. Ahead of them lay the world's greatest ocean which they planned to cross in three stages. The first leg was 3861 kilometres to Honolulu; the second, from Honolulu to Suva in the Fiji Islands, was a staggering 5148 kilometres. The final run home was the 3057 kilometres hop to Brisbane, Australia. It was not only the shortest but also the "easy one" for navigator Lyon, who suggested that even an "amateur" could not miss an island as large as Australia.

Later, for *National Geographic* magazine, the two men described their departure from the American mainland as they climbed slowly to 2000 feet:

In 12 minutes the skyscrapers of San Francisco, looking white and spectral, were swallowed up in the grey-brown pall that enshrouded the Golden Gate. Our last picture of them was as they stood, baseless and serene, like a magic city hanging in the clouds. We were to see more magic cities rising and crumbling to nothingness in the amazing cloud banks that we encountered further out. We climbed at 92 miles an hour and chuckling over our favourable start on the long air trail, we stuck a small silken Australian flag between two gasoline gauges in our cockpit. In the hours that followed, it was so beaten by the wind that only the stick remained.

The first six hours of flight were uneventful. Warner was able to confirm that they were on course by listening to the US Army's radio beam, until the signal faded 1120 kilometres out. Kingsford Smith flew while Ulm kept the ship's log. "We're as happy as hell. Everything is going as smooth as silk," he wrote, although Lyon might have used different words. He found the Fokker's vibration enough to "shake your teeth loose". To relieve their boredom the crew passed humorous notes around, some spiced with colourful adjectives.

About 1300 kilometres from Honolulu Warner was able to communicate with the Matson liner SS *Maliko* which was equipped with a radio compass and passed a series of check bearings. When Warner eventually picked up the Hawaiian radio beacon, they were within a couple of miles of his plotted position. Their first sight of land was the peak of Mauna Kea poking above the clouds. Beneath it lay the island of Hawaii.

Descending towards the island of Oahu they were met by a formation of Army aircraft which escorted the *Southern Cross* to Wheeler Field. The flight from Oakland had taken 27 hours and 25 minutes.

Late the following day the Fokker was ferried to Kauai where it required the 1400-metre expanse of Barking Sands for the maximum-load take-off for Fiji. Kingsford Smith had worked out that in the cool of the morning it should be of sufficient length for the Fokker's heaviest ever take-off. For the leg to Suva they would carry the absolute maximum fuel load of 5928 litres. It gave them a nil-wind safety margin of about 960 kilometres or six hours cruising flight.

A 5.22 a.m. on June 3, they took off easily with room to spare. Shortly after, they encountered turbulence. Ulm watched tensely as his companion struggled to minimise its effect, aware that until they had burned off fuel the buffeting could easily cause a structural failure. Once clear of the islands the turbulence stopped and both men relaxed. Navigator Lyon wrote:

> Our plan was to fly until abreast of the Phoenix group of islands which were only 200 miles off the course, then check the fuel and see if we could make it. If we were sure we could not do so, we had planned to make a forced landing on Enderbury Island at daylight but to send out an SOS before doing so.

An hour later they ran into a succession of storms that were to batter them for the rest of the flight. Kingsford Smith recalled:

> The dark curtains closed in on us, beset us from every side, and merged into a great belt of swishing water. We were flying at 600 feet, and over-loaded as we were, this rain blown by choppy gusts, was a specially unwelcome turn in the weather. Visibility shrank, the rain became thicker, and at 11:50 we were flying blind and climbing to get out of the deluge.

After several hours they broke into the clear and Ulm took over while the exhausted and soaked Kingsford Smith slept at the controls. When storms reappeared Kingsford Smith again took over. Ulm wrote in his log: "The storm seems all around us now. Smithy is at the controls. Thank God he is the flier he is ... Rain bloody rain all around and that ripsnorter of a wind!"

At about 7 a.m. they broke out into relatively clear skies and Lyon was able to do a new calculation which indicated they were only 1120 kilometres from Suva. Their respite was brief as shortly after they entered another area of storms which cut the Fokker's ground speed back even further. They had been airborne nearly thirty hours and were physically and mentally exhausted. Kingsford Smith appeared depressed and an equally gloomy Ulm wrote in the log: "Very doubtful whether we can make Suva or not."

Sensing the despondency up front, Lyon passed forward a note. It stated that he and Warner had voted to nominate Smithy for the next President of the United States considering the way he had battled through the night. Moments later they got another boost. The weather cleared sufficiently for Lyon to get a fix which showed that they were still on course and had just enough fuel to reach Suva.

Late that afternoon Kingsford Smith brought the *Southern Cross* in for a landing at Suva's tiny Albert Park sports ground. With the boundary fence coming up fast, and the Fokker not equipped with brakes, Kingsford Smith brought the aircraft to a halt by executing a deliberate ground loop. The bush pilot manoeuvre was timed to perfection and left the Fokker undamaged.

Stone deaf and dizzy from their thirty-four and a half hour ordeal the crew stumbled groggily to the ground, unable to hear that Fiji's British Governor was inviting them to a ceremonial lunch. "Yes Sir, isn't it," a confused Kingsford Smith shouted in reply.

Two days later they took off from Naseli Beach, the only suitable take-off run in Fiji. For the final leg to Brisbane, Kingsford Smith wore a ceremonial whale's tooth — a good-luck gift from a Fijian chief. The charm seemed to have little effect, for soon after departing, their vital earth inductor compass failed and they encountered the worst weather of the Pacific crossing. For most of this time it required the combined strength of both pilots to keep the Fokker under control. Kingsford Smith wrote:

> The visibility dwindled to a mile, then down to a few yards, then to nothing. Torrential rain began to drum and rattle on the windshield. I began to climb to get above it. Raking gusts jolted the plane so that we had to hold on to our seats. We were tearing though a black chaos of rain and cloud at 85 knots (156 km/h), our very speed increased the latent fury of the storm. We plunged on with no idea whatever of where we were. Any attempt at navigation was useless. We were circling, plunging, climbing, dodging the squalls as

the poor old *Southern Cross* pitched and tossed wildly about. For four solid hours, from eight until midnight, we endured these terrible conditions.

The weather improved after midnight but they struck more storms approaching daylight. Having been unable to do any worthwhile navigation throughout the night, Lyon could only guess at their position. He suggested they fly a due-west heading, knowing that they could not fail to make landfall with the whole of Australia only a few hours ahead.

The *Southern Cross* eventually crossed the Australian coast at Ballina, New South Wales, 175 kilometres off course! An hour and a quarter later they landed at Brisbane's Eagle Farm airport where thousands waited to greet their home-town hero. The first trans-Pacific flight had taken eight and a half days, during which the crew of the *Southern Cross* had been airborne for 83 hours and 15 minutes. Kingsford Smith was at the controls for 52 of those hours and Ulm for the remainder.

The following day they flew to Sydney where 300 000 people greeted them at Mascot Aerodrome. The men were bombarded with welcoming speeches by a bevy of distinguished citizens and politicians though, as Ulm wryly pointed out: "There were many wanting to shake our hand who had earlier called us idiots, and demanded we return by ship."

Asked by a journalist for his impression of his "Australian boss", navigator Lyon reported: "He is a hellish stickler for perfection ... I wouldn't want to fly with him too often. He's a tough boss. Although I like the man personally, and greatly admire his skill, he can be short tempered — even a bit hard to get along with. He's a real individualist."

Among a host of congratulatory cables was one from their American benefactor, Allan Hancock. It read:

I am delivering to the California Bank of Los Angeles for transmission to the Commercial Banking Company of

Sydney a bill of sale transferring to Kingsford Smith and Ulm together with release and discharge of all your indebtedness [approximately US$20 000] to me. I beg you accept this gift as a token of our mutual friendship, and as my tribute to you and the *Southern Cross* and also to commemorate the magnificent achievement of yourselves and brave American companions in bringing our two countries closer together. Andrew Chaffey joins me in saying "Advance Australia!"

The Pacific had been conquered, but clearly it could at best be considered an experimental victory. The time involved and the hazardous flying conditions made mounting a passenger service unthinkable. And a trans-Pacific airmail or freight service could not be considered until aircraft were available that could carry a profitable payload as well as the required fuel.

Believing that their Pacific flight would attract investors at home, Kingsford Smith and Ulm turned their attention to forming a new domestic airline. They also had plans for initiating an airmail service to New Zealand.

Over the next six years Kingsford Smith's fortunes fluctuated. He set an unparalleled array of pioneering and record-breaking flights in an effort to promote aviation and gain government backing for airmail services. However, the airline he and Ulm formed in 1930 — Australian National Airways — folded after three years following the loss of the *Southern Cloud*, — one of its Avro 10 (British-built Fokker) airliners. The partners suffered another setback when, after pioneering the airmail route to England, their proposal was rejected and the contract was awarded instead to Qantas and Britain's Imperial Airlines.

Following the failure of their airline, the two friends dissolved their partnership and Kingsford Smith, faced with bankruptcy, was forced back into the barnstorming business to make ends meet. Ironically, he was in the Australian capital, Canberra, giving $2 joy rides in the

Southern Cross when he heard that he had been awarded a knighthood for "services to aviation". When a journalist asked "Sir Charles" if he would now give up barnstorming, Kingsford Smith tersely replied: "Like hell I will. I've got obligations. There's food needed for my family, you know, and my wife depends on me to earn it."

Two years later Kingsford Smith was again planning to fly the Pacific — this time eastward from Australia to the United States. Although lacking the riveting attraction of his pioneering Pacific conquest six years earlier, the second trans-Pacific flight was in many ways a greater personal achievement. Instead of a four-man crew and the three engines of his fabled Fokker, Kingsford Smith was to place his trust in a lone crewman and the single 500-horsepower Pratt and Whitney Wasp engine of his Lockheed Altair, named *Lady Southern Cross* for his wife Mary.

The catalysts to his decision to make a second trans-Pacific flight were five white feathers and mounting debts. The decision was made after he was forced to withdraw from the MacRobertson England–Australia Air Race, just three weeks before the start on 20 October 1934. Attracting an international field of competitors the race attracted world-wide attention. Kingsford Smith had been a short-odds favourite to win the event and his retirement brought protests and critical newspaper reports throughout Australia. He also received a pile of abusive letters. Five of the envelopes contained a lone white feather — the traditional symbol of cowardice. Deeply hurt, Kingsford Smith lashed out: "What the hell do these people know about the circumstances? Nothing. Absolutely nothing ... I've done some foolish things in connection with the big race. I admit them. But I'm no squib."

The airman's popularity had been taking a pounding since it was announced that he was to enter the Mac-

Robertson affair in a Lockheed Altair monoplane. In those days ties were still close with "Mother England" and the news that Kingsford Smith was to compete in an American aircraft caused a storm of protest over his "unpatriotic" decision not to use a British machine.

The fact of the matter was that Kingsford Smith had been unable to find a suitable British aircraft for the race. De Havilland, who were constructing three purpose-built DH88 Comet racers for British crews entered in the MacRobertson, offered to build a fourth for Kingsford Smith. However, only three sets of variable pitch propellers were available and de Havilland advised the Australian that his Comet would be equipped with fixed pitch airscrews — a critical disadvantage.

Kingsford Smith explained in *Smith's Weekly* the reasons behind his decision to purchase an American machine instead of the second rate Comet:

> I would not have a dog's chance against them (the other Comets), conceding them more than 400 miles in range on the long hops in the race. There was no other British job comparable with the Comet ... I chose a plane which I think will give me the best possible chance of winning. I'm unpatriotic? Bunkum!

Following the delivery of his Lockheed in July 1934, Kingsford Smith was delayed getting an Australian Certificate of Airworthiness which allowed the aircraft to be flown with the overload required for a long-range fuel system. Kingsford Smith frankly conceded that the problem was of his own making. Despite several warnings, he had neglected to obtain the proper documentation from America's Department of Commerce. He wrote:

> I botched things up at the Lockheed factory. I made no mistake about the machine — she's the goods. But I did make two bad mistakes while I was at the Lockheed factory. I admit them. Darn'em, I'd be in England, all ready for the race, but for them. Civil Aviation were very good to

me. On the facts in their possession they could not issue me with a routine certificate of airworthiness.

The MacRobertson race was three weeks away when the vital test results at last arrived from America, and Kingsford Smith and his navigator, P.G. "Bill" Taylor, were finally able to take off from Sydney to ferry the Lockheed to England.

The final blow came at Cloncurry — their first refuelling stop — when serious cracks were discovered in the Altair's bulbous engine cowling. With insufficient time remaining to get a new one manufactured and still reach England in a fit shape to start the race, Kingsford Smith had no alternative but to withdraw from the MacRobertson event.

Disappointment throughout Australia prompted a storm of quite outrageous criticism. The most vocal and cruel critics suggested that Kingsford Smith had lost his nerve and was scared to pit his prowess against the world's best.

Believing that he had once again to prove his courage to the Australian public, Kingsford Smith retaliated by announcing his intention to make an eastbound crossing of the Pacific — thus becoming the first person to fly the ocean in both directions. He explained:

> I'm human enough to want Australia to think well rather than badly of me. And about this "squibbing" business (being a coward). Have a look at the map, you squib critics. See whether an England–Australia flight looks — looks I say — any worse than a flight across the Pacific.

Concerned that Kingsford Smith was overreacting, and worried about the dangers of him undertaking the Pacific flight in a single engine aircraft, the editor of *Smith's Weekly* sprung to the airman's defence. In an editorial which commenced "Dear Kingsford Smith" he wrote:

> You say that you are making this Pacific flight to rehabilitate yourself with your fellow Australians. Such a flight

carries with it tremendous risks alongside which the England–Australia route is a mere nothing. Need you take them? Australians do not demand such a gesture from you. They know you as the greatest airman the world has produced — from what you have done already.

There were, however, other reasons for Kingsford Smith deciding to conduct the flight. One was the matter of clearing the debts he had accumulated with his aborted race entry. To do that Kingsford Smith needed to return the Altair to the United States. He explained:

I could not sell the bus here, because it cannot get a commercial ticket. And what return could I show my backers? It is primarily because of them that I'm tackling the Pacific flight. They are going to be paid. If I pull this job off there will be money for them, and for me.

Another reason was his continuing dream of starting an airmail service to New Zealand. In this respect he suggested: " The favourable publicity of a successful flight won't do any harm to my claims for the introduction of a trans-Tasman airmail service under my control."

Kingsford Smith asked P.G. Taylor to accompany him on the trans-Pacific flight. Formerly a pilot with Australian National Airways, Taylor had already acted as navigator for Kingsford Smith on three trans-Tasman flights in the *Southern Cross*. Taylor recalled:

The pilot-navigator partnership suited us both very well at this time. He apparently was satisfied to accept and steer the courses I put on the compass without questioning my reasoning and calculations; and because of the very great respect I had for him as a pilot I accepted with complete confidence his handling of the aeroplane.

For the trans-Pacific flight the *Lady Southern Cross* required yet another increase to its fuel load, and Kingsford Smith called on the engineering genius of Wing Commander Lawrence Wackett, RAAF, later to become Australia's best-known aircraft designer. Wackett found space to cram three extra fuel tanks, which increased the fuel load by 437 litres, bringing it up to a total of 2340 litres. Space was at such a premium that Wackett tucked 91 litres of the fuel in a tank under Kingsford Smith's seat!

Checking their fuel consumption on the flight from Sydney to Brisbane — their jumping-off point — Kingsford Smith and Taylor were appalled to find that fuel flow was well above the official factory figure. Calculations based on their Sydney–Brisbane fuel consumption indicated that the Altair had insufficient tankage for the forthcoming flight!

In Brisbane the pair conducted a series of fuel consumption air tests using an array of engine power settings. To their great relief these tests provided them with a much improved maximum range power setting. It would allow them to cover the critical 5148-kilometre leg from Fiji to Honolulu into a 37 km/h headwind, with two hours in reserve.

Seven hundred people were on hand to see Kingsford Smith and Taylor depart from Brisbane on 22 October 1934. Seconds before Taylor closed the perspex canopy of his navigator's cockpit a woman rushed from the crowd and handed him a white rose "for luck". Taylor wrote: "All seven thousand miles across the Pacific I protected that rose and as long as it was there I felt that our engine would keep going."

As the two airmen took off, heading out across the Coral Sea towards their first refuelling stop in Fiji, a half a world away the contestants in the MacRobertson were thundering over Europe and the Middle East. No doubt Kingsford Smith and Taylor reflected wistfully on the camaraderie and excitement of that race as they began their long, lone combat with the vast expanses of the great ocean.

Initially the flight was conducted on top of a heavy cumulus cloud cover. Nearing Fiji conditions deteriorated and they flew in cloud and rain. The sun had set and light was fading as they reached Suva where, as in 1928, Kingsford Smith made a hair-raising landing in tiny Albert Park.

The following day, with tanks almost dry, the Australians flew to nearby Naseli Beach to take on a maximum fuel load for the critical leg to Honolulu. They faced strong crosswinds for their take-off from the beach. Their first attempt to get away was aborted when, as the Altair's tail came up, Kingsford Smith had insufficient rudder control to prevent the wind from swinging them into the surf.

A week passed before the wind dropped and Kingsford Smith was able to get the *Lady Southern Cross* off safely at dawn from the hard, low-tide beach. Throughout the day Taylor's superb navigation kept them on course. It was plain sailing. In Hawaii radio operators recorded their position reports, plotting the airmen's steady progress towards the islands.

At nightfall they were 2600 kilometres out and flying at 8000 feet when they hit a cloud and torrential rain. Kingsford Smith recalled: " I should have known that it was all too perfect and something was bound to happen … I climbed to 14 000 feet and it was worse. I didn't like it a bit. What to do? Turn and run back? "

Kingsford Smith briefly switched on the landing light to try and assess the cloud situation. Moments after turning it off again, his airspeed indicator needle abruptly dropped back to zero — "evidently the (pitot) tube was choked with rain water". Taylor related what happened next:

> Quite suddenly there was a general lessening of sound and it seemed that we were slowing up. I looked at the airspeed indicator and found to my astonishment that it was indicating only 90 knots, after the steady 125 indicated airspeed at which we had been cruising. We were near stalling speed and it was obvious that Kingsford Smith was having trouble controlling the aeroplane.

Then I felt her go suddenly into a spin. The night became a whirling madness with the needle of the turn indicator hard over, the rate of climb indicator showing a rapid descent, and the needle of the altimeter winding its way down the height scale.

In America's *Liberty* magazine Kingsford Smith recalled the terror of spinning at night in cloud and finding himself unable to recover. He wrote:

I set frantically to work but got no results. Terrifically frightened I felt a hot searing anger at myself for being unable to do what a beginner is first taught to do — bring a plane out of a spin. The instinct to fight was so strong that I pressed both feet on one rudder pedal, braced my back against the seat and pushed grimly. Either the controls were going to break or that machine had to come out of the spin.

When Kingsford Smith yelled, "I'm sorry Bill but I can't get her out," Taylor grabbed the duplicate set of controls in the navigator's cockpit in a fruitless effort to assist in the recovery. Kingsford Smith explained how the *Lady Southern Cross* finally recovered at 6000 feet.

I kept up the agonising pressure until my back was nearly broken. Aeons of time passed as we spun on around and down. Then slowly the needle wavered and came back to central. We were not spinning now but in a steep dive. I gradually eased back on the stick. The airspeed indicator came back to life but it read only 95 knots and we were still losing altitude. Knowing it was impossible to reach Honolulu like that I asked Bill if he thought he could find Fanning Island.

With less turbulence at the lower level Kingsford Smith was able to maintain control while making a complete check of the cockpit instruments. He went on:

Almost at once I shouted, vilifying myself. In switching on the landing lights I had accidentally switched on the motor which winds down the wing flaps. It was their powerful braking effect that had caused the loss of speed which had thrown us into that all but fatal spin.

During the spin the flaps also had drastically affected the airflow over the Lockheed's rudder and made the normal recovery actions ineffective. Once they were retracted the Altair again performed perfectly. Taylor retrieved his scattered navigation instruments and as Polaris — the North Star — and Sirius came into sight he took sextant readings.

During the night the weather cleared and, aided by Taylor's superb astro-navigation, the *Lady Southern Cross* clung tenaciously on track across the Pacific. The following morning they descended to 200 feet above the water so that Taylor could take a really accurate low-level sextant sighting of the sun, using the natural horizon. From it he deduced a position line for the final run into Honolulu, and their landfall on the Hawaiian Islands came on track and on time. Taylor recalled:

> I just sat there, filled with a curious sense of gratitude that we had been given the conditions to find these islands, that the engine had never shown a sign of failure in the 25 hours of flight (from Fiji); and the most wonderful sense of anticipation for our arrival at Honolulu.

A large crowd was on hand for their landing at Wheeler Field. Following an official reception they were whisked to Honolulu with a police motor cycle escort in attendance and given the largest suite at the Royal Hawaiian Hotel.

The following day Kingsford Smith offered to take the Mayor of Honolulu for a flight over the city in the *Lady Southern Cross*. Three minutes after take-off the engine failed and the Australian was forced to make a hair-raising downwind, dead-stick landing. Taylor recalled:

> The entire fuel system of this flying tanker was empty. It was simple. They were out of fuel, in three minutes flying time after we had landed from Fiji. The significance of this situation began to creep up my spine.

Convinced that the Lockheed's two hours fuel reserve could not have been consumed on the flight from Fiji, the airmen wisely decided to have the plane's fuel system checked before heading off on the 3861-kilometre leg to the US mainland. Their caution was rewarded when US Army Air Corps engineers discovered that the fuel had leaked away through a large crack which had developed in the fuselage gravity tank. The repair job, which necessitated removal of the wings, took four days.

Shortly after sunrise on 4 November, following an uneventful 15-hour flight from Hawaii, Kingsford Smith and Taylor landed at Oakland Airport, nearly two hours ahead of schedule. The engine had hardly stopped before newsmen brandishing microphones and note pads jumped up on the wing, anxious to interview the crew of the first plane to arrive in America from Australia.

They had averaged 248 km/h over the 11 765 kilometres — 88 km/h faster than the *Southern Cross* six years earlier. Once again Kingsford Smith was hailed as a hero. But even though the flight brought him more world headlines it produced no financial backing for the Tasman service. Expounding the problem that faced many of aviation's great pioneers, Kingsford Smith philosophised:

> The successful aviator who performs some startling feat will always have the microphones and newspaper men around him. There will always be an excess of publicity, so that his name will spread to the ends of the world with the speed of radio. But when it all ends, and the captains and the kings depart, he is left high and dry, stranded in a financial desert from which he must find his own way out.

The following month Kingsford Smith was in Los Angeles, unsuccessfully attempting to sell his Altair, when he heard the news that his friend Charles Ulm had vanished near Hawaii. Ulm and his crew had set out from Oakland in the Airspeed Envoy *Stella Aus-*

tralis on a trans-Pacific survey flight, hoping to attract backers for Ulm's newly formed airline, Great Pacific Airways.

After helping organise the fruitless search, Kingsford Smith left the *Lady Southern Cross* unsold in California and returned to Australia to concentrate on forming a company to start a trans-Tasman airmail service. Although the New Zealand government was keen on the idea, neither the Australian government nor private enterprise seemed interested in providing backing.

In May 1935 Bill Taylor joined Kingsford Smith and radio operator John Stannage aboard the Fokker *Southern Cross*. Ironically, Kingsford Smith had been asked by the government to make a one-off trans-Tasman airmail flight, carrying special mail commemorating the Jubilee of England's King George V and Queen Mary. Loaded with 182 kilograms of postal bags they took off from the RAAF Base at Richmond.

Over 700 kilometres out they turned back after a propeller shattered, forcing them to shut down the starboard engine. Limping home on the two remaining engines, they seemed destined to ditch when the overworked port motor started to lose oil pressure.

Taylor saved the day. Several times he struggled out along supporting struts beneath the wings, battling the slipstream to siphon oil from the useless starboard motor and transfer it to the ailing port engine. For his gallantry Taylor was awarded the Empire Medal — the highest possible award for civilian bravery. (In 1946 Taylor was knighted for his contribution to aviation. Besides pioneering the Indian Ocean from Australia to Africa in 1939, he also surveyed the South Pacific in a Consolidated Catalina flying boat, establishing airline routes from Australia to Mexico and Chile.)

Late in 1935 Kingsford Smith returned to the US and flew the *Lady Southern Cross* from California to New York, from where it was shipped to England. Sick and broke, he was hoping desperately that just one more record-breaking flight would attract backers for his trans-Tasman dream.

On 20 October 1935 Kingsford Smith and his mechanic, Tommy Pethybridge, took off from Lympne Airport near London. They were out to break the England-Australia speed record set by Britons C.W.A. Scott and Campbell Black in the de Havilland Comet during the MacRobertson race, exactly one year earlier. The attempt ended after a few hours when hail damage forced them to return to London.

Two weeks later, on 6 November, they took off again. At Allahabad Kingsford Smith and Pethybridge were four hours behind the record but still confident they would pick up time on the last half of the flight, where Scott and Campbell Black had been slowed by engine problems. Soon after, bound for Singapore, pushing hard for the record, and probably exhausted, Charles Kingsford Smith and Tommy Pethybridge vanished at night over the Bay of Bengal close to the island of Aye, just off the coast of Burma.

Ironically, just two weeks later, the Pan American Airways Martin M.130 flying boat *China Clipper* took off from San Franciso Bay, loaded with airmail, on the inaugural trans-Pacific airline service. A year later Pan American was carrying passengers across the great ocean. The vision of Charles Kingsford Smith and his comrade Charles Ulm was finally fulfilled.

Kingsford Smith's friend and noted Australian journalist Norman Ellison wrote a perfect epitaph for his friend "Smithy, the world's greatest pilot". Quoting from a book about World War I fliers, he said: "They lived like hawks and poets and paladins, and died the quick death of dragonflies."

13
France's great record breaker

The great oceans of the world were the ultimate challenge to the early pioneers, whose conquests were the milestones that measured the progress of early aviation. By 1930 the only real trans-oceanic goal remaining was an east-west crossing of the Atlantic to New York City, a mirror image of Lindbergh's 1927 flight. For, although a German Junkers W33 had made an east–west crossing in 1928, it had ended with a crash-landing on an island off Canada and missed New York by 2000 kilometres. It was not for want of trying that no one had completed the difficult against-the-wind flight from Europe to America. In 1927 two British aircraft had disappeared. Ray Hinchcliffe and P & 0 steamship millionairess the Honourable Elsie Mackay had vanished after taking off from Cranwell, England in the Stinson monoplane *Endeavor.*

Only six months earlier Princess LoewensteinWertheim at sixty years of age had been determined to become the first woman to cross the Atlantic. She hired two experienced flyers, Frederick Minchin and Leslie Hamilton, and a Fokker monoplane *St Raphael*. Before take-off from Upavon, Wilts the aircraft was blessed by the Archbishop of Cornwall, Then, dressed in her purple leather flying suit, yellow boots and black toque hat, the eccentric passenger climbed into her favourite wicker chair, positioned behind her pilots. They were never

seen again. A few days later a wicker chair washed up
on the coast of Iceland.

But by far the most tragic and publicised failure had
been that of the Levavasseur biplane *l'Oiseau Blanc*
(White Bird). The pilot, French war ace Charles
Nungesser and his one-eyed navigator, Francois Coli,
were given a monumental farewell from Le'Bourget
field outside Paris in May 1927. Among the thousands
stood Maurice Chevalier, boxer Georges Carpentier and
France's darling, Mistinguette. Politicians, artists, the
military and the workers of France watched as the two
men, dressed in yellow flying suits, climbed aboard
the ghostlike aircraft. Minutes later it staggered into
the air, then crossed the coast and disappeared into
mystery.

When Nungesser was officially declared missing the
nation went into mourning for its famous ace who had
destroyed forty-seven German aircraft and survived
seventeen crashes. It was unbelievable that "Nungesser
the Indestructible" was dead!

This then was the tragic record of the west–east
Atlantic run when the next challenger came on the
scene. And all France bubbled with the news that another of her sons, Dieudonne Costes, was taking to the
air in the slipstream of his dead countryfolk. If any pilot
was ideally suited for the task it was this brilliant chief
pilot of the Breguet Aircraft Company. His background
of technical achievement and record of long-distance
flying was unsurpassed.

Costes was born in Gascony in 1893 and as a youth
studied engineering. At the age of nineteen he enrolled
in the Blériot school for *Pilotes d'Avions* and after ten
weeks was awarded his licence. He spent the next two
years in compulsory military training at an army aviation school.

At the outset of the Great War he was sent to the
front. However, as there were many more pilots than

Arthur Geobel's Travel Air monoplane *Woolaroc* was powered by the highly successful Wright Whirlwind motor similar to that used in Lindbergh's trans-Atlantic *Spirit of St Louis*.

Showing more courage than commonsense, well-wishers line the dirt runway of Oakland's new airport as Smith and Bronte steal a march on the Dole fliers.

Headline-maker Mildred Doran at the window of her Buhl Airsedan. American newspapers called her "a flower of American womanhood".

Friends bid Mildred Doran farewell before closing the rear door. The Buhl was painted a patriotic red, white and blue.

The Breese monoplane *Aloha* was the sixth aeroplane to start but only the second to successfully get away from Oakland.

The mangled remains of Irving's overloaded *Pabco Pacific Flyer* following its second abortive attempt to take off.

"Martin Jensen, where the hell have you been," cried his wife, when the exhausted fliers finally reached Honolulu. From left: Schulter, Marguerite Jensen, Martin Jensen.

Umberto Nobile was one of the world's leading designers of lighter-than-air dirigibles.

Nobile's airship *Italia* moored at King's Bay prior to its final flight. The rear motor gondola (in which Pomella perished) and the main crew cabin can be clearly seen.

In the USA in 1920, besides piloting the Moffett-Starkey Aero Circus Avro 504, Kingsford-Smith also took his turn as a wing-walker and hanging from the biplane's landing gear.

The *Southern Cross* flies low over Fred Giles' biplane *Wanda* at San Francisco's Mills Field. Giles, from Brisbane, had withdrawn from the Dole race and was preparing to fly the Pacific alone. Fortunately his wild scheme was never realised.

Friends farewell the crew of the *Southern Cross* at Oakland Airport. Navigator Harry Lyon is second from left. Radio Operator James Warner stands with hands crossed. Charles Ulm (far right) and Charles Kingsford-Smith both wear boots and leather helmets for warmth in the Fokker's open cockpit.

The crew of the *Southern Cross* discuss their trans-Pacific triumph on Melbourne radio. From left: Warner, Kingsford-Smith, Lyon and Ulm.

Taylor, Stannage and Kingsford-Smith (left to right) after surviving the Tasman drama. Above them is the offending engine. Taylor's precarious walkway runs behind the propeller toward the cockpit.

Kingsford-Smith and Taylor arrive at Wheeler Field, Hawaii in the Lockheed *Lady Southern Cross* during their 1934 west-east Pacific flight.

France's greatest long-distance flier, Dieudonne Costes (front cockpit), and his mechanic, Maurice Bellonte.

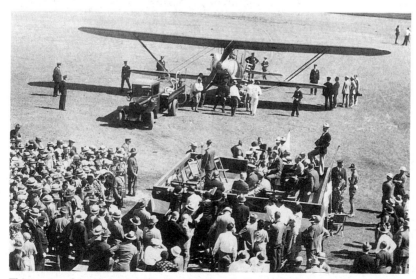

Thirty-seven hours after leaving Paris the scarlet Breguet XIX biplane *Point d'Interrogation (Question Mark)* were greeted by a huge crowd at New York's Curtiss Field.

This little-known second Ryan NYP, purchased by a Japanese newspaper after Charles Lindbergh's epochal trans-Atlantic flight, was used as a design-guider for Japan's first trans-Pacific machine — the K-12.

Inspired by Lindbergh's *Spirit of St Louis*, Japan's Kawanishi K-12 was almost twice the Ryan's size. Underpowered, it lacked the necessary performance and range to fly the Pacific.

A tiny Junker A-50 seaplane similar to the one flown by Seiji Yoshihara in a gallant but foolhardy trans-Pacific attempt.

Seiji Yoshihara was miraculously resuced by a passing ship after ditching his Junkers 1300 kilometres out to sea.

The elegant Emsco monoplane *City of Tacoma* was the fourth aircraft purchased by Bromley to fly the Pacific.

Miss Veedol suffered only minor damage during Pangborn's superb no-wheels landing following their non-stop trans-Pacific triumph. Inset: Pangborn (right) and Herndon.

In 1932 the Japanese Junkers W.33 *No3 Hochi Nichi-Bei* vanished after radio contact was lost six hours after take-off.

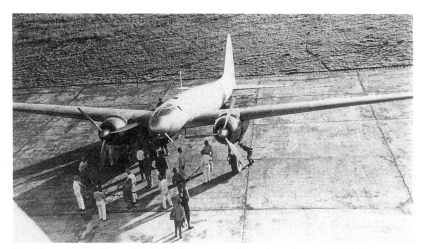

The elegant Tachikawa A-26 had long glider-like wings. Its two 1000-horsepower Nakajima engines gave it a top speed of 435 kilometres per hour. For maximum range it cruised at 298 kilometres per hour.

One-eyed airman Wiley Post (right), for once not wearing his eye patch, and navigator Harold Gatty before commencing their around-the-world flight.

Wiley Post with his Lockheed Vega *Winnie Mae* prior to making his solo around-the-world flight in 1933.

Post designed the first aviation pressure suit. Looking more like a deep-sea diver, he used it to introduce the world to pressurised stratospheric flight.

The trappings of success. Amelia Earhart with her Cord Cabriolet car and the Lockheed 10-E Electra provided by Purdue University.

Amelia Earhart examines the loop antenna of the Bendix radio compass that was installed in her Electra. Its performance was to be critical on her final flight.

Amelia Earhart poses with Hollywood stunt pilot Paul Mantz (left) and her two navigators, Harry Manning and Fred Noonan, before her first (westbound) around-the-world attempt which ended in Hawaii.

Pancho Barnes, pictured here after setting a new women's speed record in her Travel Air Model R Mystery Ship, epitomised Hollywood's image of a rip-roaring pilot.

Pancho Barnes (centre) chats with Amelia Earhart (right) and May Haizlip during America's 1929 Women's Aerial Derby.

It was scenes such as this which caused Pancho Barnes to establish the Motion Picture Pilots Association to prevent the exploitation of pilots by Hollywood film producers. Here Paul Mantz spins down for the cameras.

Howard Hughes, here at the controls of his mammoth Hughes flying boat, hired Pancho Barnes to help with the flying sequences in his epic film *Hells Angels*. She called him "a cheapskate who chiselled everyone".

Pancho Barnes and one of her four husbands pose with General Jimmy Doolittle, the first member of The Happy Bottom Riding Club.

"She was my friend," wrote Chuck Yeager, the man who first broke the sound barrier. Yeager was a regular at Pancho Barnes place. They are pictured here at a reunion shortly before the airwoman's death.

aircraft, he spent the first three months digging trenches. When Costes finally took to the skies over the carnage of the Western Front it was as a machine gunner and during this episode he lost two fingers from a shell splinter over the enemy lines. He was eventually assigned an aircraft and by war's end had shot down five German aircraft and seven balloons. He was cited for gallantry on seven occasions and was awarded the *Légion d'Honneur*.

In the 1920s Costes worked as a commercial pilot. His first record attempt, in 1925, ended in disaster. He and another pilot, Robert Theirry, were trying for a world long-distance record when bad weather forced them to detour over Germany. They crashed into a mountain and Theirry was killed. Costes was imprisoned for flying over Germany without a permit. On his return to France he was offered the senior flying post with Bruguets and accepted immediately.

Accompanied by Captain Pregnot, a year later he finally set a new point-to-point long distance record with a monumental flight from Paris to Siberia.

In 1927 he and Joseph le Brix, flying the Breguet biplane *Nungesser-Coli* which was named in honour of their dead comrades, made the first non-stop crossing of the South Atlantic. From Paris they flew to Senegal, on the west coast of Africa, and thence to Brazil. The pair continued with a triumphal tour of South and Central America, finally crossing the United States to California. By boat they carried on to Japan, then flew the Breguet from Tokyo over the Orient and back to Paris. There they were greeted as France's new heroes of the air.

Early in 1929 the Breguet company unveiled their latest model of biplane. They also manufactured a one-off special long-range version. Painted a scarlet red, it was christened *Point d'Interrogation* (Question Mark). On its rudder was emblazoned the tricolour of France superimposed with the letters "G.R." (Grand Raid) designating its long-range performance. Powered by a 650-horsepower Hispano Suiza engine the chubby biplane was capable of remaining in the air for a staggering fifty-two hours.

Costes had the experience and now the aeroplane as well. The first east-west Atlantic crossing now seemed a mere formality. The newspapers carried the news that Costes and the *Point d'Interrogation* were preparing for the great challenge of the Atlantic. All France was talking about the flight, and according to the experts the only thing to stop Costes reaching America would be bad weather. How right they were.

In July 1929 he took off from Le Bourget accompanied by Maurice Bellonte, a highly experienced airline mechanic. Only a few minutes before two Polish airmen, Majors Leon Idzikowski and Kasimir Kubala, had left Le Bourget with the same objective. Both aircraft encountered foul weather as soon as they crossed out into the Atlantic. They battled on as far as the Azores where the Polish aircraft crashed, killing Major Idzikowski.

As the *Point d'Interrogation* crossed the islands it became obvious to the Frenchmen the conditions were worsening. Cloud, teeming rain and severe turbulence made control of the aircraft almost impossible. They were being driven well off their planned route. To continue would be committing suicide!

Sadly Costes turned the Breguet around and headed back to Paris. When the airmen landed they had been airborne for twenty-eight hours and had covered 5200 kilometres — only 500 kilometres less than their planned crossing! Costes' disappointment turned to angered frustration when, following the abortive flight, the French Air Ministry announced its opposition to a further attempt. Determined to keep public interest alive and demonstrate yet again the Breguet's reliability, he planned a flight that would force the timid authorities to withdraw their opposition.

On 27 September 1929, Costes and Bellonte took off from Paris in an all-out assault on the world's non-stop distance record. A number of correspondents and concerned government officials thought the pair were making an unauthorised attempt on the Atlantic. However, the *Point d'Interrogation* headed east over Europe. The scarlet biplane landed at Moulard in Manchuria fifty-one hours and thirty-nine minutes later having covered 7905 kilometres. In one hop the Frenchmen had crossed Europe and Asia ... and still had two and a half hours fuel remaining. The news staggered the aviation world.

The only problem the airmen encountered was after landing. The Manchurians took one look at their red aircraft and decided that it must be part of the Bolshevik forces. Nervous peasants sent word to the nearest police post while the exhausted airmen slept in a nearby fortified farmhouse. When the pair set out next morning to search for fuel at a nearby town, they were soon overtaken by Chinese police who asked for their passports.

Polite, but obviously suspicious, the policemen told Costes that the nearest fuel depot was three days walk away at Tsitsihar, and that they would accompany the airmen there.

In continuous rain and snow, the party forded rivers and swamps and were all-in when they arrived at the little town. There their escorts phoned the local governor, Marshall Chang Hsueh-liang, with the news that they were holding two supposed French fliers, whom they suspected were really Bolshevik spies.

The Frenchmen were detained awaiting orders as the frustrated Costes later recounted:

> We were in a fever of impatience and had begun to despair of ever getting out. Five days passed. Then the Prefect of the town came to us all smiles and helpfulness. The Mar-

shall had been playing golf with the English Consul in Mukden and had told him the story of how two airmen, who said they were French, had landed near Tsitsihar. Their game was interrupted while the Consul and the Marshall sent telegrams everywhere, for the former had already been trying for three days to locate us.

A caravan of two cars and three horsedrawn wagons was finally organised to transport the airmen and their fuel on the nightmare journey back to their aircraft. The vehicles soon became bogged and the job was eventually completed on the backs of a caravan of coolies.

On their return flight from the East, Costes shaved seven hours off his 1927 record. Hardly had the excitement died down than the airman shattered another world record, this time for endurance. Accompanied by airline pilot Paul Codos, he circled over France for an astonishing fifty-eight and a half hours.

Thus when, in the New Year of 1930, Costes announced his intention of making another attempt at the Paris-New York flight, the authorities could do nothing but refrain from objecting. He had made his point! Realising that weather was the major factor Costes set no exact date for departure. He would stand by until conditions had not eventuated, they would take-off anyway and chance it.

The methodical, meticulous Frenchman was cutting down the odds to the bare minimum. He liaised with the meteorological office daily. But as the summer of 1930 passed into early autumn, conditions were always bad on one side of the Atlantic or the other. Finally, 5 September arrived and Costes and Bellonte were forced to leave in unfavourable weather. Costes later wrote about the final days of waiting:

It was not the flight itself as much as the preparations that counted. Anyone can get into an aircraft and attempt to fly across the Atlantic, but it is the preparation which determines success or failure. We did not hesitate to make the decision to try to leave on 5 September because we knew we had done all that anyone could do for the trip. We had overlooked nothing.

Meteorological conditions were not perfect. The conditions in France were far from good. There was considerable fog over the northern part of my country and we ran into dense banks of it again in the south of England. However, we had made up our minds to leave on that day come what might. We waited for the dawn with great impatience but the fog was so thick we had to wait for it to lift.

With the aid of the airport meteorologist the airmen phoned every reporting station along the French and English coast and from their reports plotted a weather map. Ships in mid-Atlantic indicated that conditions there were favourable. For five hours they waited, searching for signs of a tiny loophole in the fog that blanketed the European seaboard through which they might steal out into the Atlantic.

At 10.30 in the morning there was a slight improvement and Costes decided to leave before it closed back in. "We took off into the face of the mists," he wrote. "Sixty square metres of cloth fabric had to lift 6300 kilos, our total weight, and carry that tremendous load through valleys, over hills, past all kinds of projections and towering heights. Our battle with the elements had begun."

They made a low-level dash for the sea as the *Point d'Interrogation*'s heavy fuel load prevented them from climbing above the banks of fog. Eventually they broke out into the English Channel north of Rouen, and in clearing skies climbed slowly to 2200 feet. The improvement in the weather was short-lived and Costes was soon forced to skim below further fog banks, then later twist and turn to avoid a succession of rain storms that reached out at them as they approached Ireland.

Five hours out, the red Breguet was sighted passing over Ireland heading into clearing skies. An hour later the liner *Berengaria* reported to New York Marine Radio

that she had received a radio message from the Frenchmen stating that "everything is okay".

But just two hours later the airmen flew into a series
of Atlantic storms that necessitated frequent changes of
course to stay clear of their savage turbulence. Costes
knew that to risk his aircraft in the violent air pockets
generated by the storms, could easily cause the wings
to break off. They were already strained to the limit
lifting the huge overload of fuel.

They were pushed steadily north of track and at one
stage feared they might have to head over Iceland to
find a clear way through. The constant diversions were
adding hundreds of kilometres to the flight, though with
5200 litres of fuel on board, there was little worry that
the aircraft would run out of gas short of America.

By nightfall they were detouring south again to miss
yet another mass of clouds. They flew on in pitch darkness with fog below blanketing the ocean and cloud
above blotting out the stars. Costes battled sleep, listening to the steady beat of the motor and forcing his eyes
to continually search the instrument panel. The
Breguet had a duplicate set of controls in the rear
cockpit and for short periods Bellonte who had recently
gained a pilot licence, relieved the tiring pilot.

Throughout the night, ships in the Atlantic picked up
messages from the fliers reporting their position and
weather conditions. These were relayed to New York
and from there to Paris where Costes' wife kept a vigil
by her telephone.

Madame Costes, an elegant blonde actress, was a
Russian Princess whose family had managed to escape
the revolution. She and the airman had met two years
earlier and married after a whirlwind courtship. Newsmen waited all night outside her Paris apartment and
interviewed her early next morning. She looked pale
and tired, which was not surprising as she had lain

awake watching her husband the night before he left and had not slept since.

"I went to bed last night to dream of him in the great loneliness of the black night over the sea, but how could I sleep?" she declared theatrically to reporters. "I had a telephone beside me, and every word from Maurice Bellonte's wireless and from the many watching ships came to me hour after hour."

As dawn broke far out over the Atlantic, Costes computed their position to be thirty-five degrees north, forty-six degrees west. Well south of course. He turned *Point d'Interrogation* onto a north-westerly heading aiming for the eastern tip of Nova Scotia. For another seven hours the airmen dodged a succession of storms. Aided by strong tailwinds and with much of its fuel load used up, the Breguet "tore along towards the coast".

As the *Point d'Interrogation* reached the North American coast the airmen's enthusiasm was dampened by the conditions that lay ahead. Over the coast of Nova Scotia they encountered by far the worst storm of the whole flight. Determined not to lose sight of the coast, which they needed to follow for several hundred kilometres, they had to twist and turn along its jagged line. It would have been a simple task had not the low clouds and pouring rain forced them down as low as thirty feet above the waves. At times visibility was reduced to a few hundred metres.

Costes recalled the worst moment of the flight:

We came to one bend in the coast and turned it; we flew on, skirting a precipice. Suddenly there loomed up out of the mist another precipice on our port side. We were caught between the steep banks of a river — what river, I do not know. It was a tight place.

Bellonte was at the controls at that time and he had to think fast. Fortunately, having flown thousands of miles, the ship was light. Bellonte gave her the gas and shot upward. It is not pleasant to think how close we came to those cruel, jagged rocks.

The scarlet biplane touched down at New York's Curtiss Field thirty-seven hours seventeen minutes after leaving Paris. Twenty thousand Americans broke through police cordons to carry the Frenchmen shoulder high from their aircraft. One New York paper described the scene: "They constituted perhaps the wildest crowd in the history of Long Island's aviation fields. They shouted, they leaped up and down in excitement, they broke through police cordons as through so much thread, waving French and American flags and calling out to the flyers in both languages."

The Parisians celebrated by decorating the city as for a mardi gras. The Place de la Concorde and the Place de l'Opera were packed with countless thousands, cheering, blowing horns and whistles and embracing each other. Over amplified radio Costes spoke to them via a special hook-up with Curtiss Field. The airmen received congratulations from around the world. Costes was made a *Commandant de la Legion d'Honneur*.

During World War II Costes worked as an Allied agent in occupied France. But following the end of hostilities charges were laid against the former hero that he had been working for the German Secret Service. He was tried in a Paris court in 1949 and acquitted when he finally disclosed that he had worked for the Germans but only because it gave him the opportunity to operate for the Allies as a double agent.

Dieudonne Costes died in 1973 at the age of eighty. The last and arguably the greatest of the world's long-distance fliers, Costes put his life on the line as often as any of the great pioneers ... and survived! The reasons for the success of his magnificent gambles were best summed up by America's pioneer of aviation meteorology, James H. Kimball, following the Frenchman's Atlantic triumph:

Captain Costes played his game well. He took advantage of every opportunity, reduced the element of risk and won out splendidly. Colonel Lindbergh accomplished his west-to-east flight with skill and daring. Captain Costes and M. Bellonte, in making their flight which is undeniably more difficult, succeeded because they could and did utilise the knowledge placed at their disposal.

This factor, together with their skill and bravery and a modern aeroplane, carried their flight to a highly successful close. The flight of the *Question Mark* brings to a close an epoch in trans-Atlantic flight history.

14
Eastbound from Japan

Among the great aviation feats inspired by Charles Lindbergh's epochal trans-Atlantic flight in 1927, none was more gallant than Japan's little-known crusade to conquer the Pacific. It lasted seventeen years, cost four lives and ended during World War II when, facing inevitable defeat, six Japanese airmen secretly set a dazzling record.

Lindbergh's New York–Paris flight had electrified the world. An international hero, he had become the most photographed public figure of his era. While the world bathed in the afterglow of Lindbergh's gallantry, Japan decided to emulate the phenomenon by sending one of its pilots on a non-stop crossing of aviation's last great barrier — the Pacific Ocean.

The breathtaking project was announced by the Imperial Aeronautics Association in July 1927, which declared that a Japanese pilot, flying a Japanese-built aircraft, would make the first flight across the Pacific. A longer and more demanding flight, if successful it would attract even greater world reaction than Lindbergh's effort and focus attention on Japan's emergence as the industrial powerhouse of Asia.

The Tokyo newspaper *Mainichi Shimbun* placed an order with Ryan for an exact replica of Lindbergh's long-range Ryan NYP monoplane *Spirit of St Louis*. However, its mission was not to actually fly on the 7360-kilometre trans-Pacific attempt as it lacked the

necessary range. Lindbergh's aircraft had been purpose-designed to fly only the 5760 kilometres between
New York and Paris, plus a few hundred kilometres
extra for safety — whereas a flight from Japan to
America's west coast required at least an extra 1600-
kilometre range.

Although the Japanese may at first have thought it
possible to extend the Ryan's range, it seems more likely
that its role was act as a design guide for Japan to
manufacture its own long-range monoplane. The Imperial Aeronautics Association selected the Kawanishi
company to construct two machines — one as a back-up
in case of an accident. As designer Eiji Sekiguchi commenced work, four Kawanishi pilots were selected for
the project.

What little is known concerning the design and construction of the Kawanishi K-12 trans-Pacific monoplanes is best explained by Robert C. Mikesh. Formerly
a Senior Curator of Aeronautics at Washington's National Air and Space Museum, he is America's leading
authority on Japanese aviation. Mikesh wrote:

> What happened is still a mystery. Never confirmed, and
> perhaps apocryphal, the widespread belief is that the
> concept of the airplane design amounted to creating a
> machine larger than the *Spirit of St Louis* in the same
> proportion by which the span of the Pacific exceeded the
> Atlantic. The concept in simplest terms was this: Greater
> size was to produce greater range.
>
> The Kawanishi firm's K-12 looked remarkably like an
> overfed Ryan NYP, Lindbergh's plane. It relied on a mas-
> sive landing gear to support a huge boxy fuselage. That, in
> turn, was needed to accommodate the vast quantities of
> fuel required for the long flight. It had twice the wing area
> of the NYP. Its relatively pointed nose contained a 500
> horse power BMW water-cooled engine, built under licence
> by Kawasaki. The cockpit, unlike Lindbergh's, accommo-
> dated a second crew member. It looked as if it were defying
> the laws of physics. But the plane's appearance aside,
> everything seemed set for the big Pacific crossing.

While the aircraft were being built, crew training got under way. A great circle route was chosen across the North Pacific. Arching north-east from Japan, it would give the pilots some protection by tracking close to the Kurile and Aleutian Islands, before swinging south-east to the American mainland. It was decided that the K-12 would be more easily spotted, in the event the crew was forced to ditch, if it was painted silver with red stripes on the wings. The four pilots were given intensive training in long-range flying and over-water navigation by the Japanese Naval Air Corps.

In February 1928 one of their number, Yukichi Goto, was killed when his aircraft crashed into a cloud-shrouded mountain during a long-range training flight. As one Japanese writer suggested, it was "a bad omen — the death of the veteran pilot".

Three months later the first K-12 was rolled out of the factory for flight testing. Officially called the *Nichi-Bei-Go* (Japan–US Model), it was christened the *Sakura* (Cherry Blossom). Fully loaded the machine weighed in at a massive 5125 kilograms — more than twice the weight of Lindbergh's Ryan. The finished aircraft was closely inspected by officials of Japan's Civil Aviation Bureau.

Extensive testing showed that the K-12's gross weight when loaded with maximum fuel greatly exceeded the aircraft's safe-design limit. Furthermore, its fuel capacity was found to be insufficient for the flight. Adding to Kawanishi's problems, flight tests determined that the lumbering monoplane failed to meet a performance requirement of the bureau, being unable to climb to a minimum altitude of 50 feet in a given period of time, following a take-off run of less than 850 metres.

Following lengthy arguments with the bureau, Kawanishi reluctantly agreed to modify the second K-12, including strengthening its airframe to accommodate a greater load of fuel. Unfortunately, the whole design concept was flawed and it too was eventually rejected when the Imperial Aeronautics Association's project committee determined its maximum range was only 6086 kilometres — 1609 kilometres less than required for the flight.

By this time Kingsford Smith's *Southern Cross* had successfully flown the Pacific — albeit in three stages. Finally accepting that no amount of modification could ever get the K-12 to complete a non-stop Pacific crossing, the Association formally suspended its trans-Pacific project on 7 July 1928. Bob Mikesh wrote:

> The upshot was devastating. The Tokyo government would not qualify its own preferred aircraft for civil registration or give clearance for the trans-Pacific flight. In the denouement, a red-faced Kawanishi found itself strapped with an expensive white elephant, providing an inglorious end to the firm's last private-venture, non-military aircraft. Its owners hung the aircraft over the assembly shop where for many years it gathered dust. Hung beneath the forlorn flying machine was a bitter and humourless message: "How Not to Design or Build a Special-Purpose Airplane".

As the Japanese effort came to its sad conclusion, an American team from Tacoma, Washington took up the challenge of the non-stop flight from Japan. Lumber tycoon John Buffelen and the city's Chamber of Commerce had decided that a flight from Tokyo would put their town on the map, and they were backing a Canadian-born flier named Harold Bromley. If perseverance was always rewarded by success, the 29-year-old ex-Royal Air Force pilot should have been the first to fly non-stop across the Pacific Ocean. Bromley was to have four attempts at the flight.

Visiting Lockheed's new Burbank factory early in 1929, Bromley had discovered the fuselage shell of an experimental single-engine monoplane called the Explorer. Designer Jack Northrop had started work on the long-range design in 1927 hoping it would interest Australian-born arctic explorer Hubert Wilkins for his planned trans-Polar flight. When Wilkins instead chose Lockeed's new Vega, work was stopped on the special monoplane.

Bromley realised that the design had the potential to carry enough fuel for a non-stop trans-Pacific flight and placed an order for it to be completed. Several months later, Bromley carried out full-load tests on the long, concrete-like bed of Muroc Dry Lake (near the site of today's Edwards Air Force Base). Satisfied with its performance, he flew the Explorer to Tacoma's Pierce County Airport where it was formally christened *City of Tacoma*.

On the morning of 28 July 1929 Bromley made his first trans-Pacific attempt. His Lockheed, bloated with 3414 litres of fuel, sat on top of a long wooden ramp at the Pierce County Airport. The ramp's down-hill run was to give an initial boost to help the overloaded *City of Tacoma* attain take-off speed on the relatively short, grass runway. After checking the 450-horsepower Pratt and Whitney Wasp engine Bromley opened up to full power and rolled down the ramp onto the airfield.

The Lockheed was gathering speed and had gone about 300 metres when the crowd of 10 000 saw it swerve towards rough ground. Seconds later the right landing gear collapsed and the wing was shattered. As the aircraft came to a stop with its tail perched in the air Bromley leapt from the cockpit. Miraculously there was no fire. Later, explaining that he had been blinded by fuel venting from a tank breather in front of his windshield, Bromley lamented: "Nobody is to blame but myself. I can do it if they'll give me another chance."

Tacoma's indulgent businessmen were to finance three more attempts. The next came to an end two months later when Lockheed test pilot Herb Fahy survived a terrible crash in the second *City of Tacoma*. The brand new Explorer went out of control when tail flutter caused the rudder to fall off in flight.

By May 1930 a third *City of Tacoma* was built and, with Bromley again at the controls, breezed through its initial flight testing. Lockheed could no longer afford the special insurance policy required for Bromley to conduct the full load test, so he handed over to company pilot Ben Catlin for the critical flight.

Bromley positioned himself at the planned lift-off point — 1600 metres down Muroc's dry lake-bed which was used by Lockheed for the tests. As the Explorer roared past, Catlin was still having trouble getting airborne. A kilometre ahead a four-metre high railway embankment bisected the lake bed forcing Catlin to lift his reluctant aircraft into the air.

Flying on the cushion of air known as "ground effect", the Explorer wallowed uncertainly until the tiny increase in altitude needed to cross the railway embankment brought on a stall. Dropping a wing the aircraft crashed in a ball of flame. As Bromley ran to the scene he was horrified to see Catlin, wreathed in flames, staggering out of the inferno. Before dying later the luckless airman apologised "for wrecking the ship".

Bromley's Tacoma backers were still prepared to finance one last attempt. However, it was decided to look for another make of aircraft. Bromley eventually chose an Emsco monoplane manufactured by the little-known E.M.Smith and Company. Powered by a single 450-horsepower Wasp engine, it had a maximum range of 6540 kilometres — about 800 kilometres short of the distance between Tacoma and Tokyo. As the Emsco had room for a crewman, Bromley decided to carry a navigator.

He chose a former ship's officer from Tasmania, 27-year-old Harold Gatty, who was making a lean living teaching air navigation in Los Angeles. Unable to increase the Emsco's fuel load, the two men decided to reverse the route. They were confident that tailwind on a west-east crossing would increase their speed sufficiently to overcome the shortage of fuel. In view of the bad publicity generated by the previous attempts, Bromley's backers insisted that no pre-flight publicity was given to the fourth *City of Tacoma* attempt. Consequently, the actual flight received little media attention.

After shipping the Emsco to Tokyo, Bromley and Gatty flew it to a nearby naval aerodrome. When load tests proved that the runway was too short for a full load take-off, they searched for a suitable beach, finally locating one at Sabishiro, 340 kilometres north of Tokyo. At low tide the sands stretched for almost two kilometres, yet with a full 4164-litre fuel load Bromley still required a ramp to boost the Emsco's take-off performance. For three weeks local villagers helped build a sand hill which they compacted with a steam roller before laying a runway of planks leading down to the beach.

On 15 September 1931 the improvised airstrip was ready. The generous villagers, who refused to accept any payment for their labours, lined the beach. At the top of the ramp, anchored to a big pile by a thick rope, the Emsco strained as Bromley checked the engine. When he was satisfied that the Wasp was delivering full power, Bromley dropped his hand and a man with an axe severed the rope. Trundling slowly down the ramp, the Emsco slowly gathered speed. Even with the ramp's assistance the airplane did not become airborne until it reached the end of the sands, and for several hours it required climb-power just to remain clear of the waves.

Four hours out the *City of Tacoma* entered fog and low cloud that was to persist for most of the next twenty-one hours. Minutes later the exhaust system's collector ring fractured and exhaust fumes began to seep into the cockpit. Neither of the crew realised the insidious problem even though Bromley found himself laughing uncontrollably and Gatty was having spasms of coughing.

Unable to climb above the cloud, Gatty relied on dead reckoning navigation. Bromley's task of blind-flying was not helped when the Emsco's Sperry Artificial Horizon — one of the first fitted to a civil aircraft — "turned over on its back and died". Soon after, the wind-driven fuel pump failed, forcing Gatty to spend most of his time operating the emergency hand pump to keep the engine's main fuel tank topped up. He later recalled: "The first hour was pure hell but after that I didn't feel anything."

During a break in the cloud Gatty was able to fix their position by sextant and discovered they had covered only 2011 kilometres. The anticipated tail wind had not eventuated and Gatty estimated that they were still thirty-six hours flying time away from Tacoma. It was clear that they did not have enough fuel remaining and had no option but to return to Japan.

As they headed back towards Sabishiro leaks developed in the fuel lines, which the airmen repaired with friction tape. Gatty recalled being worried that Bromley continued his fits of laughter despite the knowledge that he had again failed. As the time approached for reaching the coast they noticed a hole in the cloud. Diving down they broke into the clear just above a steamer. Gatty recalled: "I don't know who was more scared. The people on the ship or me."

A red-and-white striped lighthouse lay directly ahead. It was the same one they had passed shortly after take-off the previous day. After twenty-two hours of almost continuous blind flying, this was a testimony to the accuracy of Gatty's navigation and Bromley's flying.

Although Sabishiro beach was only twenty-four kilometres away, Bromley elected to land on the first clear stretch of beach. Just before touchdown Gatty dumped their remaining excess fuel. The moment the Emsco came to stop a clearly irrational Bromley grabbed a life raft and dashed towards the water. Gatty chased after him. A few yards from the water's edge Bromley fell down and was fast asleep by the time his navigator arrived.

When he awoke, eight hours later, Bromley was quite lucid again, and told his companion that he had taken the life raft as he had thought they had ditched in the sea. A doctor later diagnosed that Bromley had suffered from mental problems brought on by carbon-monoxide poisoning from the leaking exhaust system. Three days after they landed Gatty also collapsed from the delayed action of carbon-monoxide poisoning.

With no chance of further backing from America, Bromley and Gatty returned to America leaving the *City of Tacoma* in Japan to be sold. Two years later Bromley made a long-distance flight in a diesel-powered Lockheed Vega and there was talk of his making yet another trans-Pacific attempt. But he failed to find backers and never did manage to conquer the Pacific.

In 1931 Gatty crossed the northern fringe of the Pacific — hopping across the Bering Strait between Siberia and Alaska — as he navigated Wiley Post's *Winnie Mae* on its epic flight around the world. Years later, recalling his flight with Bromley, Gatty said: "He never made the big time but he was a magnificent pilot."

In February 1931, attention was again focused on Japanese fliers when the Tokyo newspaper *Hochi Shimbun* announced it was sponsoring a non-stop flight to America by Seiji Yoshihara. The young Japanese airman had just completed a sensational light airplane flight from Berlin to Tokyo, displaying skill and perseverance by averaging over 960 kilometres each day in a tiny Junkers A-50 Junior powered by an 85-horsepower Armstrong Siddeley Genet engine. For the Pacific flight Yoshihara planned to use the same machine equipped with floats, and he named it *Hochi Nichi-Bei* (Hochi's Japan–US).

Yoshihara took off from Haneda, near Tokyo, on 14 May, following a similar Great Circle route to that planned by Bromley and Gatty. He had covered around 1600 kilometres and was flying in fog close to Russia's Kuril Islands when the Junkers developed engine trouble. The Japanese flier ditched at sea and had been adrift for seven hours when rescued by a passing Japanese ship.

Still determined to complete the flight, Yoshihara persuaded *Hochi Shimbun* to acquire a second Junkers Junior. Christened *No. 2 Hochi Nichi-Bei* it was shipped to Shinshuri Island in the Japanese-controlled Kurils — the closest suitable point they could get to the site of Yoshihara's crash the previous month. However, before the flight could be recommenced, the aircraft was damaged during testing and Japan's Civil Aeronautics Bureau wisely suspended the flight on the grounds that the aircraft was unsuitable.

Convinced that a big financial incentive might attract a suitably equipped Japanese challenge, the Imperial Aeronautics Association again became involved. It offered a prize of 200 000 yen (US$100 000) for the first person to fly "from a point of departure in Japan south of the forty-five degree north latitude". In simple terms this meant a non-stop flight from the main islands of Japan to any land south of Canada's Vancouver Island.

Tokyo's *Asahi Shimbun* newspaper added a further 100 000 yen for the successful Japanese pilot — half that amount if a foreigner happened to make the flight. US$150 000 was a king's ransom in those depression years, so with such a huge financial catalyst it was not surprising that both Japanese and American contenders quickly surfaced.

Despite the failure of its tiny Junkers Junior, the *Hochi Shimbun* had not given up and purchased a

Junkers W33 transport. It was similar to the W33 *Bremen* that had made the first east–west Atlantic crossing in 1928. Powered by a 300-horsepower Junkers L5 engine, the all-metal monoplane was noted for its rugged construction and load-carrying ability.

The newspaper ordered Mitsubishi to equip the aircraft for long-range operations and then searched for another W33 to commence crew training. Germany's Baron von Hunefeld, who had been on board the *Bremen* during the Atlantic flight, had donated a W33 to the Imperial Aeronautics Association and this was loaned to the newspaper to train its crew.

Eiichiro Baba of the Japan Air Transport Research Institute was selected as the pilot and Commander Kiyoshi Homma and Master Sergeant Tomoyoshi Inoshita of the Navy were appointed as navigator and radio operator. The three men underwent intensive training but, by the time their W33 *No. 3 Hochi Nichi-Bei* was ready, the advent of winter in the North Pacific forced the flight to be postponed until the following year.

While the Japanese had been preparing, several American crews had arrived in Japan. Seduced by the rich cash prizes, the first attempt, by Thomas Ash on 31 May 1931, was a hastily arranged affair. He purchased the abandoned Emsco *City of Tacoma*, renamed it the *Pacific*, but was unable even to get it off the sands of Sabishiro Beach.

The next American bid was made by Cecil Allen and Don Moyle who became the third owners of the ill-fated Emsco. This time rechristened the *Crasina Madge*, the plane lifted successfully from Sabishiro Beach on 8 September. Allen and Moyle made it as far as the Aleutians where bad weather forced them to land. They took off again later only to be forced down again. This time their landing area was on an uninhabited island and a week passed before they were rescued.

The next attempts were mounted from America,

where a group of Seattle businessmen had offered US$28 000 for a non-stop flight between Japan and Seattle. Reginald Robbins, a Fort Worth, Texas barnstormer and sportsman flier Harold S. Jones, a wealthy oil man, decided to make an attempt from Seattle.

Their plan was revolutionary for its day. To increase their range they planned to refuel their Lockheed Vega (christened the *Fort Worth*) in-flight from a Ford Trimotor. Aerial refuelling was still at an experimental stage, but Robbins had used the new technique two years earlier to set a 172-hour endurance record while circling over his home town. To reduce the *Fort Worth*'s fuel consumption on the Pacific flight, Robbins replaced its 425 horsepower Wasp engine with a 220-horsepower Wright Whirlwind.

The pair took off from Seattle's Boeing Field on 8 July 1931, and when they arrived over Fairbanks, Alaska they were met by their flying gas station and took on 757 litres. Approaching Nome, where they planned to take on more fuel, the two aircraft were buffeted by severe wind squalls and Robbins was unable to get close enough to the tanker for Jones to grab the dancing hose, forcing the two exhausted Texans to land at Nome.

A month later their second non-stop Pacific attempt also failed when they lost contact with the tanker in cloud before being able to take on its vital load. A few days later another westbound attempt failed when a flier named Bob Wark was forced down at Vancouver, Canada, less then 200 kilometres from his starting point.

The approach of winter seemed to spell an end to the trans-Pacific drama, when two more American pilots, Clyde "Upside Down" Pangborn and Hugh Herndon Jnr, strutted onto centre stage. Pangborn, a stunt pilot and wing-walker, was chief pilot and part owner of the Gates Flying Circus. His playboy co-pilot, Hugh Herndon, was a wealthy Princeton dropout with a penchant for flying and the good life. Herndon's mother, an oil heiress, was anxious to see her son make a name for himself. She did not turn a hair when he asked her for $100 000 to finance a world flight.

Pangborn and Herndon had left New York's Roosevelt Field on 28 July 1931 in the Bellanca Skyrocket *Miss Veedol*, with high hopes of beating the around-the-world speed record set by Wiley Post and Harold Gatty. They gave up after their plane became totally bogged on a rain-soaked Siberian airstrip.

The pair eventually reached Japan, where they were charged with espionage and making an illegal flight. Pangborn recounted:

> We were arraigned on three counts. That we had flown over fortified areas and that we had photographed these areas. True we didn't have a flight permit with us, but we assumed it would be routine for our embassy to arrange it. As for flying over fortified areas and taking pictures, we were just tourists taking what we thought were pretty landscape shots.

The fliers were tried in Tokyo's district court, found guilty, and sentenced to 205 days hard labour or fines of US$1050 apiece. When the fines were paid, Pangborn and Herndon revealed their plan to attempt the Japan–US flight. Because of the spate of recent failures, Japan's Civil Aviation Bureau had restricted future flights to only "approved" aircraft, and it took days of haggling before approval was reluctantly given for just one "overload" take-off from Japan.

On 29 September the Americans flew *Miss Veedol* to Sabishiro Beach where they made final modifications for the flight. To extend the Bellanca's range Pangborn decided to emulate a scheme first used on a 1919 trans-Atlantic attempt by Australian Harry Hawker which involved dropping the landing gear after take-off. He explained:

> We determined that to make the trans-Pacific flight we

would have to take off with the heaviest wing loading [fuel load] we had ever attempted with the Bellanca. Even then it was marginal that we would have enough fuel to take us the 4500 miles to the US west coast even at the most economical cruising speed. Studying the problem I calculated that we could increase our speed approximately 15 miles per hour if we could rid ourselves of the drag of the fixed landing gear. On a forty-hour flight that would be the equivalent of adding 600 miles to our range, and that might make the difference between success and failure.

At Sabishiro Pangborn replaced the bolts holding the landing gear to the fuselage with a series of clip and springs attached to a cable. By pulling on the cable he would jettison the whole structure once they were safely airborne. For the landing he attached steel skid strips to the Bellanca's pot belly.

While they worked on the aircraft the two Americans were guests of the people of the nearby town of Misawa City. The mayor had publicly announced that fliers of any nation seeking such an honourable goal should be hosted in friendship. However, not all Japanese were so friendly, as the fliers discovered when their painstakingly prepared flight charts were stolen. They were certain that the culprits were members of the radically patriotic Black Dragon Society who for weeks had been violently speaking out against the Americans and their proposed flight.

Delayed a day obtaining and preparing new charts, Pangborn and Herndon were finally ready to go on 2 October. Just before he climbed on board the Bellanca, Pangborn was quite overwhelmed by a tiny Japanese boy who rushed out from the crowd and solemnly presented them with a gift of five apples.

Miss Veedol used the take-off ramp that had been built for the attempt by Bromley and Gatty. Even so, the Bellanca seemed to be having trouble accelerating as it rolled down onto the wet beach. To save weight they carried no radio, no survival equipment, not even a seat cushion, and they limited their food to hot tea and some fried chicken. Yet with 3650 litres of fuel and oil aboard, the airplane was still 1542 kilograms above its designed gross operating weight.

With its 425-horsepower Wasp engine screaming at full revs, the monoplane was only up to 96 km/h with two-thirds of the beach gone. Pangborn had estimated he required 145 km/h for lift-off. As *Miss Veedol* approached a pile of logs which marked the end of the makeshift runway Pangborn could be seen rocking the aircraft from wheel to wheel in an attempt to break the friction of the wet sand. He later recounted his thoughts at that moment: "I was determined to get off, or pile into those logs. We had permission for only the one attempt and in no way was I going to spend any more time in Japan."

They made it with less than 100 metres to spare. Flying straight ahead, wallowing on near the stall, they slowly inched up above the waves. When they had a safe margin of height, Pangborn turned slowly onto a heading of 072 degrees true — heading up towards the Aleutians.

Three hours out, on track and approaching the Kuril Islands, Pangborn was satisfied that everything was operating normally and jettisoned the landing gear. He was concerned to see that two of the gear's bracing rods had not dropped clear. Pangborn realised that they posed a real threat to a safe belly landing and knew that he would have to work them free sometime during the flight.

Devoid of 136 kilograms of landing gear and its drag, *Miss Veedol* climbed slowly to 14 000 feet, where it picked up a good tail wind. As the sun went down they began to encounter airframe icing in cloud and increased height to 17 000 feet. Clear of the cloud, conditions were smooth and Pangborn decided it was the ideal time to try and get rid of the two dangling struts.

Handing over control to Herndon he put his years of flying-circus skills to good use. Struggling against the frigid 160 km/h slipstream, the steel-nerved airman eased out of the cockpit and placed his feet on the broad strut that supported the Bellanca's wing. Holding on for dear life with one hand he used the other to remove one of the offending brace rods. Pangborn clambered back into the cockpit, warmed himself, then repeated the procedure on the other side.

Through the night it was bitterly cold. "The water in our canteens and even our hot tea froze," Pangborn recalled. His first real position check was a volcano in the Aleutians and the two men were delighted to see it loom directly below them. One of Herndon's few responsibilities was to keep the main wing tanks topped up from the huge auxiliary cabin tank. This required him to transfer fuel using a hand-operated wobble pump.

Twice he forgot the task. The first time he was able to pump fuel fast enough to keep the spluttering Wasp engine running. However, on the second occasion the propeller stopped dead and, not equipped with an electric starter, Pangborn had no alternative but to dive the Bellanca in the hope of getting the propeller to windmill in the rarefied air. Yelling at Herndon to start pumping, Pangborn steepened the dive, desperately trying to turn the propeller. They had lost 13 000 feet, and were only 1500 feet above the ocean, when the propeller finally turned over and the engine burst into life again. Herndon's carelessness had come close to costing them their lives.

During the flight the only word of their progress came from an island in the Aleutians, where an amateur radio operator radioed America that he had heard an airplane passing over above the clouds. No one was quite sure of their final destination, although Pangborn's mother was adamant that her son would chose Wenatchee as his landing site and was among thirty locals who maintained a vigil at the town's small airfield.

As Pangborn sighted the tip of the Queen Charlotte Islands, off the north-west coast of Canada, he knew the worst of the navigation was over. He had been at the controls for over thirty hours and, aware that the tricky job of belly landing lay not too far ahead, decided to catch a few hours sleep. Handing over, he instructed Herndon to hold height and heading and wake him when he saw the lights of a big city. "That will be Vancouver," Pangborn yelled.

Once again Herndon's inattention let them down. When Pangborn awoke some hours later, his cavalier co-pilot had wandered off course and missed both Vancouver and Seattle. Ahead of them was Mount Rainier. Pangborn decided to carry on inland to Boise, Idaho which would also give them a new world non-stop distance record. However, two hours later, when it became evident that the Boise area was covered in fog, he turned towards Spokane, Washington. When that destination appeared to be covered by low cloud, he decided to head for his home town of Wenatchee.

At 7.14 a.m. on 5 October 1931 the big red monoplane swooped in over the hills and circled Wenatchee's tiny airfield, dumping fuel to reduce the chance of fire. Approaching slowly, Pangborn sent Herndon to the rear of the cabin, hoping that his weight would help hold the tail down during the landing. At the last moment he cut off the fuel and ignition switches and, as the Bellanca flared close to stalling, lowered it gently onto the ground. For a moment it was obscured by a cloud of dust, then, decelerating rapidly, *Miss Veedol* slithered to a stop, teetering for a moment and then falling on its left wing-tip.

After being hugged by his mother and brother, Pangborn was stunned to be greeted by a representative of

Asahi Shimbun who presented the fliers with their $25 000 check. By some quirk of fate, the newspaper's emissary had selected Wenatchee as the *Miss Veedol*'s most likely landing point.

The *Asahi Shimbun* prize was the only money realised by the epic flight. As foreigners, they were not eligible for the Imperial Aeronautic Association's prize, and Wenatchee was too far from Seattle for them to receive the prize offered by that city's businessmen. From Pangborn's point of view worse was to follow. With relationships already strained with Herndon, their partnership quickly dissolved. As backers for the original world flight, Herndon and his mother claimed the prize money and the cash realised from the sale of *Miss Veedol*. They gave Pangborn $2500 for his efforts.

The split between Pangborn and Herndon became public a couple of months later when the Albany *Times Union* carried the headline, "HERNDON INCOMPETENT SAYS PANGBORN". In the story that followed, Pangborn disclosed that his co-pilot had known nothing of navigation because he had been courting a girl instead of studying prior to their flight. He disclosed that Herndon had been little more than a passenger in *Miss Veedol*, stating: "Out of the 200 hours we were in the air, Herndon flew at most ten of those hours."

Even though there was little financial gain for Pangborn, the non-stop Pacific flight brought other, more lasting rewards. He was honoured with American aviation's most prestigious award — the Harmon Trophy — joining other greats such as Charles Lindbergh and Jimmy Doolittle. And from Japan came news that, forgiven for his earlier transgressions, Pangborn had been awarded the Imperial Aeronautical Society's White Medal of Merit.

But the most lasting memento of *Miss Veedol*'s flight was a gift that Pangborn arranged for the Mayor of Wenatchee to send to his counterpart in Misawa City, near Sabishiro Beach. To reciprocate the little Japanese boy's touching offering of five apples, five cuttings from Wenatchee's famed Richard Delicious apples were sent to Misawa City. There they were grafted onto local trees, and within a few years cuttings and seedlings were distributed around the country. Today, Richard Delicious apples are grown throughout Japan.

Even though American's had captured the *Asahi Shimbun* prize, Japan was still determined that its pilots should make the Pacific crossing. In light of Pangborn and Herndon's success, the *Hochi Shimbun* newspaper was desperate for its team to safely complete the flight. To minimise the risk, it was decided to provide two back-up aircraft for their Junkers W33.

The luckless Seiji Yoshihara was sent to England to ferry a Saro Cutty Sark flying boat back to Japan, and two army fliers were despatched to the United States to bring back a Bellanca, similar to the victorious *Miss Veedol*. In March 1932 the *Hochi Shimbun*'s carefully laid plans suffered the first setback. Their trans-Pacific Bellanca, *Rising Sun*, crashed at New York's Floyd Bennett field during a flight test, killing its pilot Captain Yoshinori Nagoya. Six weeks later Yoshihara crashed the Cutty Sark during a test flight in Oakland.

Reduced again to only one aircraft, the Japanese trans-Pacific project finally got under way again on 10 September 1932 when the *No. 3 Hochi Nichi-Bei* departed Haneda airport for Sabishiro Beach. At 5.37 a.m. on 24 September, after taking on board a full load of fuel, pilot Eiichiro Baba took off on the long-delayed flight to the United States. Navigator Homma set course on their Great Circle route and radio operator Inoshita checked his equipment. Five hours out, Inoshita reported their position as south of Iturup Island in the Kurils. They were on course and making good time. Operators in Japan waited for the next position report from the Junkers. It never came. Baba and his crew vanished, and despite a massive sea search no trace was ever found of the missing plane.

In the five years since Lindbergh had inspired the Japanese effort, seven trans-Pacific ventures had failed. All five of the unfortunate *Hochi Shimbun*'s aircraft had crashed, costing the lives of four airmen. All that remained of the Imperial Aeronautics Society's Ryan-inspired *Nichi-Bei-Go* project was an abortion of an aircraft gathering dust beneath the roof of the Kawanishi assembly shop. But it is not in the Japanese nature to give up on a project once commenced. Over the years that followed the 1932 disaster, there were still those who dreamed of making the flight.

Following the loss of the Junkers W33 *Hochi Nichi Bei*, all further attempts had been officially suspended. However, in February 1940, the *Asahi Shimbun* came up with a breathtaking plan to set world aviation back on its heels. To mark the 2600th birthday of the Japanese Empire, the newspaper announced that it was sponsoring the construction of an aircraft to make a good-will, non-stop flight from Tokyo to New York City — a staggering 13 000 kilometres. For good measure, the aircraft would then fly to Buenos Aires.

Throughout Japan the plan sparked intense interest, not the least from Army officers who had already approached several aircraft companies with the seemingly impossible task of designing a super bomber with a range of 11 000 kilometres. Japan then still perceived Russia as its greatest threat, and the Army was keen to possess a bomber that could strike against Russian cities far to the west. Like the other aircraft builders, the Tachikawa Aircraft Company had refused the Army task. However, when approached by the *Asahi Shimbun*, Tachikawa agreed to design an aircraft for the special flight. It seems that the Army, who were also involved in the discussions, hoped to benefit from the technology that could be gained from the project.

The newspaper's specifications called for a minimum range of 15 000 kilometres, a cruising speed of at least 300 km/h and an ability to cruise at around 20 000 feet where it might benefit from the high-speed jet streams. An all-civilian team headed by Dr Hidemasa Kimura worked on the design, which centred around a high-aspect-ratio wing with a laminar flow aerofoil. These two features were employed to minimise drag. Seventy percent of the wing's internal area was to carry the massive fuel load which would more than double the aircraft's 7255-kilograms empty weight.

Early plans called for two of the aircraft to be completed by November 1941, but delays put them behind schedule. With the outbreak of the Pacific War, the project was cancelled and the uncompleted machines were put into storage.

In the summer of 1942 the Army ordered Tachikawa to resume production of the A-26. It had been decided that the aircraft's range would make it ideal for special missions between Japan and Germany. First flight tests were conducted late in 1942. Powered by two 1000-horsepower Nakajima engines, similar to those used in Japan's Zero fighter, the A-26 handled superbly. A top speed of 439 km/h was achieved at 15 000 feet and the desired fuel flows were established at an economical cruising speed of 300 km/h. Other than minor oxygen-flow problems within its sealed high-altitude cabin, the radical machine met all its design expectations.

On 30 June 1943 one of the A-26s took off from Fussa, near Tokyo, on a clandestine flight to Berlin. Besides a crew of five it carried a Colonel Nakamura who it appears had a special mission in Germany. Worried that it might be intercepted by Soviet fighters on a northern route over Russia, the A-26 was despatched first to Singapore, where it refuelled for the long flight over the Middle East and Southern Europe to Berlin.

On 7 July, somewhere over the Indian Ocean, contact

was lost with the A-26. The reason for its loss was never established. Severe tropical storms were known to be in the area. It is also possible that the unarmed aircraft was shot down, as British war records disclose that an unidentified Japanese plane was shot down over the Indian Ocean on the same date.

The remaining A-26 languished until the spring of 1944 when, as US marines landed on Saipan, and China-based Army Air Force B-29s began raiding Northern Kyushu, the strange decision was made to use it to set a new world distance record. Why, with the war situation deteriorating rapidly, the Japanese should use valuable resources on such a venture has been the subject of much speculation.

Whatever the reason, it was an opportunity for *Asahi Shimbun*, and the men who designed and built the revolutionary A-26, to prove that their aircraft was capable of conducting the flight for which it had been designed. Even though there would be no world headlines, they would know that Japanese technology had finally rivalled American and European technology. It was, perhaps, a matter of honour.

Clearly, it was suicidal to contemplate flying the mission over the original course to New York and Buenos Aires. Instead, a secret closed-circuit was chosen, far removed from the war, over Manchuria. The aircraft was flown to Hsinking (now Changchun), 400 kilometres north of the Korean border, from where it was to circle over an 865-kilometres course until it had flown the required 13 000-kilometre distance.

Japanese records are sketchy concerning its crew of military and civilian airmen. They indicate that airmen named Komata and Tanaka were the two pilots, Shimozaki and Morimatsu were the engineers, Habiro was the radio operator and Sakamoto's duty was to record details of the record attempt.

The A-26, an all-metal twin-engine monoplane,

faintly resembled the Japanese bombers that were desperately fighting a losing battle against the allied forces that island-hopped the Pacific towards Japan. But there the resemblance stopped. Its superbly streamlined fuselage and remarkably long, glider-like wings indicated that this machine was not built for war. Rather, it had all the trademarks of a purpose-built, long-range record breaker.

Six crewmen watched as ground crew pumped a staggering 11 553-litre fuel load into the aircraft's wing tanks. Then, after exchanging salutes with an Imperial Japanese Army Officer, the six climbed aboard and took off easily after a roll of only 1340 metres. If all went well over the next three days they were about to fly, non-stop, for over 17 700 kilometres.

Following take-off, the aircraft's weight of 16 690 kilograms limited its ceiling to 10 000 feet. However, as fuel was consumed the aircraft was allowed to climb until it finally reached 20 000 feet. Throughout the flight, as weight decreased, the power was reduced to maintain the minimum required fuel flow.

The auto pilot failed early in the flight and the two pilots took turns at the controls. With no air circulating in the sealed cockpit, by the second day the crew had problems staying awake by the second day. Their discomfort was exacerbated by the oxygen masks they were forced to wear. Although sun streaming through the plexiglass made the interior uncomfortably warm, condensation from their breathing formed ice on the windows and metal frames.

By the start of the third day aloft the A-26 had flown 13 760 kilometres in forty-eight hours. On the ground a team monitoring the flight disagreed with the crew's assessment of their fuel remaining. Later in the day the officer in charge of the ground team ordered them to land at the completion of the nineteenth circuit. It seems likely that he believed that the error in fuel calculation was due to the crew becoming too exhausted to concentrate fully.

In the early evening of 4 July 1944 the A-26 landed safely after a flight of 57 hours and 11 minutes. It had flown a staggering 16 492 kilometres. Furthermore, when the tanks were checked it was found that 798 litres of fuel remained — enough to have flown an additional 1800 kilometres! The actual distance the Japanese airmen had flown had exceeded the Great Circle route distance to New York by more than 4828 kilometres — not to mention the reserves that remained in their tanks.

In Japan their unofficial world record was not announced. The country's military leader, General Tojo, had other things on his mind. Facing inevitable defeat, he was to resign two weeks after the flight.

Following the end of the war, Tachikawa's brilliant A-26 was among a number of Japanese aircraft shipped to the United States to be studied by aviation experts. No one was aware of its stunning record flight and, sadly, it was later reduced to scrap.

In September 1946 its record was eventually exceeded by the Lockheed P2V-1 *Truculent Turtle*, which flew 18 068 kilometres across the Pacific from Perth, Australia to Columbus, Ohio.

On 12 August 1960 — thirty-three years after it started its crusade — Japan finally conquered the Pacific. The trial-and-error years of tragedy and frustration were forgotten in the celebrations marking Japan Air Lines' inaugural non-stop DC-8C service from Tokyo to San Francisco.

Fifteen years later another airline event was to recall the efforts of *Asahi Shimbun* and its A-26. On 12 November 1975, the Boeing Aircraft Company put on a special trans-Pacific flight to demonstrate the intercontinental ability of its new 747-SP long-range jumbo. The "Special Purpose" jumbo was the brainchild of Pan

American Airways which had turned to Boeing for a
solution. Pan Am required an airliner to carry a full
payload non-stop across the Pacific between New York
and Tokyo.

When the 747 landed at Tokyo's Haneda Airport after
a thirteen and a half hour flight, reporters clustered
around one of its 181 VIP passengers. They were eager
to hear the verdict of a 71-year-old Dr Hidemasa
Kimura, head of the Tachikawa A-26 team which thirty-
five years earlier had designed an aircraft capable of
connecting the two cities — with 6437 kilometres to
spare. Closing his eyes momentarily, thinking back to a
contest so nearly won, he mused, "It was a long wait."
Then smiling brightly, he added, "But a very comfortable ride."

15
Twice around the world with Wiley Post and *Winnie Mae*

They made a strange-looking couple. He was stocky, with rough-hewn features and a shock of bushy hair that frequently flopped over the stark white patch that covered his left eye. The girl looked half his age. She was slim and pretty, and she nervously clutched his gnarled hand. The minister glanced up from his Bible, looking into the man's single bright eye. "Do you, Wiley, take May to be your lawful wedded wife?"

Throughout the ceremony the Oklahoma preacher could not help but wonder about the couple. They were strangers to the area and, guessing by her age were probably eloping. The tanned crinkle-faced man had the look of the oilfields about him. His tall, dark-haired young bride had the clear eyes and soft drawl of a rancher's daughter.

Still, the minister remembered, it was hard times in the dust bowl of the mid-west and he'd married many a couple passing through on their way to a new life in the promised land of California. Maybe that was what this surprise wedding ceremony was all about. Or maybe they'd come across the Texas border, escaping the wrath of a father who refused to give his consent to this union! The minister was right on the second count.

May's Texas-rancher father had indeed refused to let his seventeen-year-old daughter marry the 29-year-old

Oklahoma farm boy. He didn't give a damn if they were in love. No daughter of his was going to waste herself on a daredevil barnstorming pilot. Those flyers were all mad! Broke today and dead tomorrow.

Thus the couple had no option. The ex-oilfield roughneck and his sweetheart had jumped into the windy cockpit of his beat-up old Curtiss biplane and eloped by air. They had only just crossed the Oklahoma border when the ex-World War I trainer developed engine trouble. The pilot of six months made a forced landing between the rows of corn stooks in a field near the farming community of Graham. He didn't even wait to repair the engine. Grabbing the young woman by the hand he set off to find the local preacher and make her Mrs Wiley Post.

Wiley Post was a name — unknown outside Oklahoma in 1927 — that only four years later would become a household word around the globe, when the uneducated, self-taught pilot flew around the world.

More than any other pioneer airman, Wiley Post epitomised the American folk hero. His rise above his humble beginnings virtually guaranteed it, for he was the poor uneducated boy who reached the top. His story fitted the American belief that their country was the "Land of Opportunity", where the strength of one's back counted as much as one's background; and where success was the reward for determination and guts, and was not restricted to those raised and educated to prosperity.

Fulfilling the American dream, he became a nation's hero, a common man to whom Americans could relate. Their other great hero, Charles Lindbergh, was cool and aloof, ill at ease in public.

Wiley was born in 1898 in Grand Saline, Texas, the son of a Scots father and an Irish mother. When he was nine years old the family moved to a Chickashe, Oklahoma farm. A poor student, he finished at eighth grade and helped his father on the farm. Though no scholar, Wiley showed a natural aptitude for mechanics and could repair anything from a sewing machine to a harvester.

In 1913 Wiley was at a county fair when he saw his first aeroplane, a crude Curtiss Pusher biplane. He recalled the moment years later: "To this day I have never seen a bit of machinery on land, sea or in the sky that was to take my breath away as did that old Pusher." As the teenager watched exhibition pilot Art Smith spin, loop, dive and spiral overhead, he decided on the spot that he would one day be a famous flyer. During the long buggy-ride home he talked of it non-stop to his bemused father.

For the next twelve months Wiley scrimped and saved until he had enough money to take a mechanical course at the Sweeney Auto and Aviation school in Kansas City. For the next three years he worked around garages at any job he could find to develop his mechanical skills. As he explained, "I looked at each piece of machinery I worked on with the underlying thought that its principles might be applied to aviation."

In 1917, when the United States entered World War I, he tried to join the newly formed military air service but was turned down. Instead, he enlisted in the Students Air Training Corps and studied radio communications.

A year later the war was over and, with the "doughboys" coming home, jobs were hard to find. Wiley signed on as a "roughneck" on a drilling rig in a new oilfield. The work was tough, dirty and backbreaking, but by 1919 standards the wage of $7 a day was good money. It was easy enough to save the $25 it cost for his first aeroplane ride.

An ex-World War I flyer, Captain Earl Zimmerman, like many of his comrades back from the battle-skies of the Western Front, was trying to make a living from his new-found skills. lt was tough going. With a government surplus Curtiss Jenny he toured the country giving Americans their first taste of flying, for $2.50 a head. He was one of a growing band of "barnstormers", as the daredevil aerial gypsies were called. They were to be found at every county fair, rodeo and holiday picnic.

Young Wiley was not content with a quick flip around the field. He told Zimmerman he would like to see some aerobatics. It cost him ten times the normal rate but it was worth every cent. As the roughneck clung on for his life, the barnstormer put the Jenny through its paces. For most it would have been a terrifying experience but for Wiley it was an unforgettable taste of the exquisite freedom of the air. It reinforced his determination to find a way to fly for a living.

In the spring of 1924 he saw an advertisement in the local paper. "Burrell Tibbs and his Texas Top Notch Fliers' were at a nearby town. This was his chance. He walked off the oil rig and hurried to see Tibbs. Did they have a job? Anything would do, just as long as it was around aeroplanes. Tibbs, who met a score of bright-eyed young job-hunters at every show, turned Post down. The dejected young man decided that he might as well stay and watch the show. Later in the day he heard an announcement that the parachuting display had been cancelled. The troupe's jumper, Pete Lewis had been injured on his last jump.

The young roughneck saw his chance. lt was a dangerous gamble but worth the risk if it led to a job in aviation. He rushed over to Tibbs, insisting that he could do the jump. 'I don't want any pay — just give me a chance,' he implored the astonished pilot.

Ten minutes later he was climbing into the passenger seat of Tibbs' Curtiss. The crippled Lewis had helped him don the parachute and briefed him on how to pull the ripcord. "Don't forget ... count to three before you pull on the release ring," were Lewis's final words of advice. They climbed up to 2000 feet and as Tibbs throttled back Wiley climbed over the side of the open cockpit. "Then," as Tibbs recalled, "he jumped as though he had done it all his life."

His courageous gamble paid off; he was given a job with the flying circus at $50 a leap. Over the next two years he made nearly a hundred jumps. But as the nation's economy started to slump, money became short and barnstorming lost its popularity. Wiley returned to the oilfields. During his stay with the circus he had managed to get in a few *ad hoc* flying lessons, but he had not yet reached a stage where he could go solo. Money was necessary if he was to teach himself in his own aircraft. "I'd give up anything for the price of a Jenny," he said to a pilot friend as he left for the oilfield.

On 26 October 1926, his first day on the rig, an iron chip flew off a large bolt being hammered by another roughneck. It entered Wiley's left eyeball. Later in the day a doctor was forced to remove the terribly injured eye. The operation also left him partially deaf in one ear.

It was a shattering blow for the young man whose goal in life was flying. For a while he was deeply depressed. Then a few days after the accident he recalled that the pilot on his first instructional flight, Roland Pettet, had been blind in one eye! He could still become a flyer.

Day after day, week after week, Wiley practised judging distances with his monocular vision. He would spend hours guessing how far away objects were, and then check his guess by pacing out the distance. He learned to accurately judge distance by comparing the visual size of an object with the visual size of other nearby objects of known dimensions.

A month after the accident Wiley was awarded $1800 Workman's Compensation, a hundred week's pay. After settling his medical bills he had $1200 left. "My intention to get the cost of an aeroplane was realised at the expense of an eye," he wrote some years after.

He bought a Canuck biplane, a Canadian-built version of the Curtiss Jenny, which had been in a "slight crash" and cost $240. A further $300 was paid out to put it into flying shape. A friend at Ponca City airport gave him "about two hours dual flying", then Wiley Post went into the aviation business. He took on any flying job: joyriding, or transporting people or cargo anywhere at any time. He even gave flying lessons. Despite his lack of formal training Wiley was a "natural pilot". In his sensitive hands the machine became an extension of the man. As one of his students put it, "He didn't fly an aeroplane, he put it on."

The business went quite well. Once they got over the surprise of being greeted by a one-eyed pilot, his passengers liked the Oklahoman's quiet, assured manner. Sporting a trim moustache, he looked older and was more mature than his twenty-eight years. As one of his customers recalled, "He was never cocky or arrogant like most of the other flyers of the day."

But at least one of the locals didn't share the passengers' sentiments. In fact he almost put an early end to the airman's career, as another Ponca City pilot, Jack Baskin, recalled years later:

One noon I was working on my ship at Ponca City Airport and heard a plane drone over. The motor cut and I saw it land in a field of wheat nearby. I drove to where it landed, and out stepped old Wiley. "Well, here I am in a wheat field, knee high to a tall Indian," he joked. "I broke my oil line." We taped up the pipe and I cranked the motor for him, but in three or four runs across the field Wiley could not lift from the wheat.

Just then I saw him stand up in the cockpit and he shouted to me, "Look out Jack, there's a farmer coming with a long shotgun." And there was a big Polak farmer carrying a whale of a gun. Wiley gave the bus full bore and somehow managed to lift the wings above the wheat to

catch the air and he was off. The farmer let go a couple of
shells but luckily was just out of range.

That was where old Wiley learned to lift a ship from the
ground with a short run. l left pretty quick too, for the
dumb farmer was still shooting at Wiley.

The heady, thrill-a-minute but hand-to-mouth, barnstorming days continued till the end of 1928. But with
a wife to support Post searched for more lucrative and
regular work.

He camped in the outer office of Fred C. Hall, senior
partner of Hall and Briscoe, an oil company with headquarters in Oklahoma City. Post knew that Hall had
recently missed out on a rich oil lease because he failed
to get to the land owner in time. His persistence paid off
when Hall agreed to see him. He quickly convinced the
businessman that what his company needed was its
own aircraft and a permanent company pilot. He was
hired at $200 per month and given the job of purchasing
a three-passenger, open-cockpit Travel Air biplane.
Wiley and May moved into a small apartment in Oklahoma City.

Within a few months Hall was fully convinced of the
value of his latest employee and his farsighted ideas.
On Wiley's recommendation the company updated their
aircraft, trading in the slow biplane on a brand new
Lockheed Vega. The $20 000 high-wing monoplane was
the most advanced machine of its time. Returning on its
delivery flight from the factory, Post remarked happily:
"It is so sensitive and responsive to the controls that it
seems to anticipate my every move."

Hall named the aircraft *Winnie Mae* after his daughter who, like her father, had become a flying enthusiast
and shared his complete confidence in their new company pilot's ability.

A few months later the Stock Market crashed and
Hall was hit badly. He was forced to sell the Vega back
to Lockheeds, and so Wiley was out of a job. But the

aircraft's manufacturers had been impressed with the Oklahoman's ability and ideas when he had spent a week at the factory taking delivery of the *Winnie Mae*. He was offered a job as a test pilot. During his stay with Lockheed he not only tested their production aircraft but also got involved in serious experimental work.

In June 1930 Hall phoned. The oil business had improved and he asked Wiley to order a new *Winnie Mae*. Furthermore, he wanted his pilot back — this time in the capacity of company and personal pilot. Post accepted immediately.

Three months later, with Hall's encouragement, *Winnie Mae* was entered in the non-stop aerial derby between Los Angeles and Chicago. It promised to be the premier event of that year's National Air Races. One of America's brace of top racing pilots — Roscoe Turner, Bill Brock, Art Goebel and Lee Schoenhair — was expected to win. But when the first aircraft home was flagged across the line at Chicago's Curtiss Reynolds Airport, the crowd was astonished to see a white Lockheed flown by an unknown pilot. Even the judges had to consult their programs to learn his name. Wiley Post was enjoying his first taste of national fame. For the first time the news of his exceptional flying skill had spread beyond the south-west.

The win became even more exceptional when it was learnt that *Winnie Mae*'s magnetic compass had stuck on take-off in Los Angeles. Post had wasted forty minutes trying vainly to fix it, then carried on and map-read his way over the 2800-kilometre course. He came from behind to beat Goebel into second place by eleven heart-stopping seconds!

Hall was delighted with the victory and also the publicity his company gained. So when Wiley suggested an even more daring venture, the oil magnate responded with enthusiasm. At that time the record for a flight around the world was held by Germany. Their massive airship *Graf Zeppelin* had set the world back on its heels in 1929, taking only twenty-one days for its 34 400-kilometre flight. The only other aerial circumnavigation, by the US Army in 1924, had needed a team of four aircraft and had taken 175 days!

Post's plan was to take *Winnie Mae* flat out around the world and bring the record home to America. His first requirement was to find an expert navigator. Radio navigation aids were still a dream of the future and it was vital that he carry a crewman who was not only skilled in surface navigation, but also able to accurately fix position by the sun and stars.

His answer came in the form of Australian Harold Gatty, who was living in California. Gatty, a slim, reticent, thirty-year-old father of three, was a graduate of the Royal Australian Naval College. Wiley was not only impressed with the Australian's superb navigation credentials but also by his calm and efficient manner. There was no room for an emotional or excitable companion on this flight. And furthermore, Gatty had just invented a crude but efficient drift indicator that could be invaluable on the long featureless sections of the trip.

The early months of 1931 passed quickly as the two men studied all available maps, charts, airfield diagrams and weather information.Their problem was to find a route with suitable landing fields, spaced within range of the Vega's 2100-litre long-range fuel tanks. Insufficient airfields around the earth's equatorial belt forced them to settle on a shorter 24 000-kilometre flight path around the northern hemisphere over North America, Europe, Russia and Siberia.

Although the United States was not on diplomatic speaking-terms with Russia, an approach through a trading organisation brought immediate results. The Russian government would be glad to help the flyers.

Their departure from New York's Roosevelt Field was delayed a month by unfavourable weather. Although

international weather forecasting was in its infancy, Dr
James Kimball of the US Weather Bureau studied all
the charts and reports he could get hold of each day. It
was a long, frustrating wait for the flyers who had to be
ready to leave at a few hours notice.

Finally, shortly after midnight on 23 June, Kimball
phoned Post with the news that the weather out over
the Atlantic seemed suitable. "It could be a good time to
go," he suggested.

At 5 a.m. the heavily loaded *Winnie Mae* was airborne. Gatty's terse log recorded the early moments of
the flight: "Departed 4.55 (Daylight Saving Time). Visibility poor."

They reached the rocky runway at Grace Harbour,
Newfoundland in less than seven hours, averaging a
sizzling 294 km/h. Four hours later they were off on the
nightmare leg, the 3500 kilometres over the Atlantic to
England. In 1931 only a handful of aircraft had followed
Lindbergh's lead.

They had good reason to worry about the Atlantic
where, as usual, the weather was foul. Cloud and rain
forced Post to fly "blind" for most of the sixteen hour
crossing. For Gatty, crammed into a tiny space down the
back end of the wildly bucking Vega, it seemed a repe-
tition of his storm-plagued Pacific flight with Bromley.
His lonely navigator's table was separated from the
cockpit by the huge cabin tank. The Australian could
communicate only over a specially installed telephone.
This was a tenuous and impersonal link, especially
during the nerve-racking moments, when each man
would have welcomed the reassuring sight and touch of
his crewmate.

Although the Australian was holding up well, the
isolation was particularly unnerving when the time
came for his pilot to change fuel tanks.

To ensure that every drop of petrol was consumed, the
Oklahoman had devised a system whereby he ran each

tank bone-dry before switching to the next. To achieve this, Post had to wait until the roaring Wasp engine spluttered and coughed from fuel starvation, before turning the fuel-tank selector. The first few times nearly gave Gatty heart failure. But as the flight progressed he became more used to, if not comfortable with, the sudden loss of power.

Despite the weather, they set a record for the Atlantic crossing. When they touched down at the Royal Air Force's Sealand Aerodrome near Liverpool at 7.45 a.m., the flyers had averaged 217 km/h. They refuelled, ate breakfast, then headed for Berlin, making a brief re-fuelling stop at Hanover. When they landed at Temple-hoff Airport late that afternoon, a huge crowd had assembled to welcome them.

The world's press had suddenly caught up with the significance of the flight, and their progress made front-page news. Utterly exhausted after thirty-five hours without sleep, the airmen took a nine-hour break. It was just as well, for they would need all their strength, and their wits about them, for the 2560 kilometres to Moscow.

The eleven-hour flight was made in terrible con-ditions. Headwinds and pouring rain battered the *Win-nie Mae*. Their ground speed was back to a snail's-pace 165 km/h. Even the taciturn Gatty was moved to make this entry in his log: "Heavy rain, hedgehopping, no visibility." And minutes later, "Hell! Rain and more rain. Strong headwinds. Toughest part of the flight so far."

Post was later to remark that they would never have completed this, or the Atlantic leg, had the Vega not been equipped with the latest in blind-flying instru-ments. Primitive by modern standards, they were ade-quate to allow him to maintain height and heading during the hours of cloud flying. The machine even had a rudimentary artificial-horizon-indicator which, though far from perfect, aided the pilot in the ennervating task of holding the wings level in the turbulent cloud.

Moscow's October Airport was deserted for their arrival but later that night the airmen were feted at an elaborate banquet at the Grand Hotel. Toast after toast was proposed, accompanied by the inevitable glasses of vodka. Post and Gatty, acutely aware of an impending dawn take-off, wisely responded with water. When their genial hosts had finally finished their congratulatory gesture, and the exhausted pair were able to struggle up to bed, there was only time for two hours sleep.

When they arrived at the airport next morning there was a frustrating delay. The Russian refuellers had put on too much fuel for the take-off from the rough field. Precious time was wasted as the overload was slowly syphoned from the Vega's tanks. When they finally left for Siberia, foul weather had closed in along their route.

They made two stops during the 5840 kilometres to Khabarovsk. At the first stop, the small town of Novosibirsk, the two flyers decided to catch some sleep. They had spent an exhausting eleven hours since leaving Moscow. Unfortunately, the beds were not only rock hard, but also infested with bed bugs. It was the same story at Khabarovsk, where they spent the night before setting out to cross the Bering Sea to Alaska. Siberia was living up to its harsh reputation and had few facilities for unexpected visitors.

But at least the Russian authorities, if unable to provide them with comfort, were quick to help when they hit trouble. When the Vega became totally bogged in the muddy airfield at Khavaroosk, it seemed unlikely they would be able to move until the weather cleared and the field dried out. And that could take days.

As they ruefully surveyed their mud-trapped Vega, the two men heard a clamour, and looked up to find a band of helpers with a team of draft-horses slithering across the field. As the teamsters yelled and cracked their long whips, the straining team dragged their strange load out of the cloying mud and well away to higher and dryer ground. The flyers were able to carry on as scheduled — the next stop Alaska and the North American continent!

But they had to fight every metre of the way. The seventeen hours between Khabarovsk and Solomon, Alaska was an epic of personal endurance. They were tired before they left on the 4000-kilometre leg and the hectic pace of the flight had finally caught up with the men. Up front, Post fought off sleep as he battled the weather. At one stage fog forced them down to a mere ten metres above the Bering Sea. A second's distraction and they would have hit the frigid water!

In his tiny prison, walled in by fuel tanks and the three radios, Gatty kept watch on their position, relying much of the time on his skilful astronavigation. A series of sightings produced one bit of good news: over the telephone the Australian delightedly told his pilot that they were at last picking up tailwinds and were averaging 275 km/h.

Arriving safely at Solomon they decided to take only a four-hour break. Having returned to the home continent, they wanted to push on as quickly as possible. The cumulative effect of lack of sleep over the previous six days was taking its toll, and they were nearing the end of their mental and physical tether. If they failed to return home soon they might be forced to make an extended stop. All they had to do was keep up the pace for another day!

The flight nearly ended on the take-off from Solomon's beach. *Winnie Mae* hit a patch of soft sand and nosed over, bending the metal propeller blades. Wiley's earlier years around farm and oil rig equipment now paid off, as the inventive ex-roughneck managed to straighten the blades using a hammer, a wrench and a large stone. But as he started up the engine to test the blades' balance there was another brush with disaster. As it burst into life the accelerating propeller struck Gatty and he was thrown to the ground. Luck was with them, for the Australian was only badly bruised. He insisted they carry on.

In snow and rain the Lockheed droned on via Fairbanks and Edmonton, where they caught a few hours sleep. But when they tried to take off from the Canadian prairie city, they found the airfield was waterlogged. Willing workers removed telephone poles and power lines so that the Vega could use the town's paved main street as a runway.

In the United States the word was out: "Post and Gatty are heading for New York." Crowds were out all along their homeward route gazing skywards trying to catch a glimpse of the white monoplane.

A vague sighting was reported over Iron Range, Wisconsin. Then they were seen over Upper Michigan. But after that came only a few vague reports, some tinged with doubt. There was no radio contact with Gatty as the world waited for news.

Cleveland went mad when *Winnie Mae* appeared 10½ hours out of Edmonton. Post and Gatty remained just long enough to fill the tanks. As they raced east, town after town reported the Vega's progress across Pennsylvania and New Jersey.

New York was bathed in the glow of a beautiful sunset as the Lockheed came in low over the harbour, escorted by a straggling formation of aircraft. Minutes later, with a triumphant final burst of power, Post touched gently down on Roosevelt Field at 8.47 p.m. on 1 July 1931 — just eight days, fifteen hours and fifty-one minutes since *Winnie Mae* had left. They had covered 24 758 kilometres at an average speed of 233 km/h air time.

A huge crowd surged around the aircraft and, unable to control the thousands of cheering New Yorkers, police battled to make a path for the flyers. The *New York Times* reported the scene:

> Mrs Post, who had waited on the field for half an hour with F.C. Hall, backer of the flight, ran forward, and the crowd surged around her pushing in on all sides and cheering. Suddenly Mrs Post burst into tears and seemed for a moment to be quite hysterical. Mr Deegan and Mr Hall took her arms and led her forward and by the time she met her husband she was calm again, although tears still streamed down her cheeks.
>
> The flyers were too exhausted to say much and Mrs Post kept looking at her husband and saying nothing at all. Her days of anxious waiting for bulletins were over and her husband's triumph complete.

The paper also reported that Charles Lindbergh and his wife had viewed the arrival from a car parked at the edge of the airfield. He did not go on the field to greet the flyers personally and left very quietly after they had landed. He was reported to have called the flight "a wonderful achievement that stands on its own merits". And then the retiring Lindy, shunning public view, disappeared into the night.

Poor Gatty had to wait another twelve hours to be reunited with his wife. Her aircraft was delayed at Pittsburg by bad weather, and she eventually completed the journey by rail.

The following day the cheers of a quarter of a million people turned New York's skyscraper-walled Broadway into a roaring canyon. As the airmen and their wives drove to an official reception, their open cars were engulfed in fluttering tickertape and paper. The city's traditional homage to the nation's heroes was like a mammoth snow-storm.

The newspapers called the flight the "greatest aerial feat of all time". Among the honours showered on Post and Gatty were Distinguished Flying Crosses from President Hoover, the first given to civilians. The Aeronautical Chamber of Commerce struck special bronze plaques. Both men were given honorary membership in the prestigious Aeronautical Association, among only three others still living at the time: Orville Wright, Charles Lindbergh and Admiral Byrd (the polar air explorer).

Their magnificent effort did much to help convince a sceptical public of the reliability of the latest aircraft. Until then American aviation had been trying unsuccessfully to shake off the barnstorming image and its high fatality rate. The long list of airmen killed flying the 1920s transcontinental airmail services had also shocked the public.

When the hullaballoo finally died down Wiley Post returned to Oklahoma to run an agency distributing aircraft in the south-west. Gatty had decided that one such flight was enough and joined the US Army Air Corps as a specialist navigation instructor.

By 1933 Post was bored. Seeking more action, he decided to repeat his world flight in the *Winnie Mae*. But this time he would do it on his own. A solo flight ... a daunting undertaking.

Months passed in preparation for the tremendous physical ordeal. He studied cockpit fatigue reactions in himself by sitting for hours in the parked *Winnie Mae*. At times he sat awake all night noting his reactions and proficiency deterioration. He purposely ate at irregular intervals to adjust his physiology to accommodate the problems he would meet crossing the world's time zones. These were the problems of jetlag faced by air-travellers thirty years later, but unknown in Post's day. He practised sleeping for short periods, with long breaks in between, as a check of his endurance and ability to "catnap". He also studied the effects of hunger in preventing drowsiness.

The Oklahoman had purchased *Winnie Mae* from F.C. Hall and had it equipped with a new Sperry invention: the first auto-pilot. Also, he installed a new piece of equipment that had been evolved by the US Army — the Automatic Direction Finder. The ADF would enable Post to use radio broadcasting stations as homing beacons, and if successful, would greatly simplify his navigation procedures.

He took off from Roosevelt Field on 15 July 1933 and followed virtually the same route as on the previous flight. It seemed almost impossible, but by the time Post returned he had trimmed nearly a full day off his previous record. He had also established an enduring record as the first pilot to solo around the world.

He was able to report the success of the new equipment and described the inevitable "bugs" that showed up. Armed with this knowledge the manufacturers modified their inventions and both were soon to become standard equipment in the nation's airliners.

During this period of Post's career his fertile brain and technical know-how reached their peak. For some time he had been convinced that aviation's future lay in the stratosphere and just below, where huge winds were known to exist. Later to become known as "jet streams", these winds could add up to 300 km/h to an aircraft's ground speed. The problem was how to fly high enough to use them. At those heights a man would die within minutes, due to the low pressure and lack of oxygen. "His theories were too advanced for aviation engineers to grasp them fully," wrote one aviation expert about Post's ideas on solving the problems of high-altitude flight.

Post designed and built three successful pressure suits, which were rather like divers' suits but worked in reverse. He had *Winnie Mae*'s engine double supercharged, and to increase performance devised a system whereby he jettisoned the wheels after take-off — and then calmly proceeded to crack open the door of stratospheric flight.

On 3 December 1934, he unofficially achieved 50 000

feet over Bartlesville, Oklahoma. Unfortunately the
barograph which recorded his altitude failed as *Winnie
Mae* climbed past 34 000 feet, so his record was never
officially ratified.

Three months later, again wearing the world's first
"space suit" he rode the jet stream from Burbank, California to Cleveland, Ohio. His average speed was 446
km/h, in an aircraft with a maximum cruise speed of
270 km/h! He had introduced the world to pressurised
stratospheric travel.

In June 1935, following four emergency landings
while attempting a transcontinental record in the jet
stream, Post sadly retired *Winnie Mae*. His faithful
aircraft was wearing out and he decided he would have
the Lockheed preserved for posterity. The historic machine was purchased by the government for the Smithsonian's National Air Museum.

America's best-loved humorist and actor, Will Rogers,
had once said, "I never met a man I didn't like". He met
Wiley Post at a dinner in 1931, and the two became close
friends. It was not surprising, for the gentle actor with
his droll homespun philosophy had much in common
with the shy, soft spoken, down-to-earth pilot. Both
shared common loves, their native Oklahoma, and flying. Their friendship blossomed when Post went to
Hollywood to star in a flying movie, *Air Hawks*, at
Columbia Pictures. Rogers became a frequent passenger in his friend's aircraft.

In 1935 the airman announced his intention to make
another world flight — in the opposite direction. It came
as no surprise that he was taking Will Rogers along as
his companion. The two had planned a leisurely aerial
tour.

Post had a new plane, a hybrid constructed from the
parts of two crashed Lockheeds — an Orion and an
Explorer. Similar to the *Winnie Mae* but with low-set

wings, the *Orion-Explorer* was flown to Seattle to be fitted with floats for the world cruise.

The specially designed pontoon-floats failed to arrive. Rogers was impatient to reach Alaska where he had arranged to interview an old trapper who lived at Point Barrow. So Wiley made do with a set of floats from an old Fokker transport. They were larger and heavier than those he'd ordered and made the aircraft nose-heavy. During the test flight Wiley noted that it was vital to keep power on during the landing or it became impossible to keep the nose up. They were far from ideal but would do in the interim.

The two friends took off on 6 August. Tucked on board was the actor's typewriter and two cases of tinned chili, their favourite food. From Juneau, Alaska, Rogers happily wired home, "This old boy Wiley turns up the right alley all the time", a reference to his companion's skill at threading his way through Alaska's mountains and fjords.

A week later they arrived at a small lagoon near Point Barrow. The airmen visited a small Eskimo sealing camp to ask the way to the town and were told it was a few minutes flying time away.

They returned to their *Orion-Explorer*, taxied out into wind, and Post opened the throttle for take-off. The aircraft had climbed out over the water when suddenly the engine stopped dead. The plane was seen to dive steeply into the shallow bay. It struck with terrific impact and flipped over on its back. The fuselage broke open and a wing was torn away. Both men were killed, Post pinned by the failed engine and Rogers thrown out into the icy water.

It appeared that, with no power to compensate for the heavy floats, Post had been unable to recover from the nose-heavy dive caused when the engine failed. An Eskimo ran twenty-five kilometres to the US government Reindeer Station with the fateful news. When he described the victims as "a man with rag over a sore eye and a big man with boots" there was no doubt as to the victims' identities.

Their bodies were brought home to a grieving nation. Even America's hoboes declared a thirty-day period of mourning for the "Immortal Cherokee Kid", as the actor was often called. Post's state funeral in Oklahoma City was the largest the state had ever seen.

Thus Wiley Post passed into aviation history. Not speeding for a record or gambling his life in a crude pressure suit exploring the edge of space, but during a casual holiday flight. Surely this was an ironic death for such a fearless pioneer.

His place among aviation's true greats was earned not merely as a long-distance flyer but, more importantly, as an airman who was ahead of his time. In particular, his experiments in high-altitude flight heralded an era when jet aircraft would carry passengers along the jet streams the Oklahoman had been the first to ride.

He was touched with genius, that rare combination of brilliant pilot, technician and designer. But to his friends and the millions who avidly followed his flights he was "Old Wiley", the simple country boy who could "fly the pants off them all". As one of his aviation contemporaries, Harry Bruno, wrote after the fatal crash:

> Wiley Post was a tough, scarred, absolutely fearless Oklahoma boy with a soul too big for any mortal frame. He was a man whose tremendous energies, whose phenomenal drive needed wings as much as aviation needed him. If ever a man belonged in the cockpit of an airplane, that man was Wiley Post.

16
Lost near Howland Island

"We are in a line of position 157–337. Will repeat this message on 6210. We are running north and south. We have only a half hour's fuel left and cannot see land." The message came loud and clear over the radio of the US Coast Guard cutter *Itasca*. The airwoman's voice betrayed anxiety. Quickly the operator switched to 6210 kilocycles and waited for her call. It never came. Her silence was shrouded in the crackling static of interference out over the vast Pacific Ocean.

It was 2 July 1937 — A day that would never be forgotten by generations of Americans. Amelia Earhart, the darling of American aviation was missing. She and her navigator, Fred Noonan, would never complete their flight around the world. The mystery and the long fruitless search had begun. Two generations later the mystery surrounding her disappearance remains unsolved and, for some, the search still continues.

Amelia Earhart's association with flying the Pacific went back to January 1935 when she made a solo flight from Honolulu to Oakland in a Lockheed Vega. Not only had she been the first pilot, man or woman, to fly solo over the daunting 3862-kilometre route, but she had done it in the remarkable time of 18 hours and 16 minutes. Conducted in perfect weather, Amelia Earhart had described the flight as a "joy ride". She wrote: "Contrasted to the Atlantic crossings, it was a journey of stars, not storms; of tropic loveliness instead of ice."

Sadly, she would find conditions less idyllic next time she challenged the Pacific.

Few pilots gained greater world attention than Amelia Earhart. Born in Kansas in 1898, she used the airplane to promote the cause of women. Greatly influenced by her mother, an early feminist, she studied medicine until deciding to become a pilot after attending an air meet in 1920.

Equipped with a new pilot's licence, Earhart tried to find work, but there were no flying jobs for an inexperienced female. She became a social worker and then, in 1928, she was hired as a crew-member for a trans-Atlantic flight. Delight turned to disgust, however, when she realised her presence was merely a publicity gimmick. Not allowed to do any of the flying, Amelia Earhart felt "like a sack of potatoes". Nevertheless, she became the first women to cross the Atlantic in an airplane and rocketed into the headlines. Earhart's strong resemblance to Charles Lindbergh led to her being dubbed "Lady Lindy" — a sobriquet she disliked.

In 1931 she married publishing magnate George Putnam, who became her manager. The following year, determined to attract the public's attention, she flew solo across the Atlantic. Trying doggedly to prove that women flyers were equal in ability to their male counterparts, she made numerous other long-distance flights. Writing, lecturing, and counselling on women's careers at Purdue University, she used her fame to promote women's rights. "Amelia has become a symbol of a new womanhood," one journalist wrote.

By 1937 she was the world's best-known airwoman. But what was personally important to Amelia Earhart was the knowledge that the hero-worship she now generated had been earned. She was no longer "Lady Lindy", the false hero concocted by a clever press agent and abetted by the news media following her 1928 trans-Atlantic passenger flight. Nor was she merely a

woman who flew. She had developed into a superb pilot
whose skill and courage were respected by her aviation
peers. Undoubtedly much of her success had been due
to her husband's wealth. But his money only assisted in
providing her record-breaking equipment. Even the
most chauvinistic of airmen could not deny that wealth
had no bearing on skill and courage. In the cockpit,
profligate women pilots faced the same dangers as
impoverished airmen, battling the elements over the
desolate oceans of the world.

Amelia Earhart's circumnavigation of the world was
to be her last flight. When asked why she was making
the flight, she replied: "Because I want to." However, her
autobiography, *Last Flight*, published by George Putnam following her death, illustrated that the reasons
went much deeper than just wanting to be the first
woman to complete such a flight. She wrote:

> Here was a shining adventure, beckoning with new experi-
> ences, adding knowledge to flying, of peoples — of myself.
> I felt that with the flight behind me I would be more useful
> to me and to the programme we had planned at Purdue.
> Then, too, there was my belief that now and then women
> should do for themselves what men had already done —
> thereby establishing themselves as persons, and perhaps
> encouraging other women towards greater independence
> of thought and action.

The aircraft chosen for the flight was a modified,
twin-engined, Lockheed L-10 Electra. Lockheed's sleek
10-passenger airliners had been in service since 1934.
Designated the 10-E (Earhart), modifications to the
specially built aircraft included more powerful 550-
horsepower Pratt and Whitney Wasp S3H1 radial engines, removal of the passenger seats to accommodate
extra fuel tanks in the cabin, and blanking out the
passenger cabin windows. It was equipped with the
latest blind-flying instruments, a Sperry auto-pilot, a

Bendix Radio Compass and both voice and morse-code radios.

The purchase of the aircraft was assisted by research funds provided by Purdue University, where she used it to conduct high-altitude tests. With a fuel capacity of 4353 litres it had a theoretical range of 6437 kilometres when flown at 4000 feet and at a true airspeed of 223 km/h — sufficient for the longest legs of her proposed flight.

Amelia Earhart took off from Oakland on 17 March 1937 heading west on a 43 450-kilometre globe-girdling route that followed close to the equator. Besides pilot and friend Paul Mantz who was hopping a ride to Honolulu, she had two navigators on board: marine navigator Captain Harry Manning and Pan American Airways' Pacific expert, Fred Noonan (who had lost his airline job because of his drinking problem). Realising that a lone pilot could not both fly and perform the exacting navigation required to island-hop across the Pacific, Earhart had developed an unusual compromise which would allow her to complete the flight alone. She explained: "I planned to drop Noonan at Howland [Island] and Manning in Australia. At the time we said here would be the occasion where it would be the males who'd do the walking home."

An hour out the Electra overtook Pan Am's Hawaii-bound Clipper service. For both Amelia Earhart and the Clipper's Captain Ed Musick, this was the first time that either had seen another plane during a trans-oceanic flight. After an uneventful 15 hour and 47 minute flight Earhart and her crew landed at Wheeler Field, Honolulu setting a new speed record for the route. However, the flight ended three days later when, bound for Howland Island, the Electra blew a tyre early during its take-off run from Honolulu. The strain caused the whole right landing gear to collapse and the aircraft was severely damaged. The crew emerged unhurt. "I'll be back," Earhart told reporters, as she and the crippled Lockheed sailed back to California.

Three months later the plane had been repaired and was ready for a second attempt. Following her abortive take-off in Hawaii, Earhart had removed some equipment to reduce the Electra's weight. One item was the 75-metre-long trailing aerial which was normally used for radio communications and obtaining directional bearings on the frequencies most commonly used by ground-based radio stations. This strange decision appears to have been based on her aversion to winding it in and out in flight, and the fact that neither Earhart nor Noonan was skilled in the use of Morse Code. Instead they had elected to rely entirely on the aircraft's fixed antennae, even though it had less range.

For the second attempt Earhart had changed the route, deciding to head eastward and thus leaving the Pacific crossing till last. Following the Honolulu crash, Manning had dropped out and she decided now to carry only one navigator, Fred Noonan. He was to be on board for the whole flight.

The pair left the American continent from Miami on 1 June, heading south-east towards the equator. Before leaving she told newsmen: "I have the feeling that there is just about one more good flight left in my system, and I hope this trip is it." She planned to be back home for the Independence Day Celebrations on 4 July, or at worst for her thirty-ninth birthday party planned for 24 July.

Their flight took them over Africa and Asia. At Bandung, Java (Indonesia) they were held up for three days as Dutch airline mechanics worked on malfunctioning "long-distance flying instruments" — as Earhart reported in a long-distance phone call to her husband. "Amelia delayed in Java", the newspapers reported on 27 June, although for once she was outheadlined by another American woman.

On the previous day Britain's Duke of Windsor — the man who gave up a throne for love — had married America's Wallace Simpson. As the Duke and Duchess set out on their secret honeymoon Earhart and Noonan finally got airborne for Darwin in northern Australia, where they landed with radio problems. Stanley Rose, the young Australian radio engineer who fixed their radio, recalled the flyers shipping their parachutes home from Darwin in a final attempt to minimise the load for the Pacific crossing. He was also appalled to note that they had removed the aircraft's trailing aerial. The next day the pair flew to Lae, New Guinea for the final dash across the Pacific. The first trans-oceanic leg would be 4113 kilometres from Lae to tiny Howland Island — the most grueling of the entire flight.

At Lae they topped up the fuel tanks to the 3596 litres which they estimated would get them safely to Howland with a little more than two hours reserves. Undoubtedly they would have preferred a full 4353-litre load but were clearly concerned about trying to lift excessive overload off Lae's 915-metre airstrip. At Lae they were delayed a day by strong headwinds along their route. Furthermore, because of radio difficulties Noonan was unable to reset his two chronometers — and the accuracy of his celestial navigation depended on their time being exactly correct. Noonan's inability to check his navigational clocks added to his problem of locating a destination that was a mere speck of sand and coral — two and a half kilometres long and 800 metres wide! The Electra was to be the first aircraft to land on its newly constructed airstrip.

Even with a first-class navigator on board it would have been an incredible feat to find the island by celestial navigation and dead reckoning alone. With a track error of only one degree they would miss their target by 64 kilometres. Even if Noonan's calculations were exactly right, it was impossible for a pilot to read and hold

a compass heading on such a razor's edge of accuracy —
particularly over such a long distance. Aware of these
hazards Amelia Earhart had enlisted the aid of the US
government. The Navy fleet tug *Ontario* was positioned
half-way along their route and the Coast Guard ship
Itasca was anchored at Howland.

Besides normal voice communications the *Itasca* was
equipped with a radio direction finder and had a beacon
that could be picked up by the aircraft's Bendix Radio
Compass. Furthermore, it had been arranged that the
Itasca would act as a visual beacon by making smoke.
Once the Lockheed came within range the ship could
guide them in. Even if they were a little off course it
would not matter ... or so it seemed!

At 10 a.m. on the morning of 2 July they took off from
Lae. In Greenwich Mean Time — which is generally
used by navigators on long flights — the time was
exactly 0000 hours (midnight). They estimated that the
flight to Howland Island would take exactly 18 hours.

"Miss Earhart's Wasp-motored Lockheed Electra
plane made a difficult take-off with ease, but it was only
fifty yards from the end of the runway when it rose in
the air," reported the New York *Herald Tribune*. In a
second, radioed report headlined "ABOARD THE CUTTER
'ITASCA' — OFF HOWLAND ISLAND" the paper told its
readers: "United States sailors and Coast Guardsmen
set watch tonight along one of the loneliest stretches of
the earth's surface to guide Amelia Earhart on the
longest, most hazardous flight of her career. The *Itasca*
and the *Ontario* awaited word of her take-off from Lae
for Howland Island, an almost microscopic bit of land
representing America's frontier in the South Pacific."

During the early hours of the flight, the Electra used
its radio callsign "KHAQQ" to report by radio every 30
minutes to operators in Lae. Seven hours out they
reported that the weather had deteriorated and they
were experiencing increased headwinds. Their position

report indicated they were only achieving a speed over the water of about 206 km/h — considerably less than planned. But the pair seemed unconcerned. All was going well and Amelia Earhart advised that the engines were operating perfectly. Through the night radio operators on the *Ontario* and the *Itasca* listened for the Lockheed's scheduled reports, but heavy static interference made reception impossible. A contributing factor was Earhart and Noonan's decision to remove the Lockheed's trailing aerial.

At 1215 GMT Amelia Earhart's transmissions broke through for a moment. Her only intelligible words were "cloudy and overcast". Spirits soared — the fliers were safe and coming in. With renewed efforts the operators broadcast homing signals for the pilot to pick up on her radio compass. But for an hour nothing more was heard. However, no one was greatly concerned for, at this stage, the aircraft was still 1600 kilometres out and at extreme radio range. Another garbled message was heard. The pilot was calling for a homing signal but, again, they were unable to establish two-way communications. At 1745 GMT, as the sun rose at Howland Island, the *Itasca*'s radio operator heard another snatch of Earhart's voice reporting that they were "200 miles out and no landfall". Thirty minutes later she broke through loud and clear reporting: "We are approximately 100 miles from *Itasca*, position doubtful. Please take a bearing on us and report in half an hour. I will transmit into the microphone." The seamen swung their direction finder in vain. For some reason they could not lock on to her signal.

For another hour intermittent calls were heard, but it appeared that the fliers were not picking up the *Itasca*'s radio nor the signal beamed to the aircraft's radio compass. At 1912 GMT Earhart called again: "We must be right on top of you but cannot see you. Our gas is running low. Have been unable to reach you by radio.

We are flying at an altitude of 1000 feet. Please take a bearing." The *Itasca* acknowledged her message and immediately transmitted a homing signal. They made several calls over the next ten minutes, but again the Electra was not receiving them. They were still unable to take a bearing on the aircraft's transmissions. Something was radically wrong for at that range they should not miss.

Again the airwoman's voice came booming through the static: "KHAQQ to *Itasca*. We are circling but cannot hear you. Go ahead on 7500 now." Frantically the operators switched frequency and sent a homing signal on 7500 kilocycles. For a moment it seemed to have worked. She called back: "Receiving your signal but unable to get a minimum ... please take a bearing on us." By "minimum" the airwoman was referring to getting a bearing with the aircraft's radio compass. When pointing at the *Itasca*'s radio beacon she would hear a minimum or silent signal. It worked on a reverse, but similar, principal to turning a hand-held transistor radio to get the best reception from a broadcast station.

At 2000 hours GMT the Electra had been airborne for 20 hours. The *Itasca*'s crew realised that the confused fliers were nearby, circling and attempting to use their radio compass. It seemed the flyers must be within spitting distance of Howland Island yet for some reason could not sight the small twist of sand. Perhaps it was because the island rose only a few feet above the sea and was impossible to spot from their low altitude. This problem would have been compounded by their scanning directly into the morning sun.

At 2025 hours GMT, twelve minutes after the Electra's fuel should technically have run out, Amelia Earhart's final urgent message was heard. The *Itasca*'s operators later reported their belief that she must have been very close because it was so loud. They also noted that her voice was high-pitched and tinged with alarm.

Her reference to a 157–337 "line of position", some believe, indicated that the fliers had finally picked up a reading on their radio compass but were not sure whether they were north or south of the station. If this was the case, with insufficient fuel remaining to solve this ambiguity of location, the pair resorted to flying a search pattern north and south along the position line.

However, there is another explanation of why Earhart used the unusual "line of position" terminology, rather than using the common aviation expression of "position line". It is quite probable that she was relaying the words used by her navigator. During his time as the senior navigator on Pan American Airway's trans-Pacific service, Noonan had worked closely with Australian navigation teacher Harold Gatty, who advised the airline on overwater procedures. One of the procedures Gatty had instituted had been conceived by British airman Francis Chichester, who in later life became the famous world-circling lone yachtsman. On a flight across the Tasman Sea, Chichester had devised an island-finding navigation technique which became known as "Chichester's Theory of Deliberate Error".

Chichester's technique had been adapted from an early sailing manual and used the term "line of position". It is unlikely that the desperate fliers had sufficient fuel remaining after sunrise to use Chichester's complete method. This would have involved putting the Lockheed well north or south of their destination — thus solving the problem of which way to turn once they reached the "line of position". However, it seems certain that, with the *Itasca*'s direction finder and their own radio compass not working, Noonan took an astro-shot of the rising sun and worked out a "line of position".

The problem they then faced would have been which way to turn to head for Howland. There would have been little recourse but to search in both directions along the line. This theory is reinforced by the part of Amelia

Earhart's final message that states, "We are running north and south."

Following meticulous research, noted British aviation historian and former RAF navigator Roy Nesbit is also of the opinion that Noonan used a sunrise astroshot. Furthermore, he believes that the problem was probably exacerbated by the simple oversight of Noonan neglecting to allow a "dip correction" to compensate for the aircraft's cruising altitude of 1000 feet.

Nesbit's findings were published in the prestigious *Aeroplane Monthly*. He wrote: "One might have expected Noonan to have known this, but he was primarily a marine navigator and he was probably mentally exhausted after working solidly for 18 hours. If he had made this oversight, it would have resulted in the Electra flying up and down a position line at least 35 miles to the west of Howland Island."

Whatever the case, the 157–337 degree position line came too late to help them locate Howland Island. Nothing more was heard from the Electra. Probably only minutes after the final message Earhart and Noonan ditched in the Pacific. Shortly after, a message went out from the *Itasca* telling the world that Amelia Earhart was missing. Within hours, a fleet of naval ships set out from Pearl Harbour and San Diego. But it would be several days before they reached the area. Meanwhile a stunned world listened to the radio for news of Lady Lindy.

Within hours of the plane going down hopes had soared when three naval operators reported picking up a morse code message which said: "Can't last much longer. Plane is sinking." Then, as a massive search slowly got under way, other garbled messages were received indicating the pair had crashed on a reef and were well.

At first the messages reinforced the public's desperate hope that their hero was still alive and awaiting rescue. However, from the outset, the experts were sceptical that radio signals could have been sent from the downed aircraft. Then, as the signals continued, the authorities became certain that they were the work of the warped minds of hoaxers — the ghouls who frequently came out of the woodwork when such events occurred. On 4 July, with a cloud hanging over America's Independence Day celebrations, newspapers dashed the nation's hopes. The *Baltimore American* reported on a press conference held by Amelia Earhart's husband and search officials:

> Putnam, grim-faced and communicating his views rarely, expressed his belief that the messages had not come from Miss Earhart's plane. The Coast Guard was more emphatic in its disparagement of the atrocity of the many signals claimed to have been received.

A desperate and distraught George Putnam even enlisted the aid of woman flier and family friend Jacqueline Cochran, who was noted for her powers of extrasensory perception. She put her mind to the problem of finding her missing friend and told Putnam that the two were alive and that the Lockheed was still floating. In desperation navy vessels fruitlessly searched the area Cochran indicated. After sixteen days the search was finally called off. Ten ships and sixty-two aircraft had covered an area of 520 000 square kilometres. Not even an oil slick had been sighted.

There was criticism that the one vessel capable of mounting an immediate rescue was not allowed to head into the search area. The *Itasca* had set sail within hours but was recalled by Washington to hold at Howland and act as a tender for seaplanes flying in from Hawaii. Unfortunately the seaplanes were delayed for several days by severe storms. When the *Itasca* was finally released, and the search had reached significant proportions, eight days had passed during which the storms had also struck the area around Howland

Island. By that time any traces of the crashed Electra lay beneath the Pacific.

Following the tragedy, there were many who refused to believe that their hero was dead. In the absence of indisputable proof, many wild and improbable theories were advanced concerning her fate. The most popular was that Earhart and Noonan were on a clandestine government mission to photograph Japanese military establishments in the Pacific.

During World War Two a number of clues supposedly surfaced that proved that the fliers had been captured by Japanese soldiers. Over the years writers of countless books and articles have kept the aura of mystery alive. Some claim she survived the war in a Japanese prison. Others that she and Noonan were executed on Saipan.

Even today there are those who believe that Amelia Earhart still lives; that she was smuggled back to the United States disguised as a Catholic nun, and lives anonymously in New Jersey, still guarding the secret of her covert mission.

Besides Roy Nesbit, several other flyers have tried to solve the problem of her disappearance and put the mystery to rest. The most noted — and dedicated — was Captain Elgin Long, an airline pilot, navigator and trained crash investigator. Having spent years researching every minute detail of the flight, he ran critical tests on the range and performance of the direction-finding equipment used by the Electra and the *Itasca*.

From the test a vital clue emerged that explained why the ship's direction-finding equipment had failed to lock onto Amelia Earhart's booming transmissions. By experimenting with identical equipment, Captain Long established that it had been turned on hours too early. By the time the Electra was within range the equipment's inefficient lead-acid batteries were too flat to allow it to operate correctly.

Like most other professional flyers, Elgin Long's exhaustive investigation finally led him to the conclusion that Amelia Earhart's Lockheed simply ran out of fuel close to Howland Island. He believes that its remains probably lie somewhere within a 48-kilometre radius of its tiny target. However, for those who need to believe in the immortality of heroes and heroines, the mystery remains unsolved and the search continues.

Amelia Earhart would have preferred that her millions of admirers, particularly the women whose cause she espoused, remembered her best for the reasons she gambled her life against the vast Pacific. She once wrote: "Women must try to do things as men have tried. When they fail, their failures must be a challenge to others."

It is unlikely we will ever know exactly what happened near Howland Island on 2 July 1937. The secret is locked on the bed of the Pacific Ocean. However, we do know that Amelia Earhart fulfilled a last wish she once expressed to her husband. "I don't want to go; but when I do, I'd like to go in my plane — quickly," she wrote.

17
The Happy Bottom Riding Club

The ashes of a dude ranch lie beneath the landing path at Edwards Air Force Base, California. Once it dominated Antelope Valley but time and the desert sands have all but erased its memory.

Forty years ago it was the haunt of the "Blow and Go Club" — the select band of USAF test pilots probing the "sound barrier" high over the Mojave Desert. By day they flew their fractious rocket-powered mounts and at night they drove to Pancho's Fly Inn to unwind with an eccentric, leathery old airwoman who endearingly called them "son-sa-bitches".

Their host, Florence "Pancho" Barnes, was more than just a desert bar owner. She was the stuff of legends. Stunt pilot, air racer, hobo, pig farmer, a salty-tongued union leader who called Howard Hughes a "cheap-skating chiseller", she spent a lifetime snubbing convention and her society background.

Pancho was a part of an extraordinary era which encompassed the formative years of aviation and the motion-picture industry. Like most extroverts she aroused an array of emotions ranging from outrage to abiding affection. Larger-than-life she was the subject of legend and gossip and it is often hard to separate the fact from the fiction in her free-wheeling career. The Blow and Go Club's most famous member, Chuck Yeager, wrote of Pancho in his autobiography: "She was my friend."

Her Fly Inn was for serious drinking. The dilapidated tables and chairs, battered piano and beer-stained pool table testified to years of boozing. The walls were covered with aviation photos and a large framed nude dominated the bar. Strictly run-down 1940s, it was paradise to pilots looking for somewhere to let their hair down.

Pancho and the pilots were buddies. They confided in her and she lived vicariously through their exploits. When it came to flying talk the airmen were equally fascinated listening to the former Hollywood stunt pilot. Furthermore, she could out-drink, out-joke and out-swear the best of them. The day's flight-testing over, they would drive to Pancho's where the nerve-racking problems of high-speed flight mellowed over a few drinks at her bar. The married pilots left the day's problems at Pancho's rather than taking them home to their wives.

When the stress of flight-testing their lethal aircraft became unbearable, the pilots held all-night drinking marathons — letting off steam in friendly brawling that left the place a shambles. Pancho encouraged it, for she was one of the gang and comfortable with their ways.

She was one of the few to be told the news on the day in 1947 when Chuck Yeager's Bell X-1 *Glamorous Glennis* broke the sound barrier — a closely guarded secret for months after. Pancho had promised a free steak dinner to the first pilot who passed Mach One and lived to tell her. Yeager collected, starting a custom she extended to the others as each fired his first sonic boom. Yeager wrote: "If Pancho's little oasis didn't exist, we test pilots would've invented something like it. I reckon I spent more time at her place than I did in a cockpit over those years."

The airmen could not have imagined the high society beginnings behind their eccentric host's rough exterior. Born Florence Loentine Lowe in 1901, Pancho's childhood in a 32-room mansion was filled with butlers, maids and doting parents. The family's wealth had been passed down by her paternal grandfather, Professor Thaddeus Sobieski Lowe. A prolific inventor and pioneer balloonist, Lowe had commanded the Union Army's Balloon Corps during the Civil War.

Professor Lowe had moved west in 1888 and helped found the California Institute of Technology. Inspired by the beauty of the San Gabriel Mountains he constructed a scenic railway along the ranges overlooking Pasadena. For nearly half a century it carried delighted Los Angelinos to the restaurants and hotels he built along its route. Lowe's inventions included America's first artifical ice machine.

Pancho's sportsman father treated her like the son he had wanted, teaching her to hunt, fish and ride. Her socialite mother believed it more important that her daughter be raised as a refined young lady and insisted that she study painting and ballet. Unable to please both parents, Pancho turned into a rebellious tomboy and, despite the efforts of a convent and two prestigious girls schools, she spent the rest of her life snubbing the conventions.

Following her graduation, Pancho, who had become a superb horsewoman, announced that she wanted to study veterinary science. Her despairing mother, looking around for a suitable husband, chose a socially acceptable Episcopalian Minister, C. Rankin Barnes. Pancho gave in even though she was not "too damned overjoyed at the prospect".

It was a disastrous mismatch. Pancho was bored stiff by her pious husband. The birth of a son did not help, nor did a breakdown caused by her mother's sudden death and the ensuing enstrangement from her father, who remarried and squandered her inheritance. Employing a nanny to look after her baby she took up with the "fast crowd", cavorting around Los Angeles as post-war America roared through the 1920s.

For a time she kept up a facade of marriage, attending occasional functions with her husband. But that too crumbled as she searched for excitement and her own identity. The couple remained legally married for another twenty years but lived separate lives. Recalling the break-up Pancho explained: "Life as a clergyman's wife was too slow for me so I left home and joined a travelling horse show."

In 1923 she used her riding skills to break into Hollywood's burgeoning silent-movie business. Renting her horses and a trained dog to the studios, Pancho eventually found work as an equestrian stand-in. One of her jobs was to perform the riding sequences for silent-screen star Louise Fazenda in the Rin Tin Tin pictures. Heavyweight boxer Jack Sharkey employed a heavily padded Florence to do his riding when he played "bad guys" in a number of westerns.

She also doubled for the evangelist Aimee Semple McPherson. A timid horsewoman, Aimee frequently appeared at rodeos and county fairs drumming up business for her Four Square Gospel Church. She employed Florence to do the hard riding. In her unconventional, yet entertaining biography, *The Lady Who Tamed Pegasus* by Grover Ted Tate, Pancho recalled:

> I would dress in an outfit exactly like Aimee's and when we were in the tunnel at the Ambassador Show Ring we would trade places. I took Radiant (Aimee's horse) around that ring so fast and with my head hunched between my shoulders, everyone thought it was Aimee who was riding. She paid me well for riding for her and I also enjoyed knowing her.

The nickname Pancho was the legacy of an adventure in 1927. Clipping her hair and masquerading as male deckhand, Jacob Crane, she worked her passage to Mexico on a banana boat that was also running guns to a group of revolutionaries. After jumping ship, she and the radio officer, Roger Chute, spent four months wandering across Mexico mixing with bandits and soldiers. The pair travelled on a white horse and a small grey donkey they had acquired. Chute, armed with a long wooden staff, led the way on the skinny white horse. Late in her life Pancho recalled in a newspaper interview:

> I told Roger that he reminded me of Don Quixote riding about the countryside of Spain tilting at windmills and rescuing beautiful ladies in distress. Looking down at me on my burro he answered that I looked a great deal like Quixote's servant-companion, Pancho (Sancho)!

Pancho recalled how Chute's misnomer stuck: "Pancho Barnes! Sort of a pleasant contradiction. Roger didn't know it but he had christened me for life as Pancho Barnes, a name that fitted me physically and spiritually."

Returning to the United States Pancho hoboed across the country hopping freight trains and sleeping in flop houses. In Austin, Texas she was arrested for vagrancy, given twenty-five cents, and told to "get out of town". Arriving back in California she searched for a new thrill and found it in aviation.

America's flirtation with flying had blossomed into a love affair following Charles Lindbergh's epic Atlantic flight in 1927. Aviation was all the rage. The nation's infatuation with the Model T had been replaced by the biplane, and a legion of itinerant fliers haunted county fairs and farmer's fields selling two-dollar circuits and five-dollar loops. The nation's new matinee idols were the flamboyant air racers who jammed America's grandstands as they raced hell-for-leather for glory and cold hard cash.

Pancho couldn't resist the glamor. Moreover, it was another opportunity to compete in a man's world. "They charged $5 for a 15 minute lesson and didn't teach you much. The only instrument you had was an oil gauge," Pancho said, recalling her flying lessons.

Her instructor, Ben Capman, quickly realised that his new student had a natural aptitude and, unlike most of his students, was not merely indulging a passing whim. Pancho soloed in six hours and purchased a Travel Air biplane.

In the summer of 1929 she was one of only 34 women among America's 4690 licensed pilots. To build hours she gave joyflights, took aerial photographs, and even flew rum runners across the Mexican border. Eventually Union Oil, cashing in on the news value of women pilots, employed her on promotional flying.

Promoting Union Oil at the 1929 US National Air Races at Cleveland, Ohio she was among 23 pilots who raced from Los Angeles to Cleveland, Ohio in the inaugural Women's Aerial Derby — the forerunner of today's Powder Puff Derby. It was a highlight of the 1929 Nationals. Unfortunately Pancho failed to finish. One of the first to land at Pecos, Texas for fuel, she collided with the car of an over-enthusiastic spectator. The event was eventually won by Louise Thaden. Amelia Earhart, also just beginning to make her mark as a pilot, took a minor placing.

The following year Pancho purchased a Travel Air Model R — a brawny monopolane produced by Walter Beech and dubbed the "Mystery Ship". It was a sistership of the machine flown to victory by Doug Davis at the 1929 Nationals. Davis' Model R had caused a sensation, and red faces among the military, by beating the Army and Navy's best pursuit planes.

Determined to make a name for herself, Pancho used her Mystery Ship to attack the women's world speed record set by Amelia Earhart. After two abortive attempts she eventually reached 314 km/h — 19 km/h faster than Amelia.

"Mrs Florence Lowe Barnes, socially prominent

woman flier, held the women's air speed record today," the *New York Sun* soberly reported. Other tongue-in-cheek newspaper articles which referred to her as a "minister's wife" must have amused Pancho. By then she had openly adopted the mannerisms and dress of the male fliers of the day. A leather flying jacket, riding britches and boots topped off with helmet, goggles and a white scarf were her trademark. For effect she smoked foul-smelling cigars which she lit with matches struck on the seat of her pants.

Pancho became a regular contestant in air races and transcontinental flights. She flew for Shell Oil, and later barnstormed the country with her own company, Pancho Barnes' Mystery Circus of the Air. During the late 1920s the enigmatic Howard Hughes, diversifying his interest from his tool company, had become involved with film-making and flying. In 1930 he hired Pancho to help with the flying sequences in his epic aviation success, *Hells Angels*.

The film was billed as "the first multi-million dollar talking picture", yet studio stunt pilots earned only $25 a day! Pancho was incensed that Hughes and other film producers could afford to pay the stars ridiculously high salaries, yet gave the fliers a pittance for putting their lives on the line. She insisted that Hughes increase the stunt pilots' pay by $100 a day.

"Howard had us flying down streets, crashing into barns, spinning right down to camera level. We had lots of pilots killed doing those cheap stunts," she recalled.

Hughes refused point blank so Pancho responded equally bluntly. Trading on the remains of her social clout, she organised Hollywood's stunt pilots into the powerful Motion Picture Pilots Association. Then she told the movie moguls to pay or else. Pancho recalled: "The studio big shots didn't like it, especially Howard Hughes. He hated it because he was a cheapskate. He chiselled everyone."

The studio heads gave in and the MPPA pilos flew in many other pictures. Although the pay had improved, the horrific accident rate remained. Whenever one of the pilots was killed, the MPPA held a lavish funeral followed by a rowdy wake at the Beverly Hills Hotel. When someone suggested that rather than miss their own funeral each pilot should be honoured before they died, the group commenced a macabre series of drunken funeral parties which included everything down to a mock interment ceremony.

"After that, if the honoree was killed, there would only be a simple ceremony of the basics of a burial," Pancho explained.

During the early 1930s Pancho, the flamboyant flier, became a part of the Hollywood social scene. Among her friends were Gary Cooper, Tyrone Power and Errol Flynn — the rising young stars of the new-fangled "talkies". She had a brief affair with the fading silent-screen heart-throb, Ramon Navarro, who showered her with gifts including a specially designed flying outfit.

"It was of light blue suede and consisted of pants, jacket and helmet. He had a pair of soft leather Brazilian boots made to go along with it and a pale powder-blue silk scarf. It was dramatic stuff and I loved it," recalled Pancho, in a rare display of femininity.

As the depression deepened, Pancho did other work to augment her diminishing flying income. At one stage she worked as a script-writer for director Erich Von Stronheim, as well known for his temper and riding crop as for his innovative films.

By 1933 she was nearly broke and was unable to afford the upkeep of the family mansion and a Los Angeles apartment building she had inherited following her father's death. Pancho sold the buildings and, turning her back on Hollywood, used the funds to purchase an 80-acre desert farm in Antelope Valley. With her she took her twelve-year-old son, William.

Whether Pancho was running away again or seeking a more meaningful challenge is not clear. Certainly she had fallen in love with the lonely magnificence of the Mojave Desert when test-flying for Lockheed in 1931. Investigating maximum weight take-offs on a new aircraft, Pancho had utilised a thirteen-kilometre stretch of the concrete-like bed of Muroc (Rogers) Dry Lake.

"When my son Billy and I first got to that place there wasn't anything around except coyotes, lizards, jackrabbits, and sidewinder snakes," she wrote, describing the wilderness of scrub and gnarled joshua trees. Pancho knew that with a lot of work, and irrigation, the desert around the lake could produce good crops. They sank wells and planted alfalfa, and then set about expanding the farm's ramshackle four-room house and constructing fences.

The US Army Air Corps had also found a use for Muroc. It made an ideal bombing range. Pancho soon had new neighbours when a 17-man detachment was based on the lake bed to evaluate the performance of army bombing. The men of the lonely outpost christened themselves "The Foreign Legion of the American Army".

Grasping the commercial potential of the military presence, Pancho shrewdly purchased a small dairy herd and provided the base with fresh milk. Next she contracted to collect their garbage which she fed to hogs and, in turn, sold back to the military as hams. As the Muroc air base grew, so too did her hog farm, until Pancho had around 3000 hogs and was making steady profits.

By the close of the 1930s the astute farmer had parlayed her original 80 acres into a 368-acre ranch. She had expanded her house, built a swimming pool, constructed a small private airfield and bought a string of riding horses.

Pancho had continued to fly over the years. Indeed there are rumours that she made clandestine flights smuggling arms into Mexico. Certainly, years later, when she flew Chuck Yeager down to Mexico in her Stinson, he recalled not only that "she was a damned good pilot", but also that she seemed to know everybody south of the border and was treated "like a queen".

When war started in Europe, and American involvement seemed inevitable, Pancho was enlisted to run a training school for civilian pilots. The government-funded Civilian Pilot Scheme (CPT) was organised to help evaluate potential military flight cadets and to train civilian pilots for non-combat duties. Pancho's airfield, with its excellent flying weather and proximity to Muroc, was an ideal location.

Following Pearl Harbour, Muroc burst at the seams as hundreds of young men arrived to train for war. Lonely, and with nowhere to go, they began drifting over to Pancho's where she let them ride, swim and swap yarns. Soon they were coming in droves and the entrepreneur in Pancho saw a new opportunity.

In quick succession she built a restaurant, two bars, a rodeo corral and a twenty-room motel. She erected a big dance hall and employed hostesses to dance with the men, cautioning them: "Hustling on the job will get you rapid transportation elsewhere."

She named her establishment The Pancho Oro Verde Fly Inn Dude Ranch but to the men at Muroc it was simply Pancho's Place — "a real jumping joint". To the budding young pilots Pancho herself was a big attraction. They crowded the bar hanging on her every word as she told tales of gun-running, barnstorming, and sharing the limelight with the movie stars and aviation heroes.

Eventually the ranch became known as "The Happy Bottom Riding Club". Pancho gave various versions of the origin of the name. The most persistent was that it was inspired by her longtime friend, General Jimmy Doolittle, a frequent visitor to the ranch who was presented with the club's first membership card. Following a long ride on one of her horses, Pancho said that Doolittle had joked: "It gave me a happy bottom."

In 1942 Pancho and the Reverend Barnes were finally divorced. In the years that followed she would marry and divorce another three men in a fruitless attempt to find a lasting relationship.

With the post-war jet age Muroc became home of the Air Force Flight Test Center. It was later renamed Edwards AFB in memory of Captain Glenn Edwards who was killed while testing a flying wing. A different breed of fliers now crowded into Pancho's. Her new pals were the test pilots taking aviation to the edge of space in jet and rocket-powered experimental aircraft. She was fascinated by their exploits. However, it was a mutual admiration society as the airmen were equally intrigued by the tough old woman who could drink them under the bar and, it seemed to them, had done everything worth doing and knew everyone worth knowing.

Even though most of the pilots' wives disapproved of the free-wheeling establishment, their husbands still went there. Pancho's attitude did not help. She allowed few women to see the warmth behind her tough, rip-roaring exterior. Yeager's wife Glennis believes it was because Pancho wished she were a man that she wanted nothing to do with women. Glennis Yeager was one of the few wives Pancho seemed to like, though she suggested Pancho merely put up with her "because I was part of a package that included Chuck".

In 1953 the Air Force needed Pancho's land for extensions of Edwards AFB and the US government filed a condemnation suit to get it. Soon after, the Happy Bottom Riding Club was declared "off limits" to service personnel on "moral" grounds. Pancho battled it out in her own inimitable style. Acting as her own attorney she filed a $1.5 million suit against a senior air-force officer and in court eloquently told the judge:

"Plaintiff's grandfather, T.S.C. Lowe organised the first military aerial war unit in the world which is now the United States Air Force, and he was its first commander-in-chief," also protesting that, as a member of true Pasadena society, she was "greatly chagrined" when her ranch was put off limits.

"What I was doing was raising hell with them. It was a matter of principle. They condemned my place and I fought it. I would have won that case and a lot more but the presiding judge died. He was mad at the government for the way they were pushing me around and him around," she explained years after.

In the middle of the battle Pancho's play mysteriously burnt down. After two years of wrangling, Pancho won a $415 000 settlement. She tried to start again at another location but it was too late. By the time her new Gipsy Springs Ranch was opened, the old gang was gone. Fast cars and modern highways were speeding a new generation of Edwards pilots to the bright lights of Las Vegas and Los Angeles.

An indomitable figure she battled a serious bout of breast cancer and in her seventies was living alone, with her dog, in a mobile home in her beloved Mojave Desert. She started work on an autobiography, kept in touch with a few aviation friends, and was a star attraction at the annual Barnstormers' Reunions.

A chip-off-the-old-block, son Billy became a successful pilot and eventual owner of Barnes Aviation. Fortunately Pancho did not live to see the day he was killed during an airshow at Edwards AFB — crashing his P-51 only a few hundred yards from the site of her old Fly Inn.

In March 1975, more than 20 years after her battle with the air-force brass, she received a symbolic peace offering. It came in the form of an invitation to have lunch with the wives at the Officers Club at Edwards AFB. She never turned up. Some time earlier, no one quite knows when, she had died alone in her desert home.

A few days later her son Billy and her friend and biographer Grover Ted Tate flew over Antelope Valley. They scattered the ashes of Pancho Barnes over the site of The Happy Bottom Riding Club.

Bibliography

Aeronautical Chamber of Commerce, *The Aircraft Year Book*, New York: Van Nostrand (numerous volumes from 1920 to 1937).

Crouch, Tom 1977, *Charles A. Lindbergh: An American Life*, Smithsonian Institution, Washington DC.

Dornan, Geoffrey 1951, *Fifty Years Fly Past*, London: Forbes Robertson.

Earhart, Amelia 1937, *Last Flight*, New York: Harcourt & Brace.

Ellison, Norman 1957, *Flying Matilda*, Sydney: Angus & Robertson.

Grahame-White, Claude and Harper, Harry 1913, *With the Airmen*, London: Hodder and Stoughton.

Gwynn-Jones, Terry 1991, *Wings across the Pacific*, New York: Orion Books.

Kingsford-Smith, Charles 1937, *My Flying Life*, Philadelphia: David Mackay.

Levin, Hugh 1989, *Milestones of Aviation*, Smithsonian Institution: National Air and Space Museum, New York.

Lindbergh, Charles A. 1927, *We*, Sydney: Cornstalk Publishing Company.

Nobile, General Umberto 1961, *My Polar Flights*, London: Frederick Muller.

Oakes, Claudia M. 1978, *United States Women in Aviation through World War I*, Washington DC: Smithsonian Institution Press.

Santos Dumont, A. 1904, *My Airships*, London: Grant Richards.

Viking Press 1930, *Andree's Story: The Complete Record of His Polar Flight, 1897*.

Viking Press 1971, *The Romance of Ballooning*, New York.

Yeager, General Chuck and Janus, Leo 1986, *Yeager*, Hutchinson of Australia.

Extensive use was also made of old flying magazines, newspaper clippings, research documents and other papers in the archives and reference library of the Smithsonian Institution: National Air and Space Museum, and the Library of Congress, in Washington DC.

Index